ETERNAL WARRIOR

ETERNAL EMPEROR

GREG PAK | ROBERT GILL | GUY MAJOR

CONTENTS

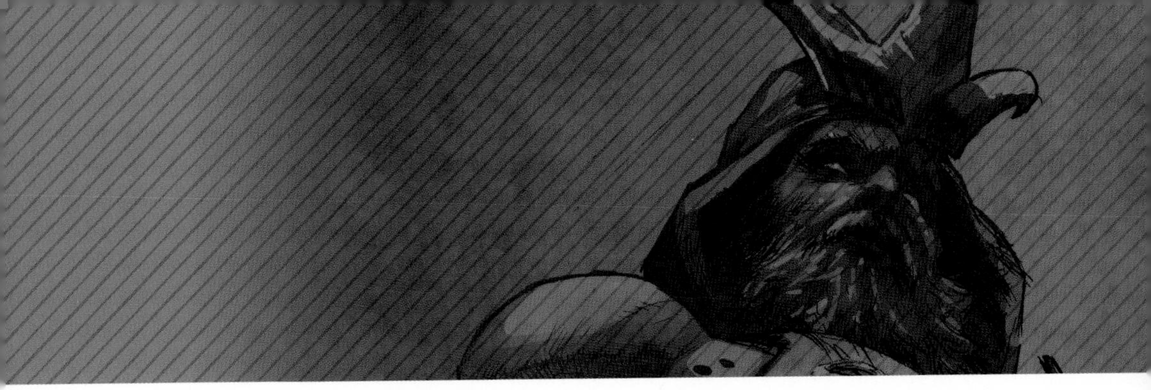

Collection Cover Art: Clayton Crain

Peter Cuneo
Chairman

Dinesh Shamdasani
CEO and Chief Creative Officer

Gavin Cuneo
CFO and Head of Strategic Development

Fred Pierce
Publisher

Warren Simons
VP Executive Editor

Walter Black
VP Operations

Hunter Gorinson
Director of Marketing, Communications
& Digital Media

Atom! Freeman
Sales Manager

Travis Escarfullery
Production and Design Manager

Alejandro Arbona
Associate Editor

Josh Johns
Assistant Editor

Peter Stern
Operations Manager

Robert Meyers
Operations Coordinator

Ivan Cohen
Collection Editor

Steve Blackwell
Collection Designer

Rian Hughes/Device
Trade Dress and Book Design

Russell Brown
President, Consumer Products,
Promotions and Ad Sales

Jason Kothari
Vice Chairman

Eternal Warrior®: Eternal Emperor. Published by Valiant
Entertainment, LLC. Office of Publication: 424 West 33rd Street,
New York, NY 10001. Compilation copyright © 2014 Valiant
Entertainment, Inc. All rights reserved. Contains materials originally
published in single magazine form as Eternal Warrior #5-8
Copyright ©2014 Valiant Entertainment, Inc. All rights reserved. All
characters, their distinctive likenesses and related indicia featured
in this publication are trademarks of Valiant Entertainment, Inc.
The stories, characters, and incidents featured in this publication
are entirely fictional. Valiant Entertainment does not read or accept
unsolicited submissions of ideas, stories, or artwork. Printed in
the USA. First Printing. ISBN: 9781939346292.

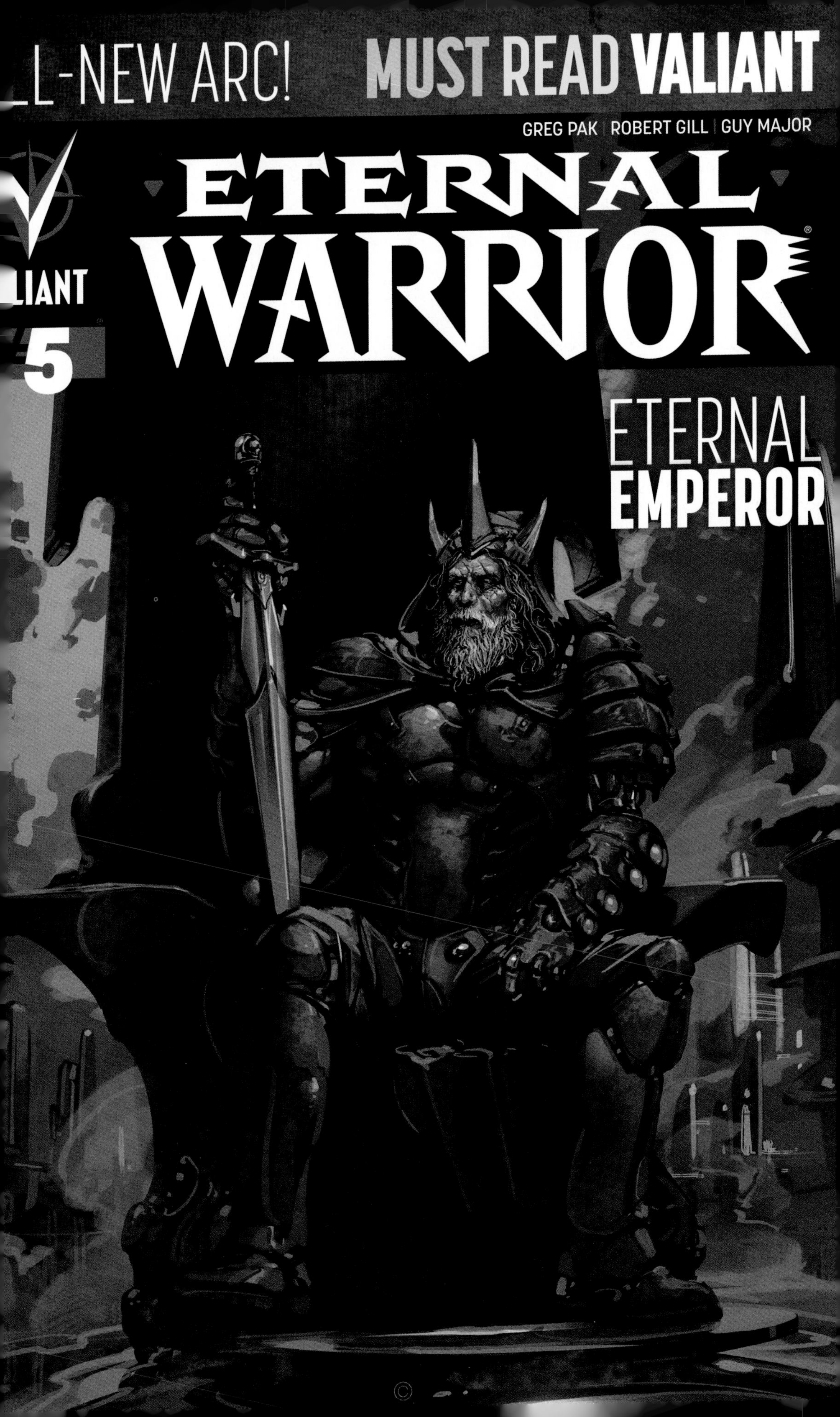

LL-NEW ARC!
MUST READ VALIANT
GREG PAK | ROBERT GILL | GUY MAJOR
VALIANT
ETERNAL WARRIOR
#5
ETERNAL EMPEROR

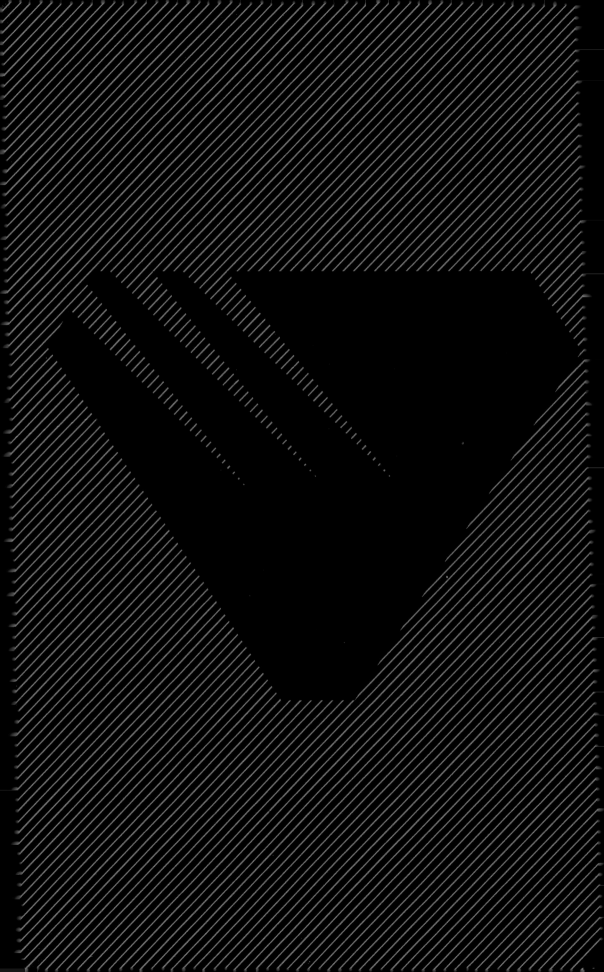

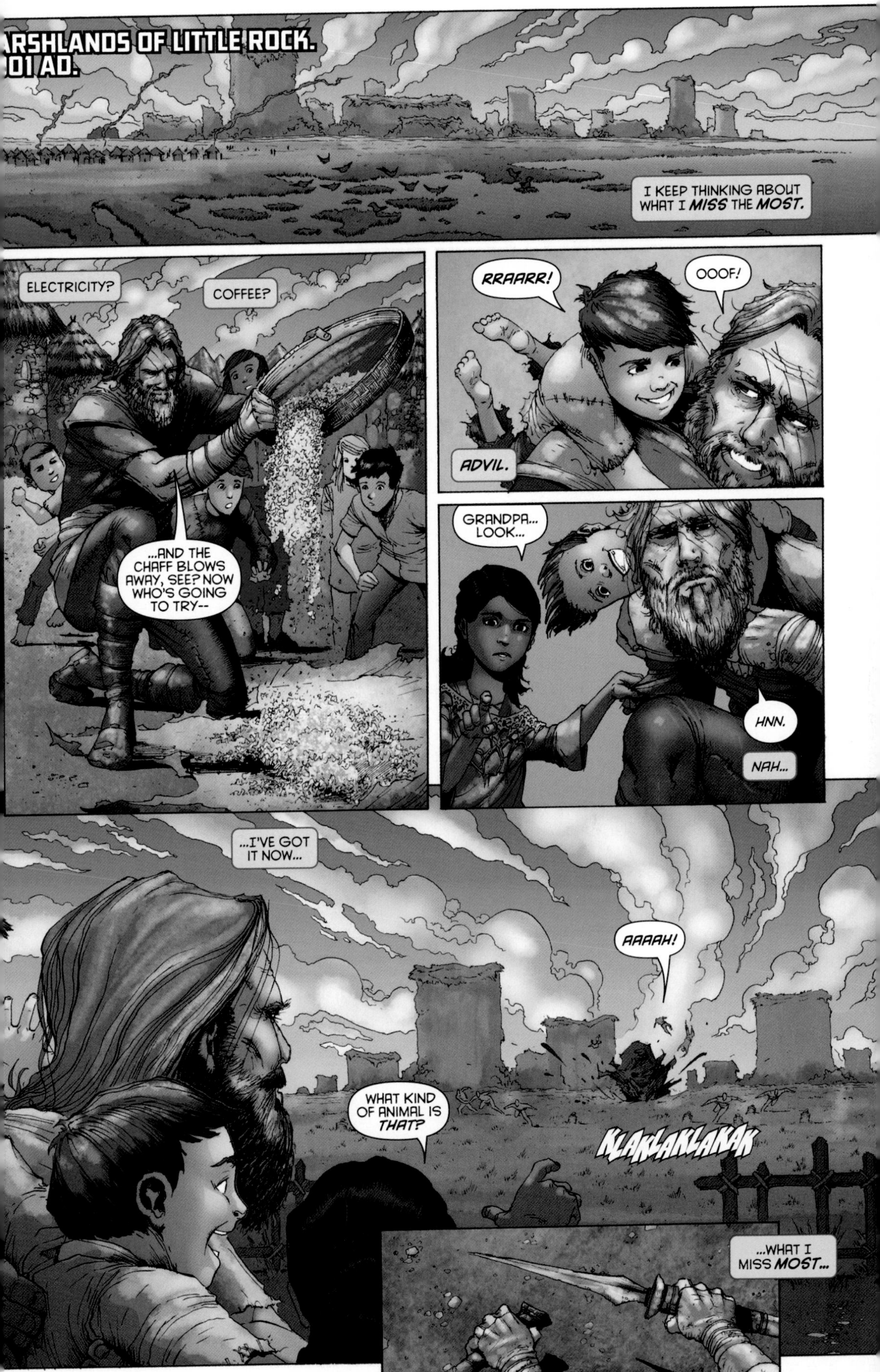

RSHLANDS OF LITTLE ROCK.
01 AD.
I KEEP THINKING ABOUT WHAT I MISS THE MOST.
ELECTRICITY?
COFFEE?
...AND THE CHAFF BLOWS AWAY, SEE? NOW WHO'S GOING TO TRY--
RRAARR!
OOOF!
ADVIL.
GRANDPA... LOOK...
HNN.
NAH...
...I'VE GOT IT NOW...
AAAAH!
WHAT KIND OF ANIMAL IS THAT?
KLAKLAKLAKAK
...WHAT I MISS MOST...

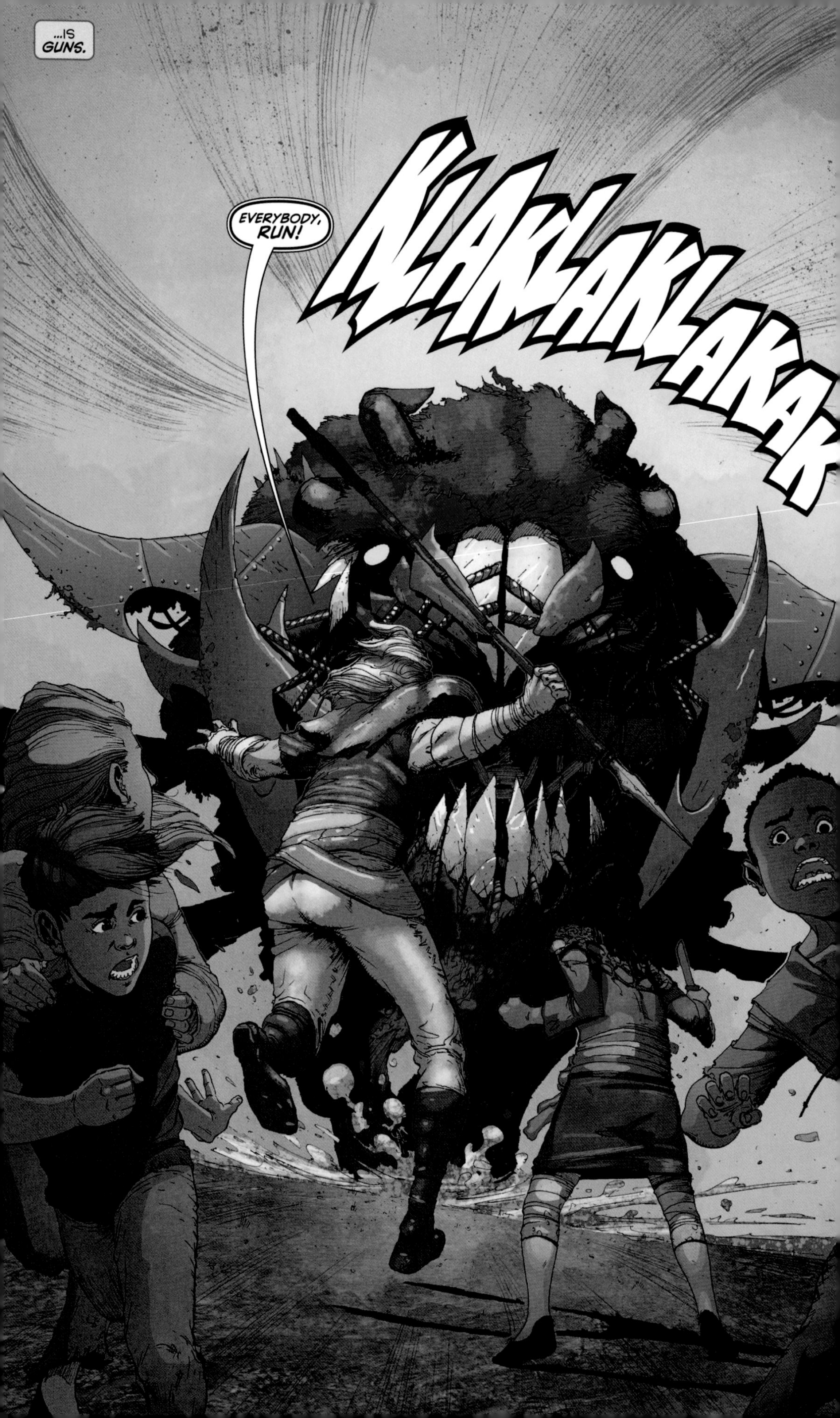
...IS GUNS.
EVERYBODY, RUN!
KLAKLAKLAKLAKAK

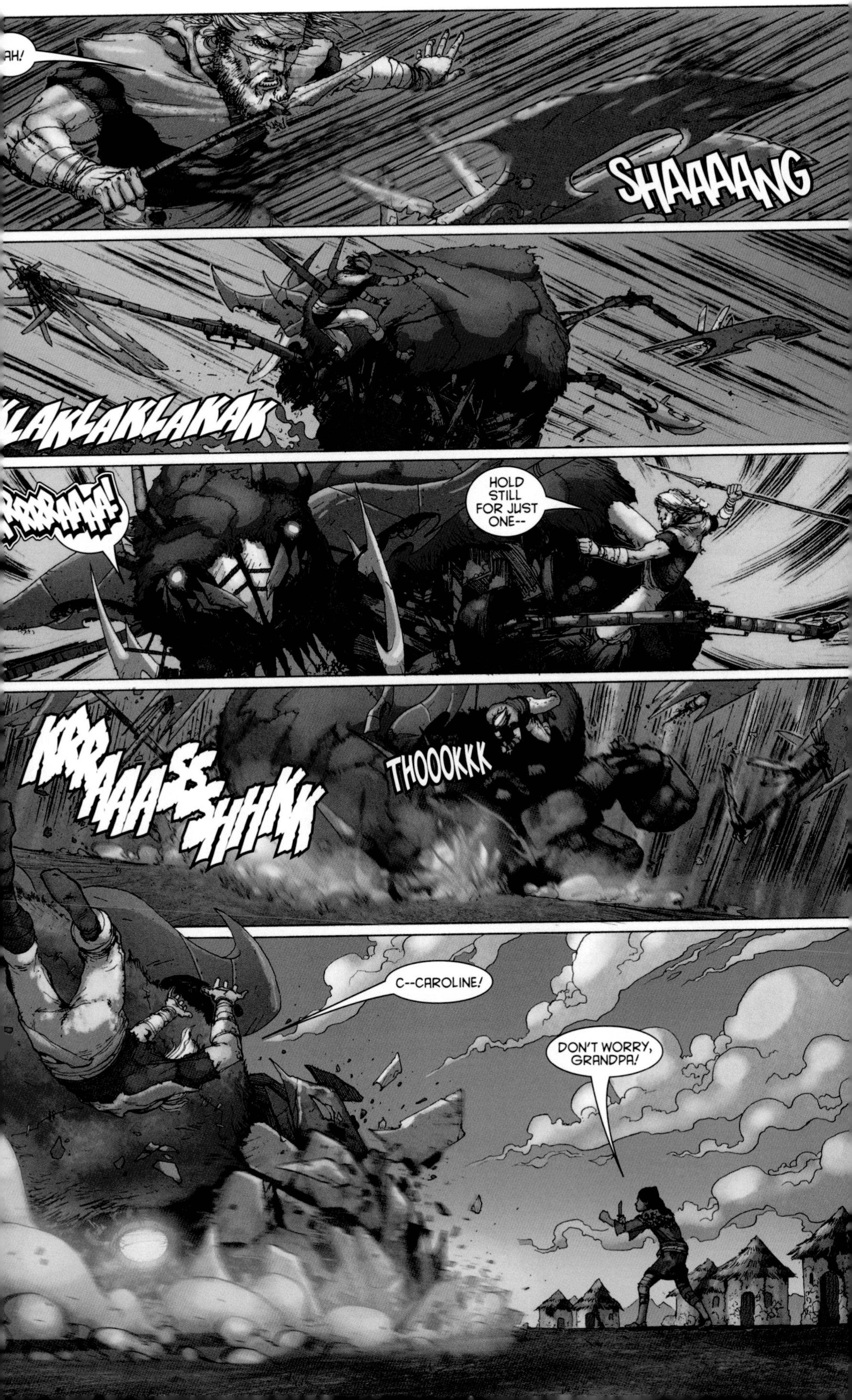

AH!
SHAAAAANG
KLAKLAKLAKLAKAK
RRRBAAAA!
HOLD STILL FOR JUST ONE--
KRRAAA-SSHHKK
THOOOKKK
C--CAROLINE!
DON'T WORRY, GRANDPA!

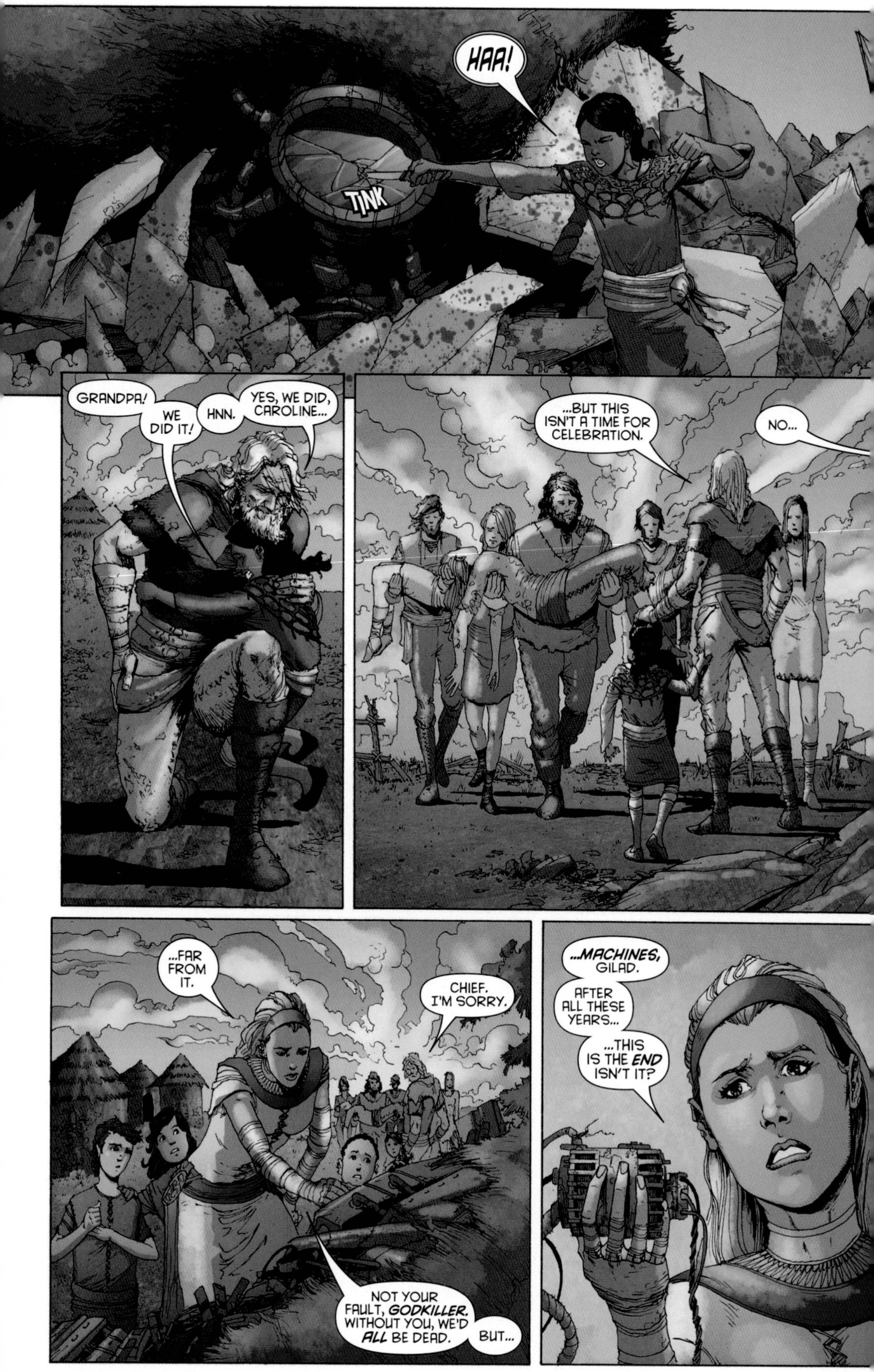
HAA!
TINK
GRANDPA!
WE DID IT!
HNN.
YES, WE DID, CAROLINE...
...BUT THIS ISN'T A TIME FOR CELEBRATION.
NO...
...FAR FROM IT.
CHIEF. I'M SORRY.
NOT YOUR FAULT, GODKILLER. WITHOUT YOU, WE'D ALL BE DEAD.
BUT...
...MACHINES, GILAD.
AFTER ALL THESE YEARS...
...THIS IS THE END ISN'T IT?

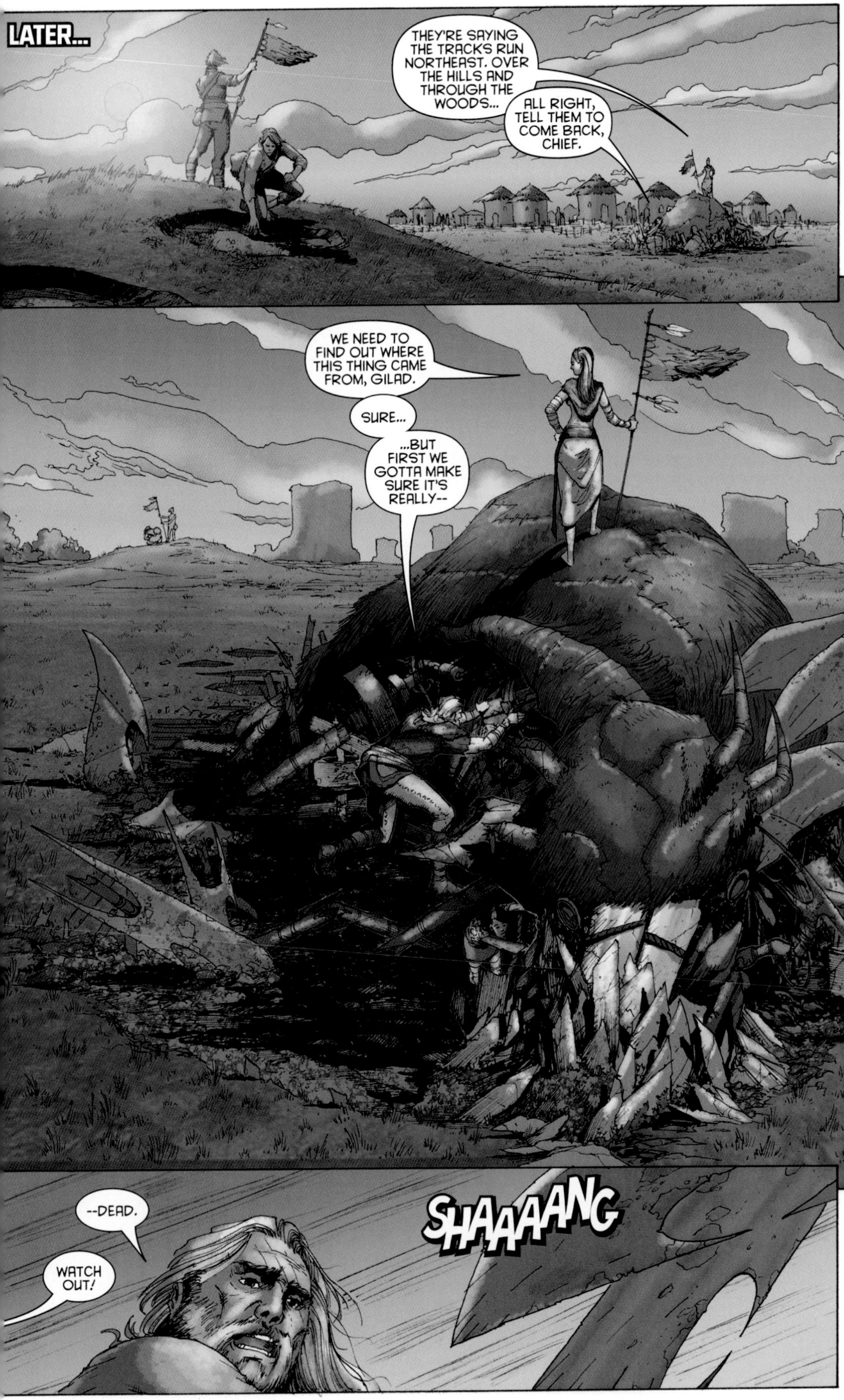
LATER...
THEY'RE SAYING THE TRACKS RUN NORTHEAST. OVER THE HILLS AND THROUGH THE WOODS...
ALL RIGHT, TELL THEM TO COME BACK, CHIEF.
WE NEED TO FIND OUT WHERE THIS THING CAME FROM, GILAD.
SURE...
...BUT FIRST WE GOTTA MAKE SURE IT'S REALLY--
--DEAD.
WATCH OUT!
SHAAAAANG

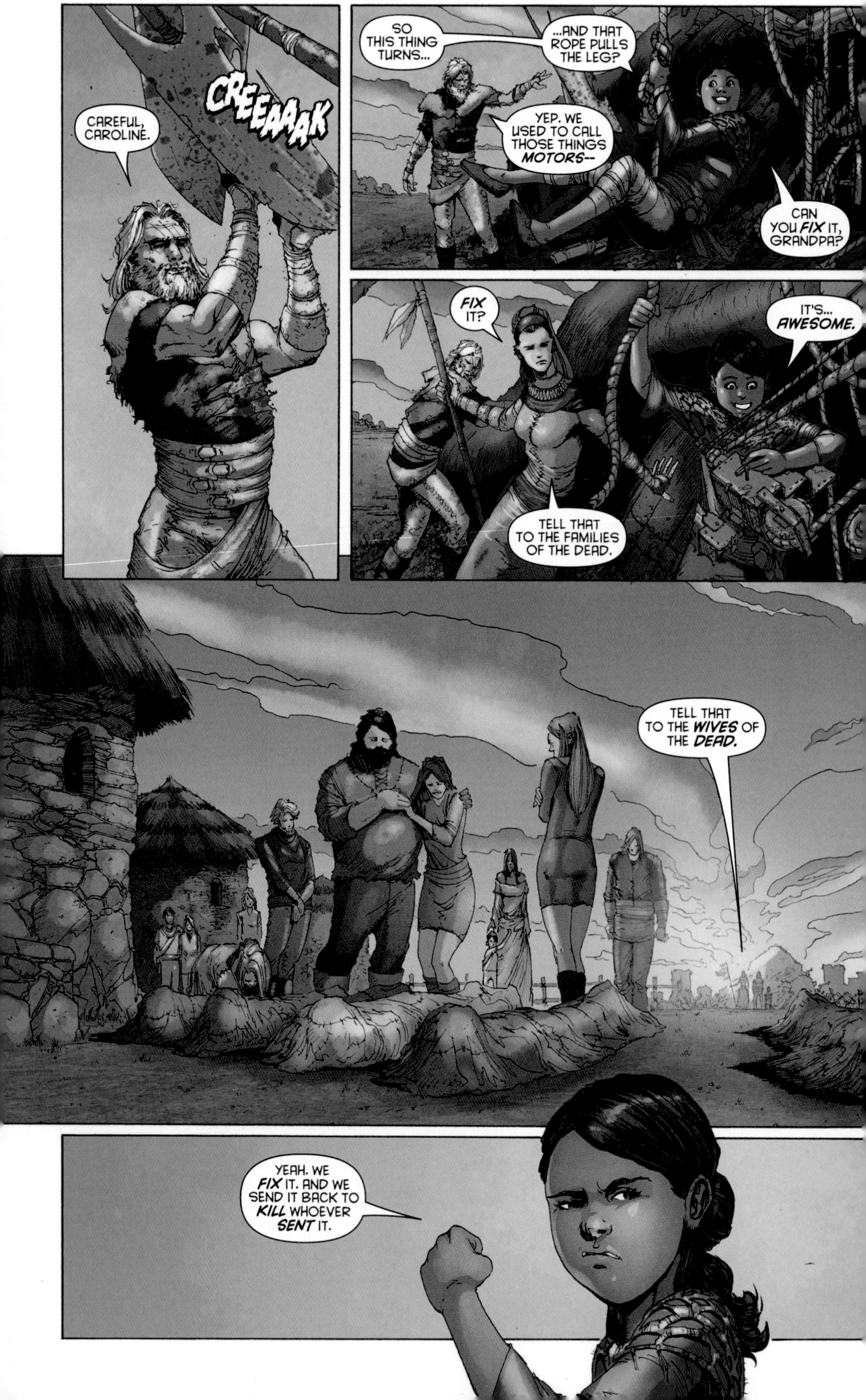
CAREFUL, CAROLINE.
CREEAAAAK
SO THIS THING TURNS...
...AND THAT ROPE PULLS THE LEG?
YEP. WE USED TO CALL THOSE THINGS MOTORS--
CAN YOU FIX IT, GRANDPA?
FIX IT?
IT'S... AWESOME.
TELL THAT TO THE FAMILIES OF THE DEAD.
TELL THAT TO THE WIVES OF THE DEAD.
YEAH. WE FIX IT. AND WE SEND IT BACK TO KILL WHOEVER SENT IT.

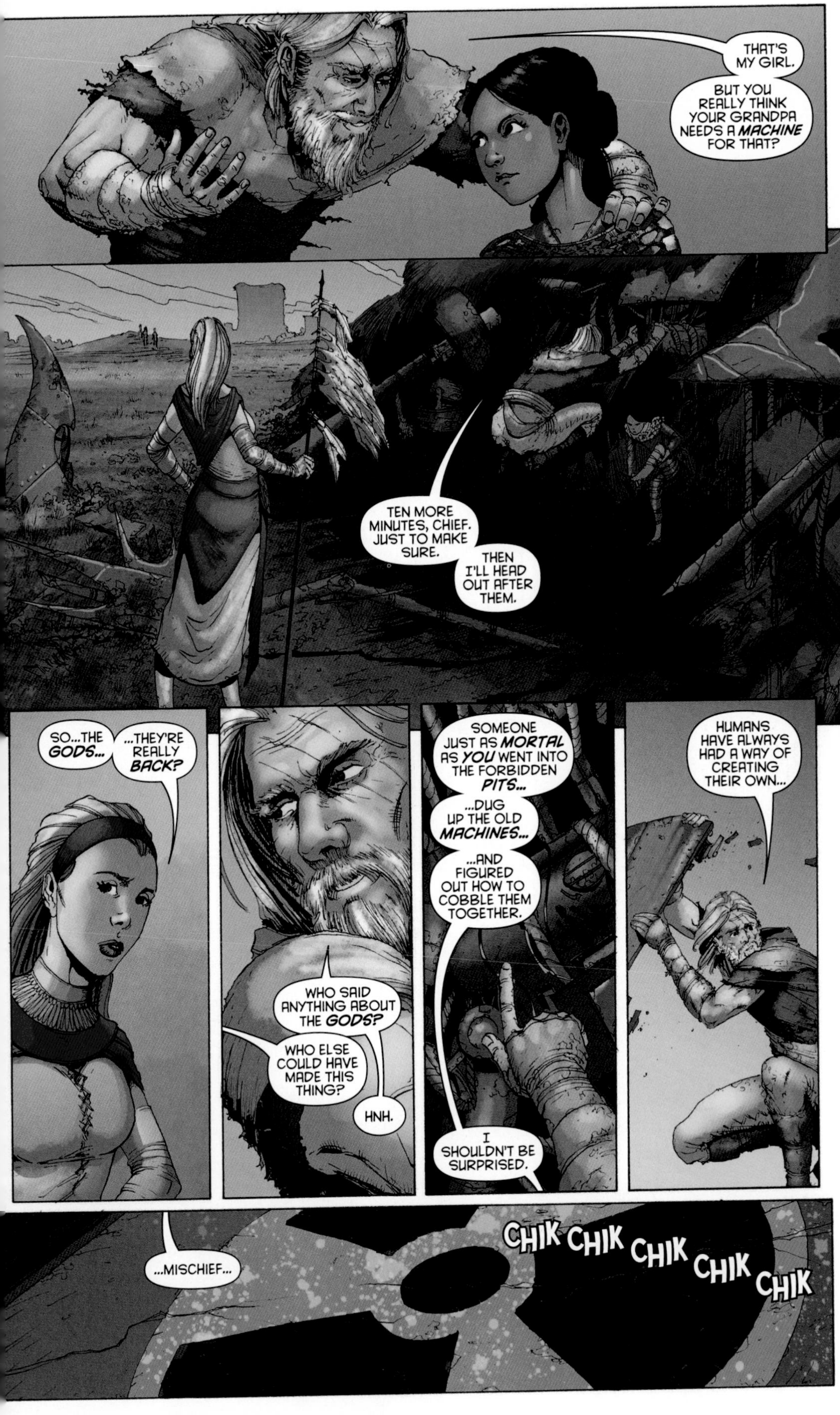
THAT'S MY GIRL.
BUT YOU REALLY THINK YOUR GRANDPA NEEDS A *MACHINE* FOR THAT?
TEN MORE MINUTES, CHIEF. JUST TO MAKE SURE.
THEN I'LL HEAD OUT AFTER THEM.
SO...THE *GODS*...
...THEY'RE REALLY *BACK?*
WHO SAID ANYTHING ABOUT THE *GODS?*
WHO ELSE COULD HAVE MADE THIS THING?
HNH.
SOMEONE JUST AS *MORTAL* AS *YOU* WENT INTO THE FORBIDDEN *PITS*...
...DUG UP THE OLD *MACHINES*...
...AND FIGURED OUT HOW TO COBBLE THEM TOGETHER.
I SHOULDN'T BE SURPRISED.
HUMANS HAVE ALWAYS HAD A WAY OF CREATING THEIR OWN...
...MISCHIEF...
CHIK CHIK CHIK CHIK CHIK

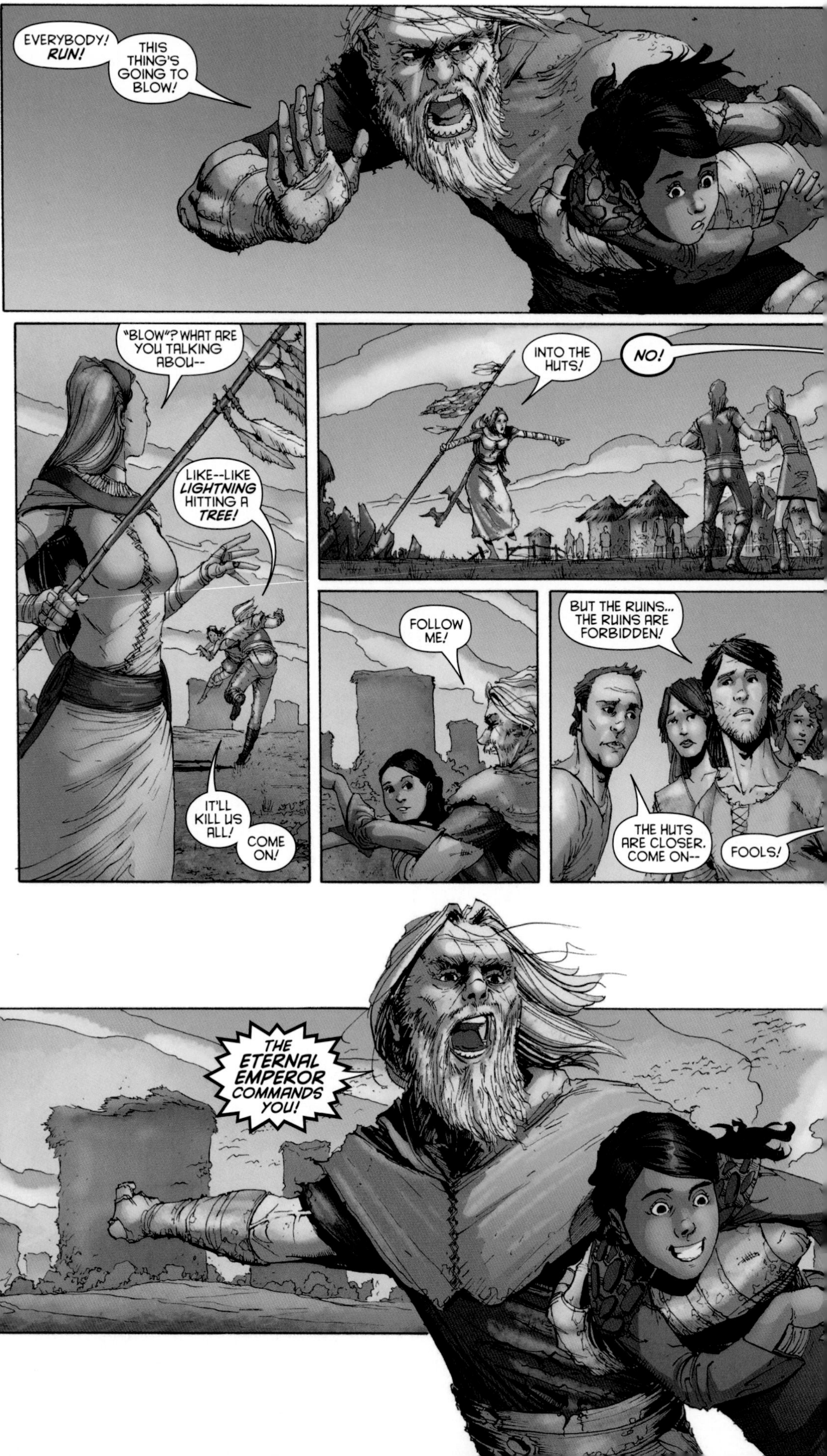
EVERYBODY! RUN!
THIS THING'S GOING TO BLOW!
"BLOW"? WHAT ARE YOU TALKING ABOU--
LIKE--LIKE LIGHTNING HITTING A TREE!
IT'LL KILL US ALL!
COME ON!
INTO THE HUTS!
NO!
FOLLOW ME!
BUT THE RUINS... THE RUINS ARE FORBIDDEN!
THE HUTS ARE CLOSER. COME ON--
FOOLS!
THE ETERNAL EMPEROR COMMANDS YOU!

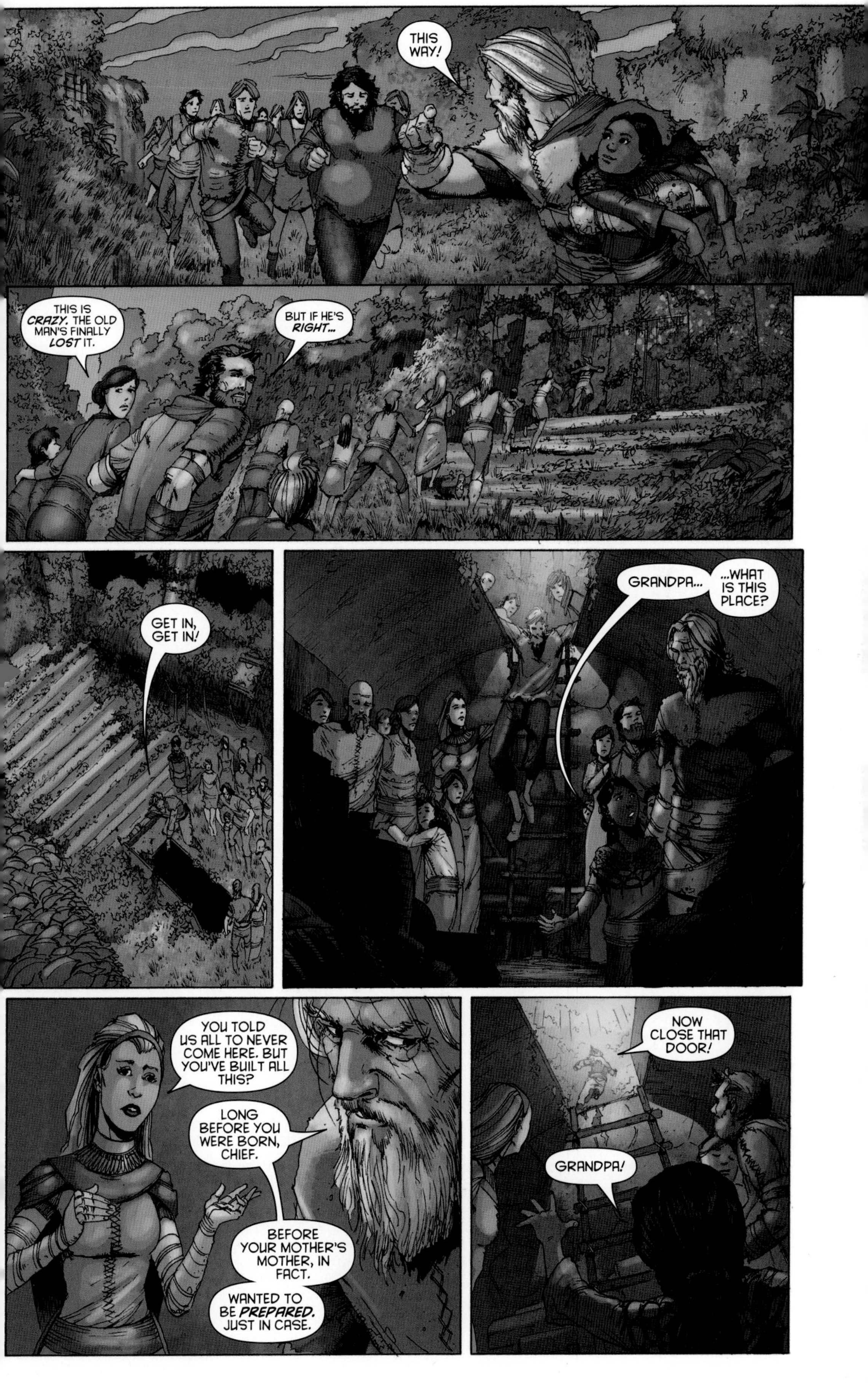
THIS WAY!
THIS IS *CRAZY.* THE OLD MAN'S FINALLY *LOST* IT.
BUT IF HE'S *RIGHT...*
GET IN, GET IN!
GRANDPA...
...WHAT IS THIS PLACE?
YOU TOLD US ALL TO NEVER COME HERE. BUT YOU'VE BUILT ALL THIS?
LONG BEFORE YOU WERE BORN, CHIEF.
BEFORE YOUR MOTHER'S MOTHER, IN FACT.
WANTED TO BE *PREPARED.* JUST IN CASE.
NOW CLOSE THAT DOOR!
GRANDPA!

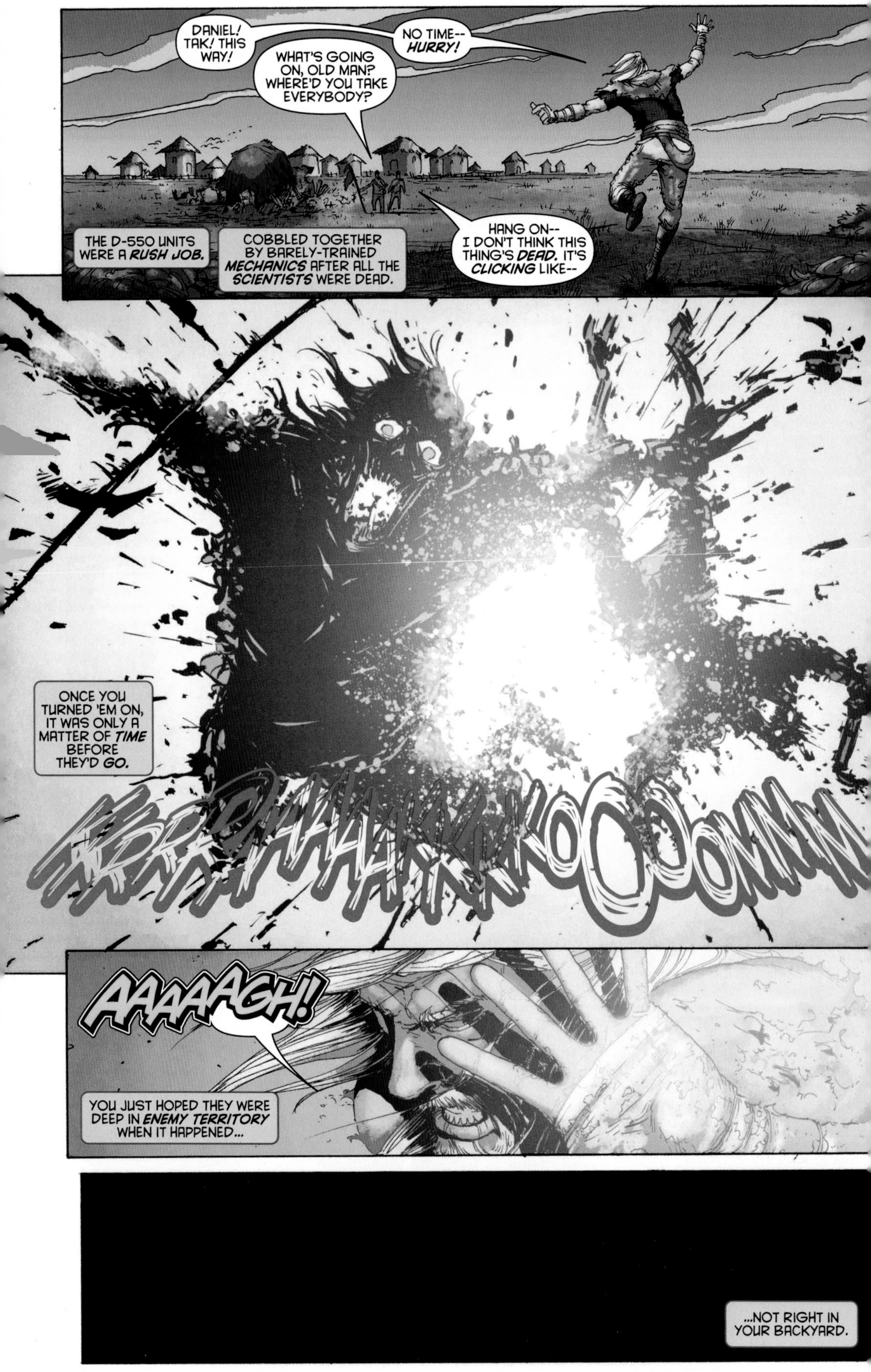
DANIEL! TAK! THIS WAY!
NO TIME-- HURRY!
WHAT'S GOING ON, OLD MAN? WHERE'D YOU TAKE EVERYBODY?
THE D-55O UNITS WERE A RUSH JOB.
COBBLED TOGETHER BY BARELY-TRAINED MECHANICS AFTER ALL THE SCIENTISTS WERE DEAD.
HANG ON-- I DON'T THINK THIS THING'S DEAD. IT'S CLICKING LIKE--
ONCE YOU TURNED 'EM ON, IT WAS ONLY A MATTER OF TIME BEFORE THEY'D GO.
AAAAAGH!
YOU JUST HOPED THEY WERE DEEP IN ENEMY TERRITORY WHEN IT HAPPENED...
...NOT RIGHT IN YOUR BACKYARD.

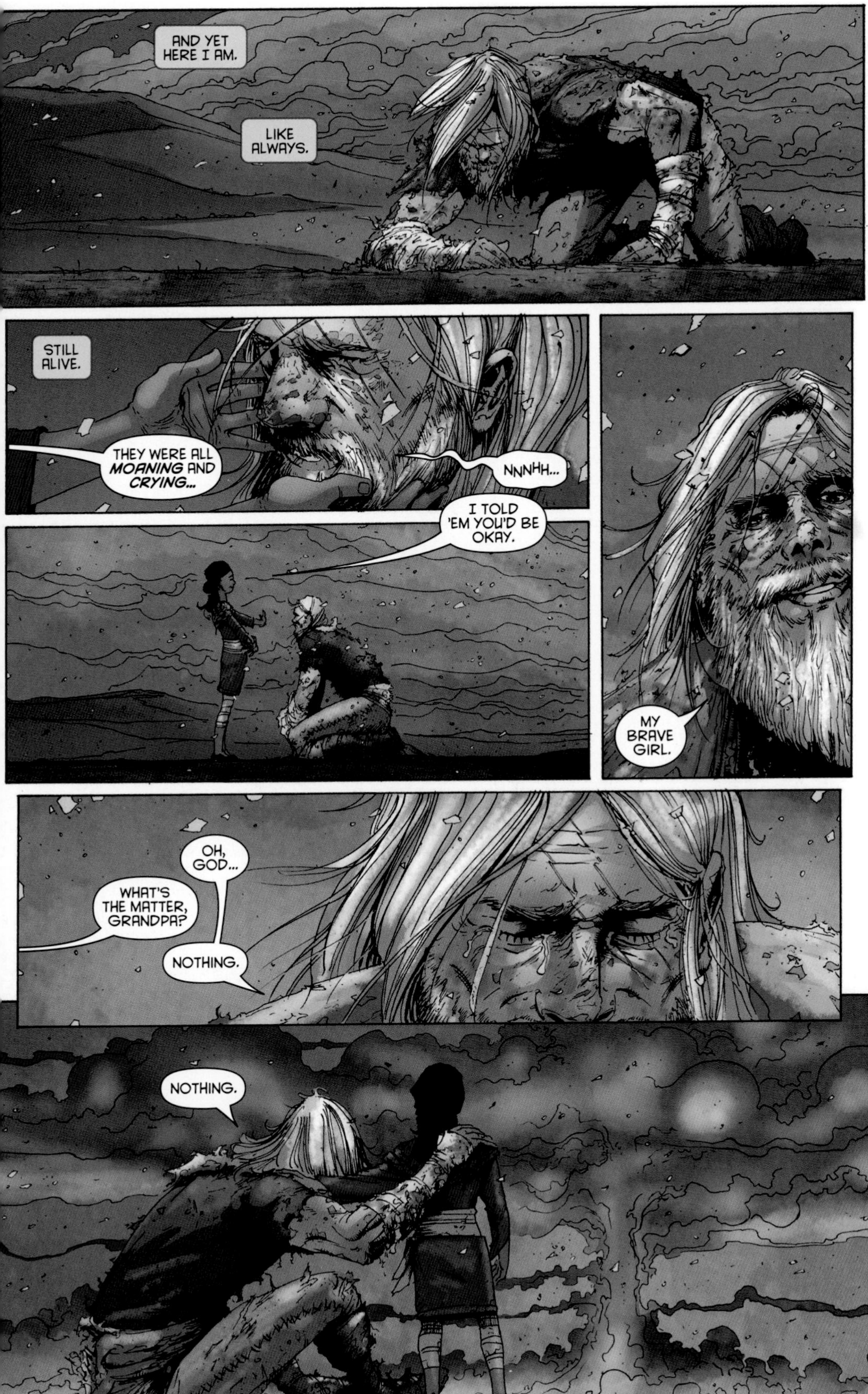
AND YET HERE I AM.
LIKE ALWAYS.
STILL ALIVE.
THEY WERE ALL *MOANING* AND *CRYING*...
NNNHH...
I TOLD 'EM YOU'D BE OKAY.
MY BRAVE GIRL.
OH, GOD...
WHAT'S THE MATTER, GRANDPA?
NOTHING.
NOTHING.

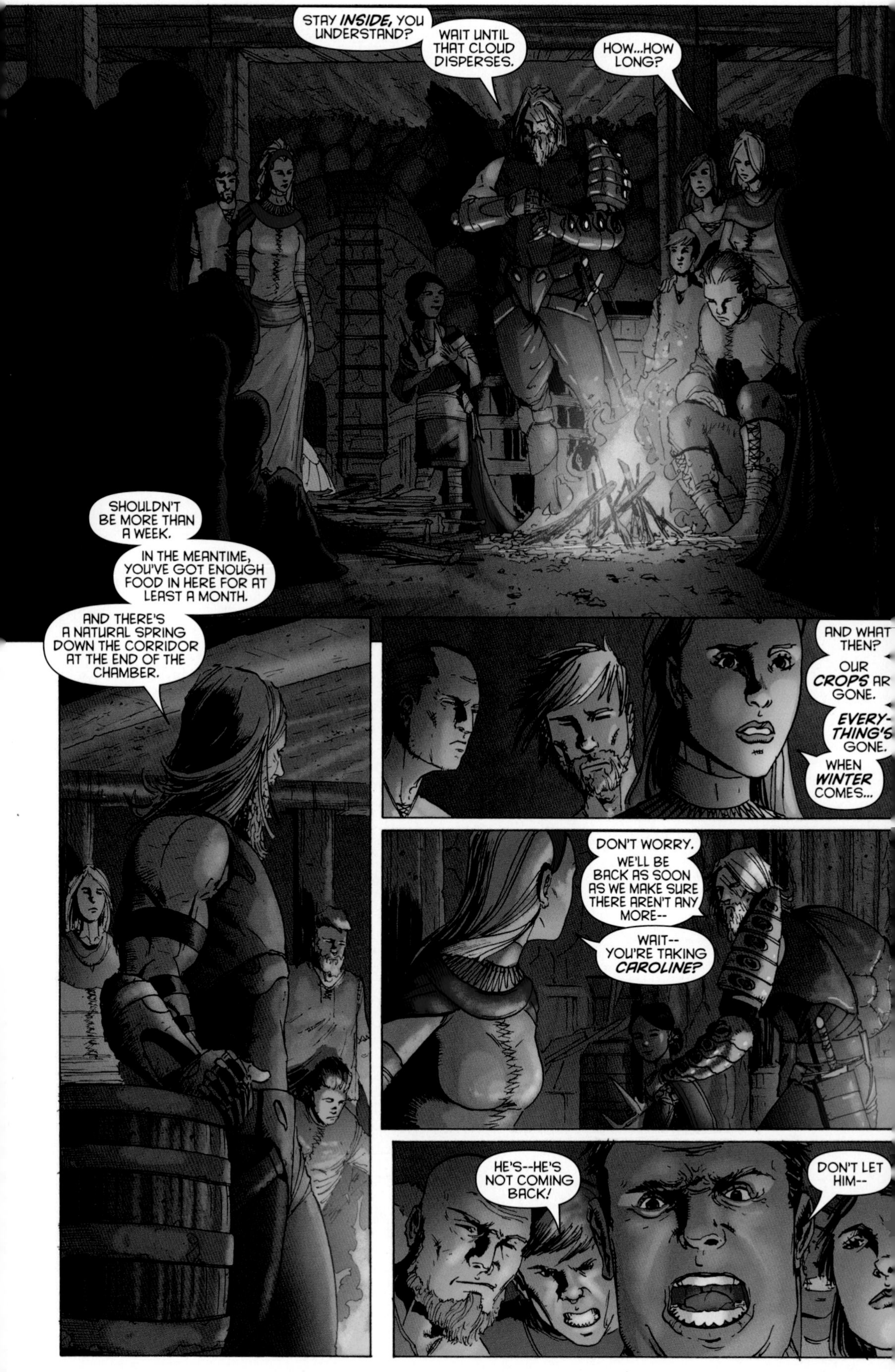

STAY INSIDE, YOU UNDERSTAND?
WAIT UNTIL THAT CLOUD DISPERSES.
HOW...HOW LONG?
SHOULDN'T BE MORE THAN A WEEK.
IN THE MEANTIME, YOU'VE GOT ENOUGH FOOD IN HERE FOR AT LEAST A MONTH.
AND THERE'S A NATURAL SPRING DOWN THE CORRIDOR AT THE END OF THE CHAMBER.
AND WHAT THEN?
OUR CROPS AR GONE.
EVERY-THING'S GONE.
WHEN WINTER COMES...
DON'T WORRY.
WE'LL BE BACK AS SOON AS WE MAKE SURE THERE AREN'T ANY MORE--
WAIT-- YOU'RE TAKING CAROLINE?
HE'S--HE'S NOT COMING BACK!
DON'T LET HIM--

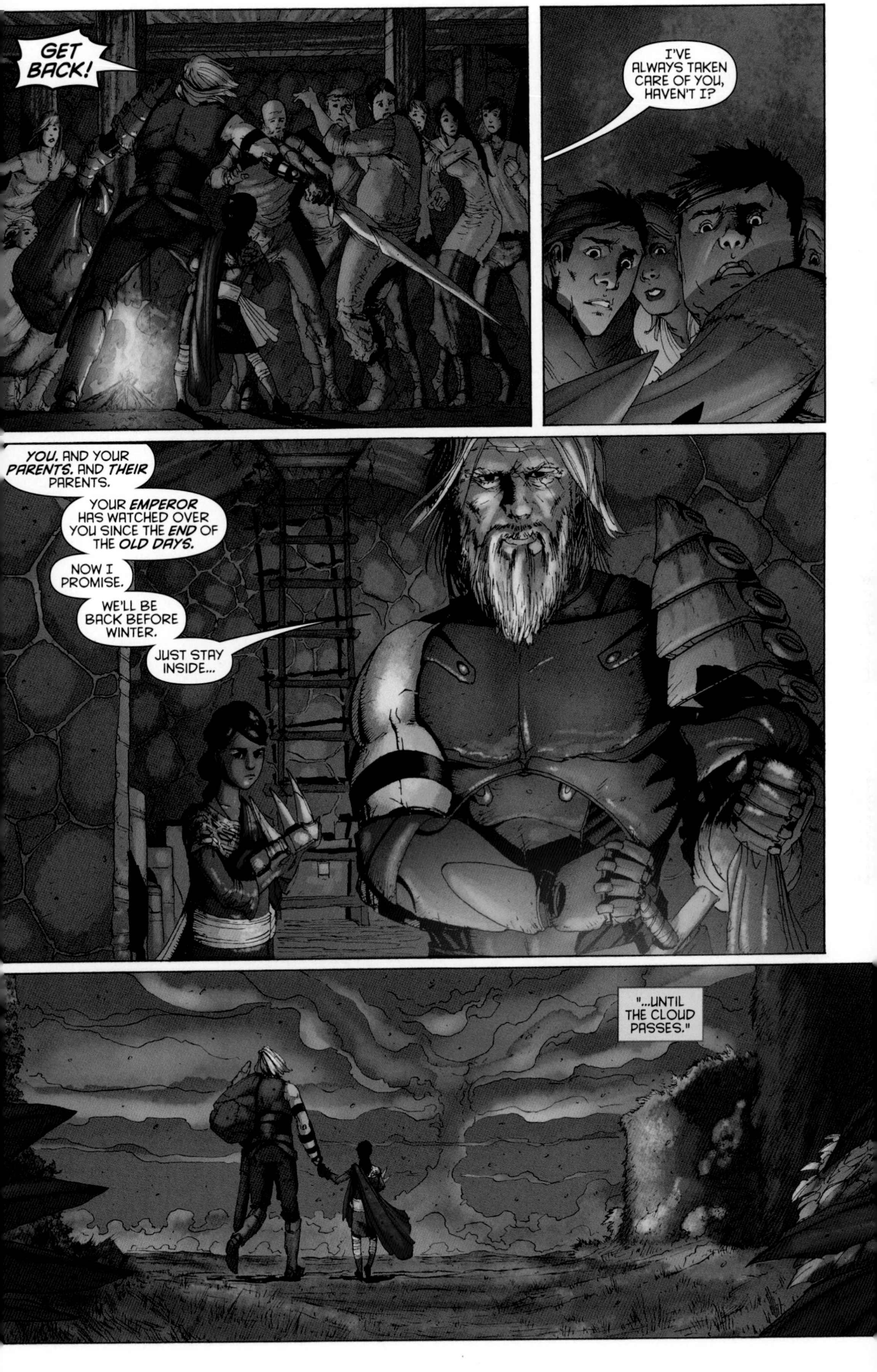
GET BACK!
I'VE ALWAYS TAKEN CARE OF YOU, HAVEN'T I?
YOU. AND YOUR PARENTS. AND THEIR PARENTS.
YOUR EMPEROR HAS WATCHED OVER YOU SINCE THE END OF THE OLD DAYS.
NOW I PROMISE.
WE'LL BE BACK BEFORE WINTER.
JUST STAY INSIDE...
"...UNTIL THE CLOUD PASSES."

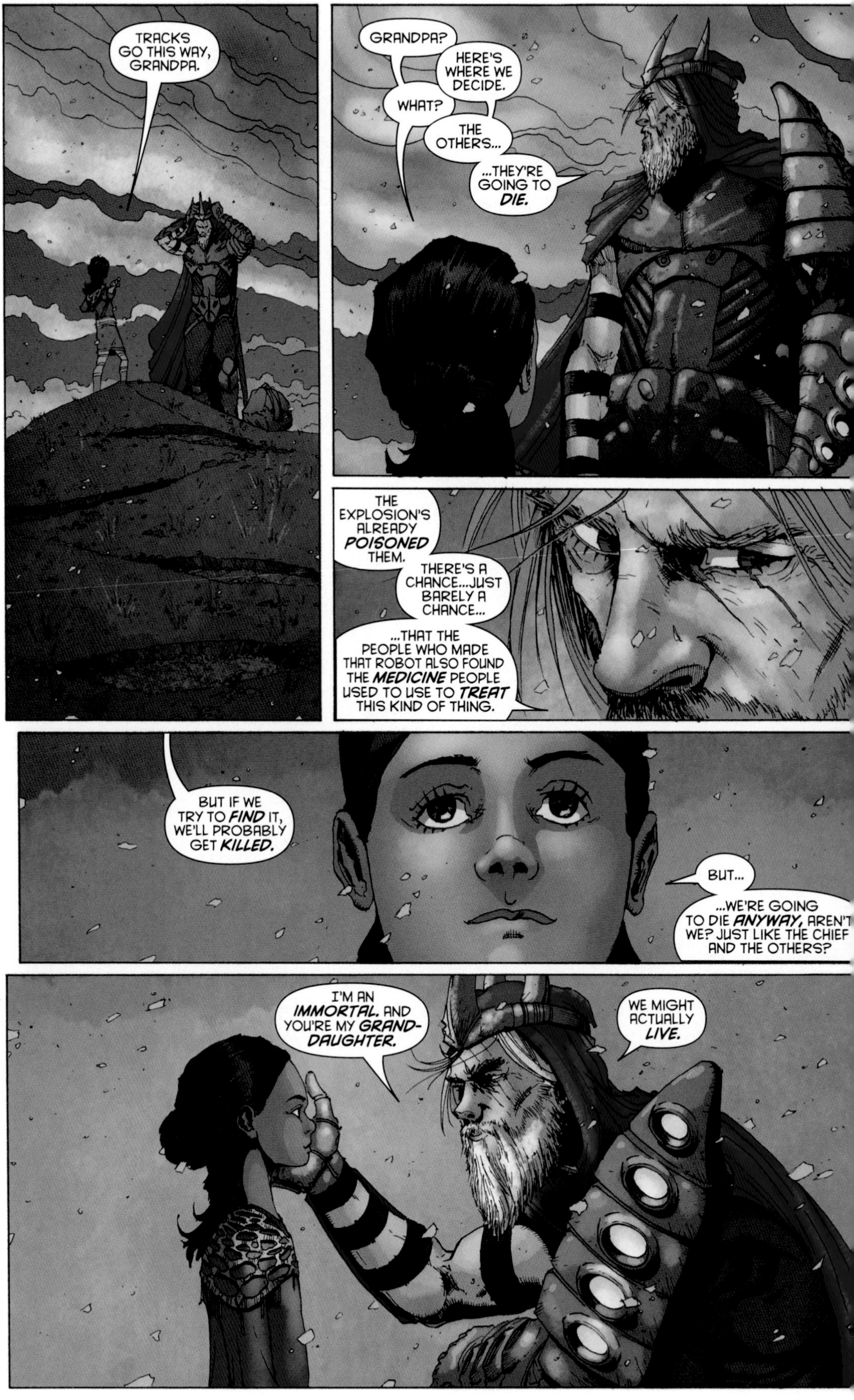
TRACKS GO THIS WAY, GRANDPA.
GRANDPA?
HERE'S WHERE WE DECIDE.
WHAT?
THE OTHERS...
...THEY'RE GOING TO *DIE.*
THE EXPLOSION'S ALREADY *POISONED* THEM.
THERE'S A CHANCE...JUST BARELY A CHANCE...
...THAT THE PEOPLE WHO MADE THAT ROBOT ALSO FOUND THE *MEDICINE* PEOPLE USED TO USE TO *TREAT* THIS KIND OF THING.
BUT IF WE TRY TO *FIND* IT, WE'LL PROBABLY GET *KILLED.*
BUT...
...WE'RE GOING TO DIE *ANYWAY,* AREN'T WE? JUST LIKE THE CHIEF AND THE OTHERS?
I'M AN *IMMORTAL.* AND YOU'RE MY *GRAND-DAUGHTER.*
WE MIGHT ACTUALLY *LIVE.*

NO GUARANTEES. BUT IT'S A CHANCE.

WHAT DO YOU SAY?

IF WE GO SOUTH, ALONG THE COASTLINE, IT'LL BE EASIER TO MAKE IT THROUGH THE WINTER.

WE CAN START OVER. SOMEWHERE SAFE.

WE... ...WE PROMISED, GRANDPA.

YEAH.

WE DID.

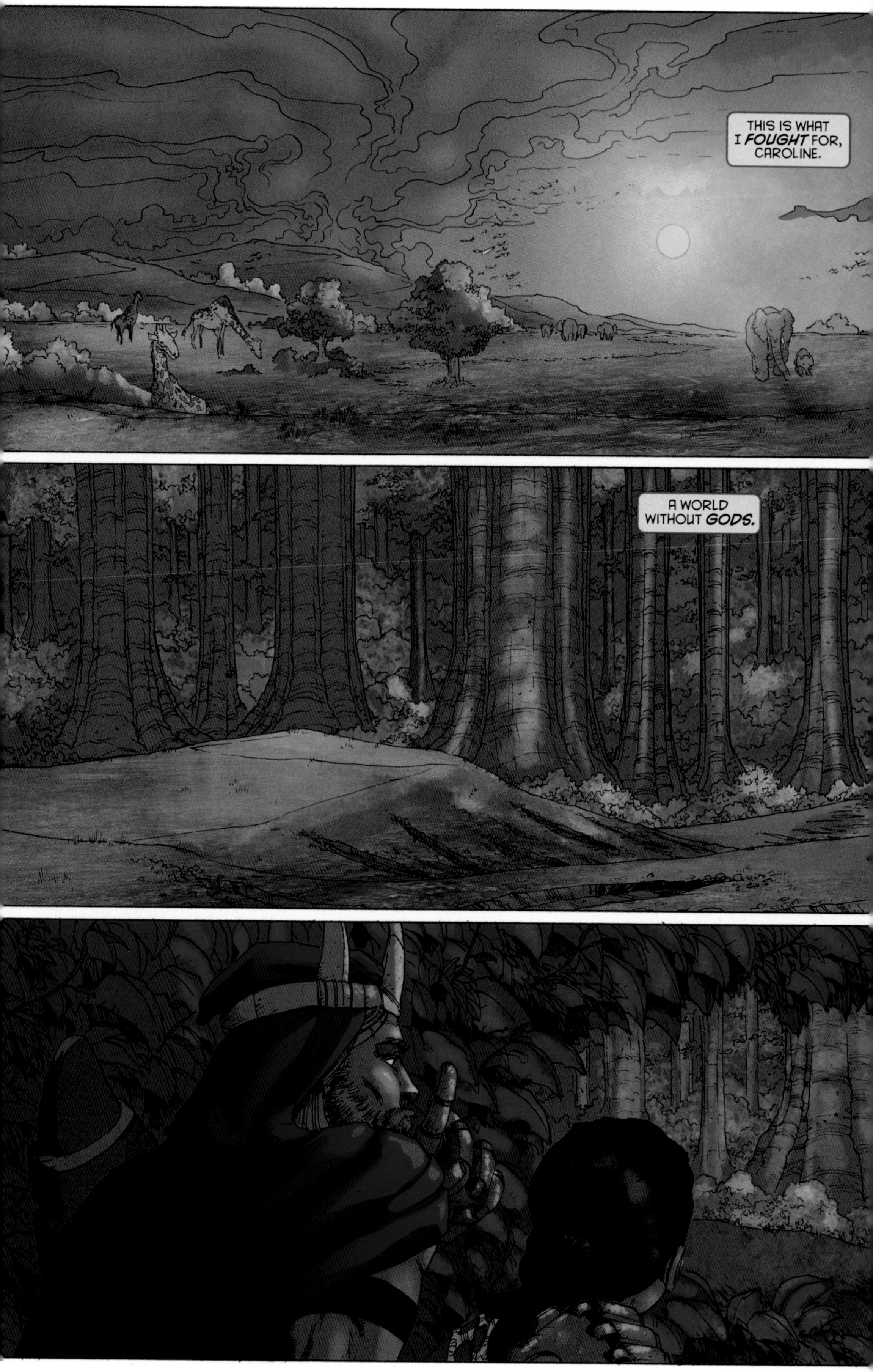
THIS IS WHAT I *FOUGHT* FOR, CAROLINE.
A WORLD WITHOUT *GODS*.

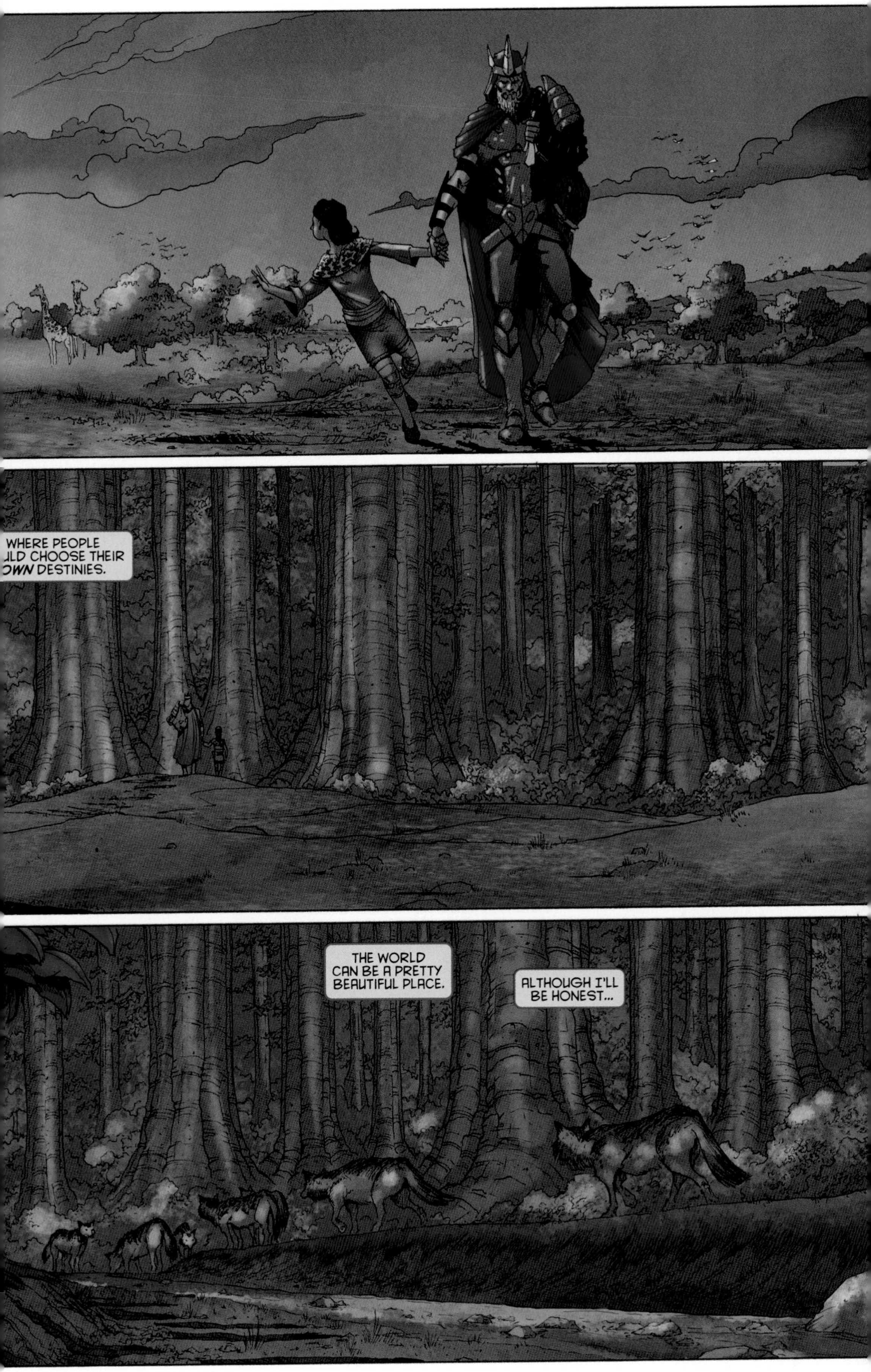
WHERE PEOPLE LD CHOOSE THEIR OWN DESTINIES.
THE WORLD CAN BE A PRETTY BEAUTIFUL PLACE.
ALTHOUGH I'LL BE HONEST...

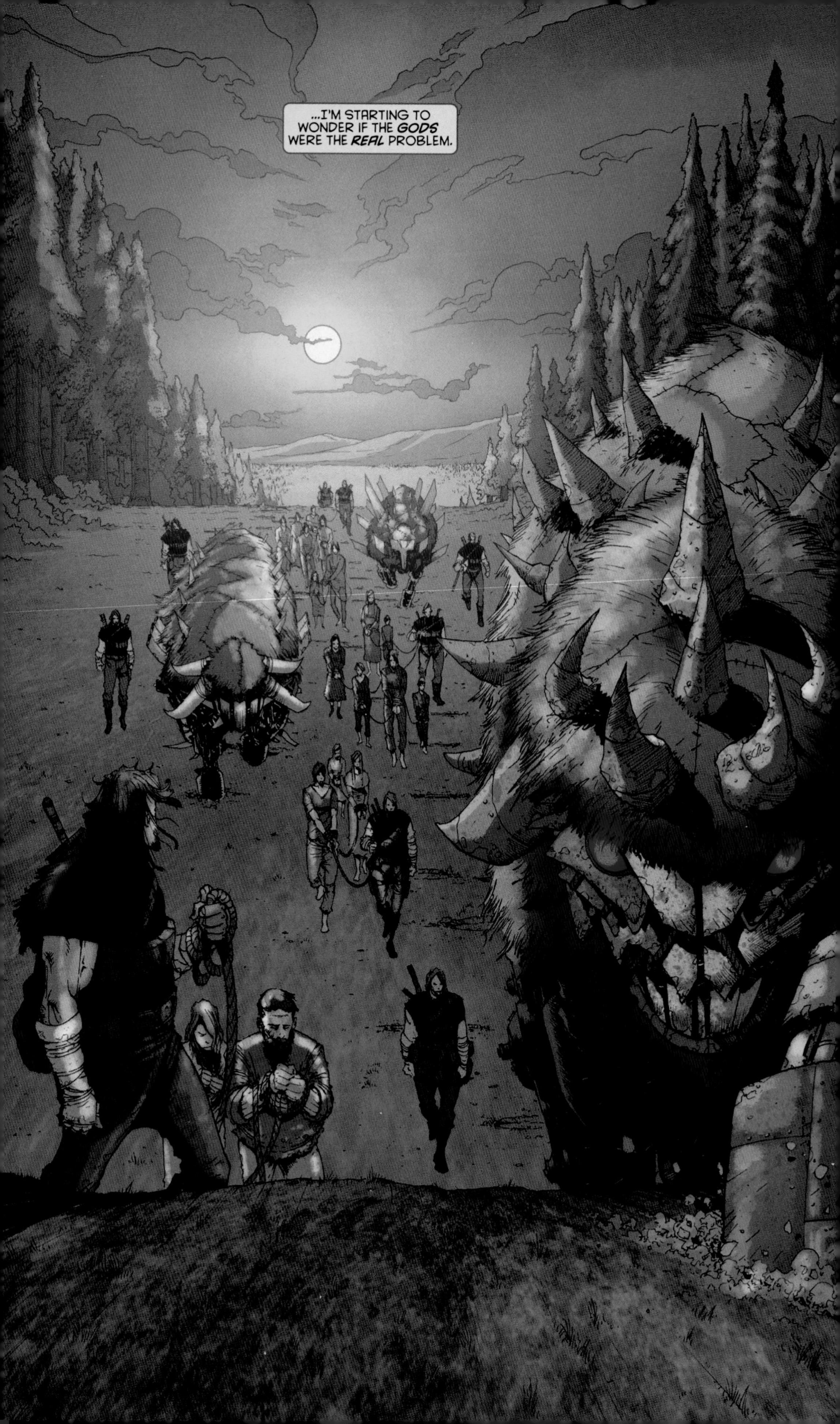
...I'M STARTING TO WONDER IF THE GODS WERE THE REAL PROBLEM.

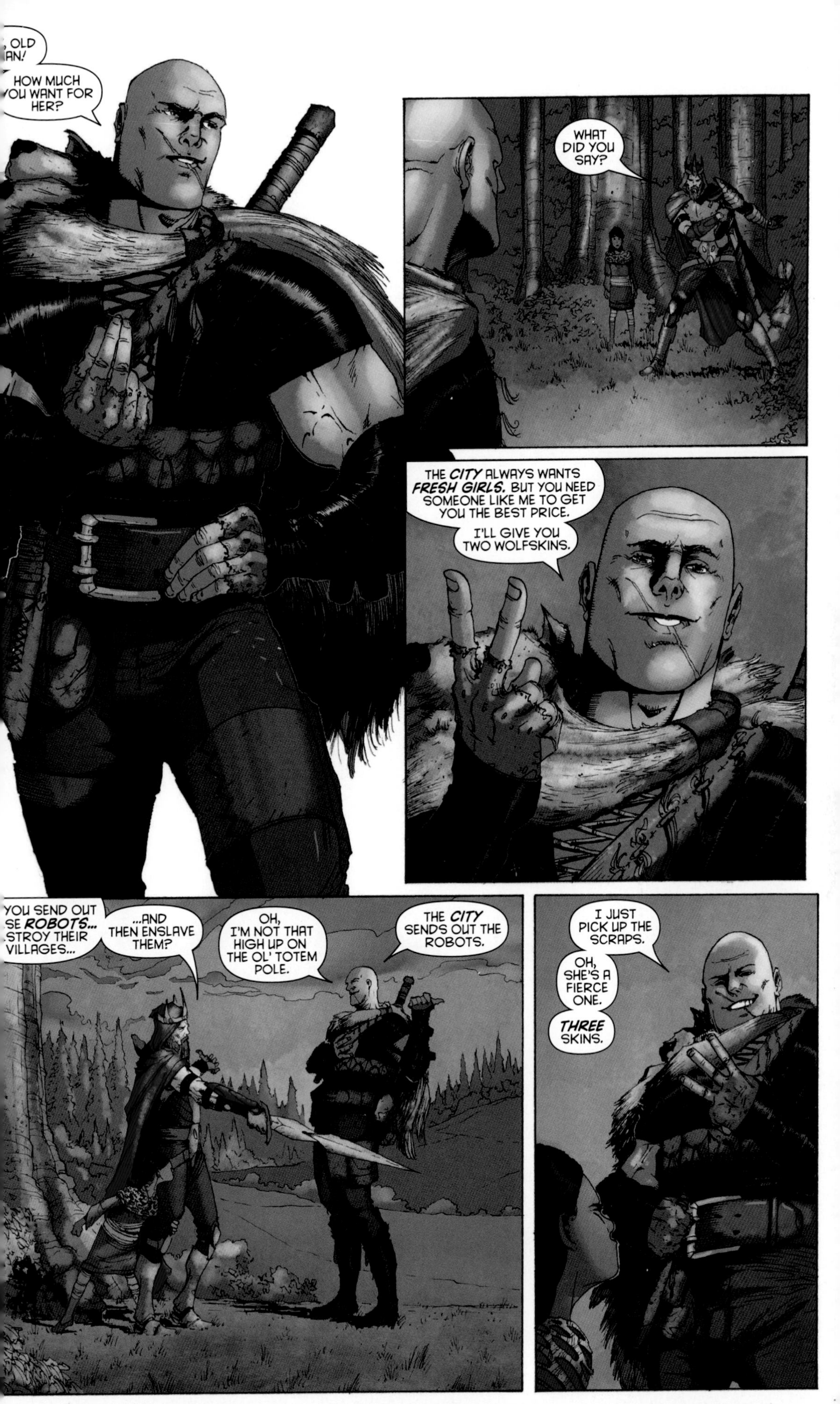
, OLD
AN!
HOW MUCH
YOU WANT FOR
HER?
WHAT
DID YOU
SAY?
THE *CITY* ALWAYS WANTS
FRESH GIRLS. BUT YOU NEED
SOMEONE LIKE ME TO GET
YOU THE BEST PRICE.
I'LL GIVE YOU
TWO WOLFSKINS.
YOU SEND OUT
SE ***ROBOTS...***
STROY THEIR
VILLAGES...
...AND
THEN ENSLAVE
THEM?
OH,
I'M NOT THAT
HIGH UP ON
THE OL' TOTEM
POLE.
THE *CITY*
SENDS OUT THE
ROBOTS.
I JUST
PICK UP THE
SCRAPS.
OH,
SHE'S A
FIERCE
ONE.
THREE
SKINS.

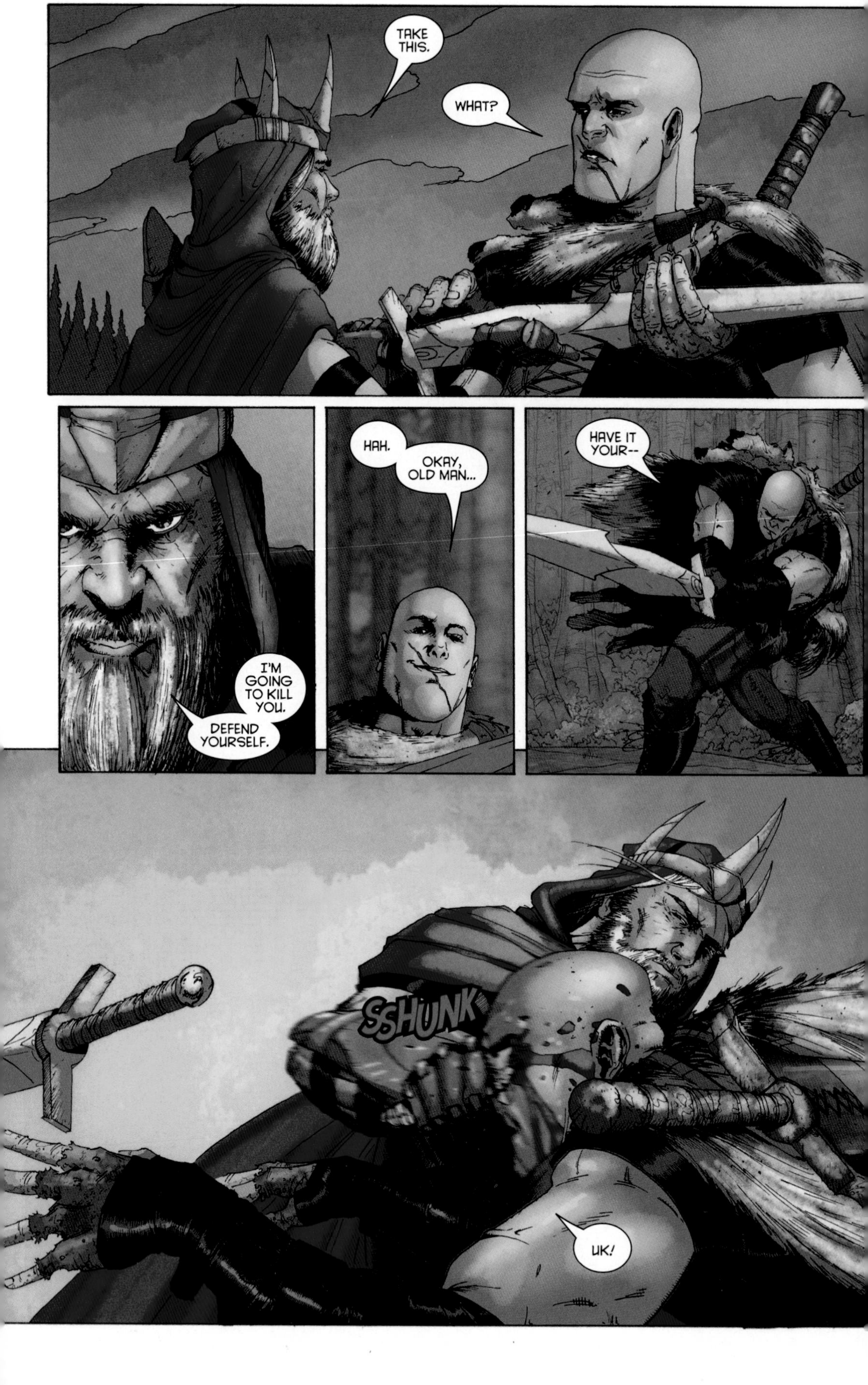
TAKE THIS.
WHAT?
I'M GOING TO KILL YOU.
DEFEND YOURSELF.
HAH.
OKAY, OLD MAN...
HAVE IT YOUR--
SSHUNK
UK!

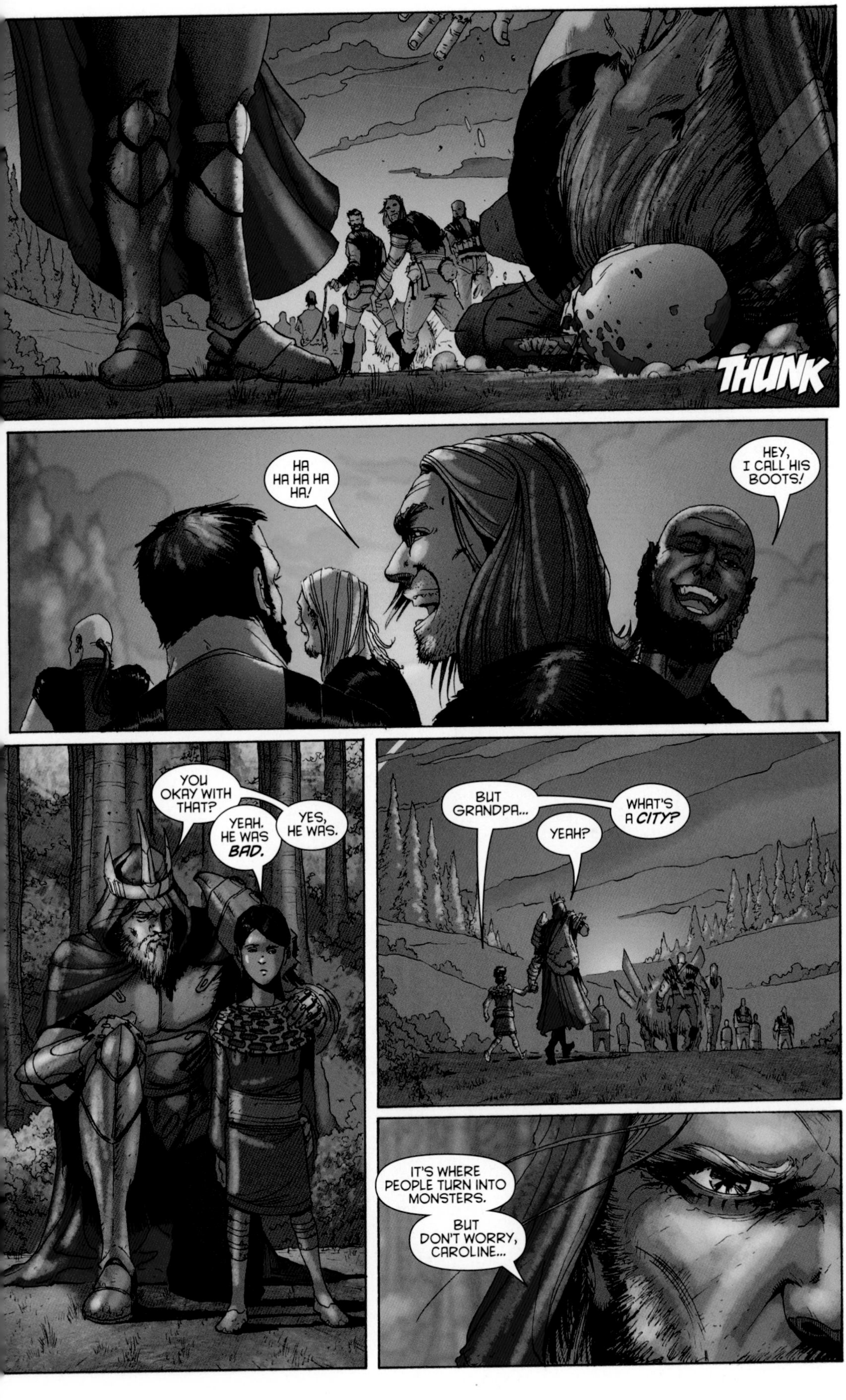
THUNK
HA HA HA HA HA!
HEY, I CALL HIS BOOTS!
YOU OKAY WITH THAT?
YEAH. HE WAS BAD.
YES, HE WAS.
BUT GRANDPA...
YEAH?
WHAT'S A CITY?
IT'S WHERE PEOPLE TURN INTO MONSTERS.
BUT DON'T WORRY, CAROLINE...

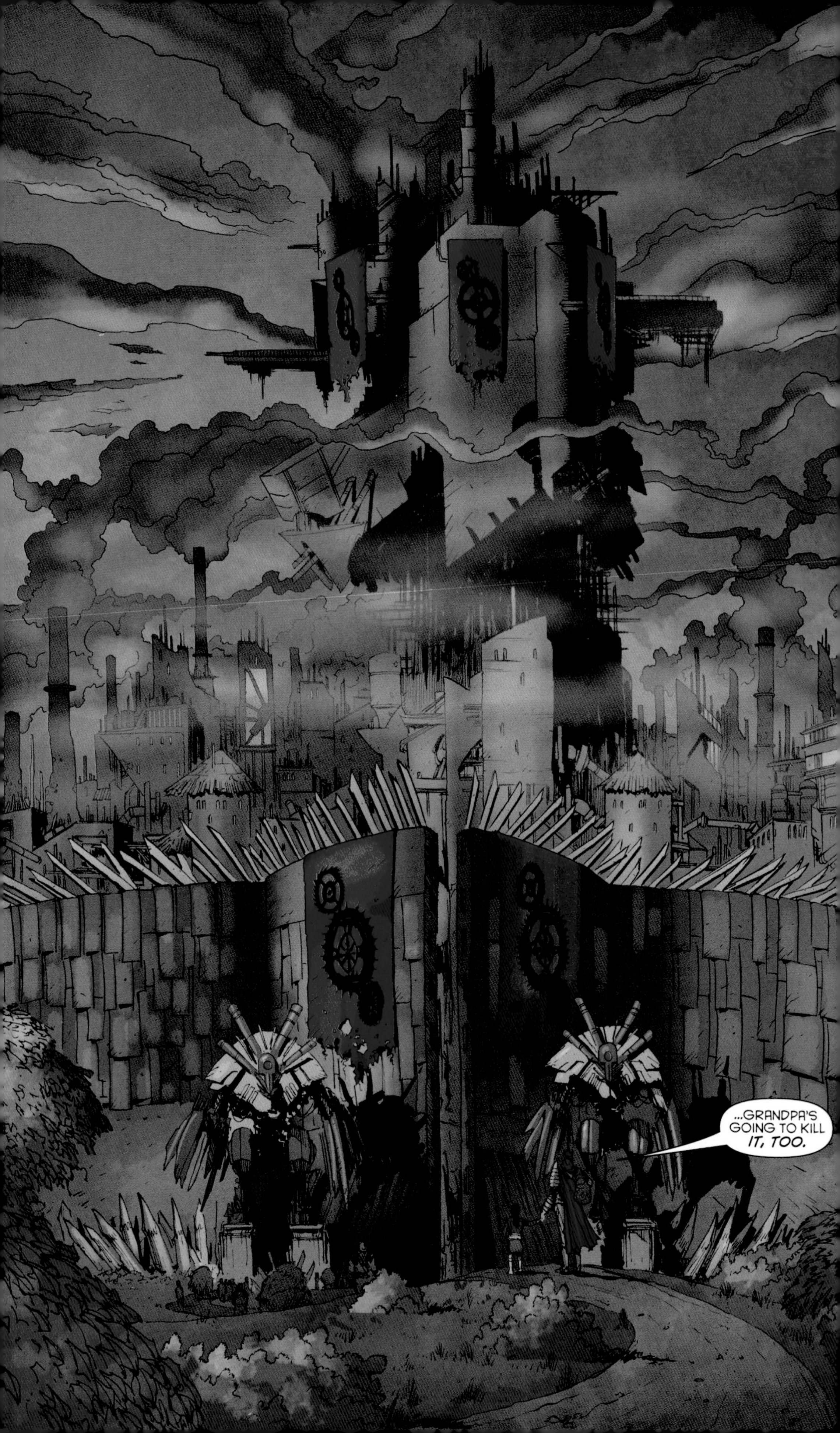
...GRANDPA'S GOING TO KILL *IT, TOO.*

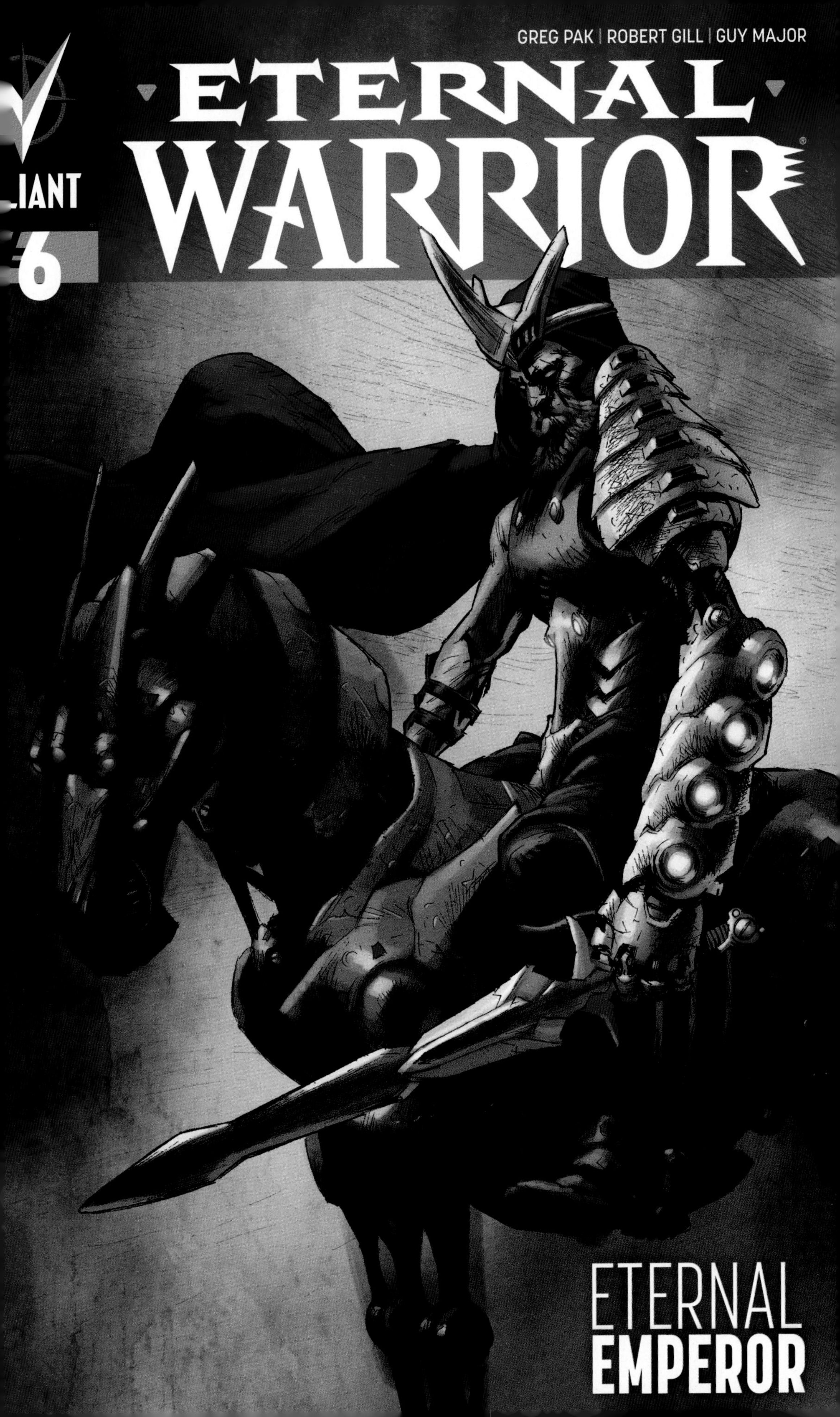
GREG PAK | ROBERT GILL | GUY MAJOR
ETERNAL WARRIOR
6
ETERNAL EMPEROR

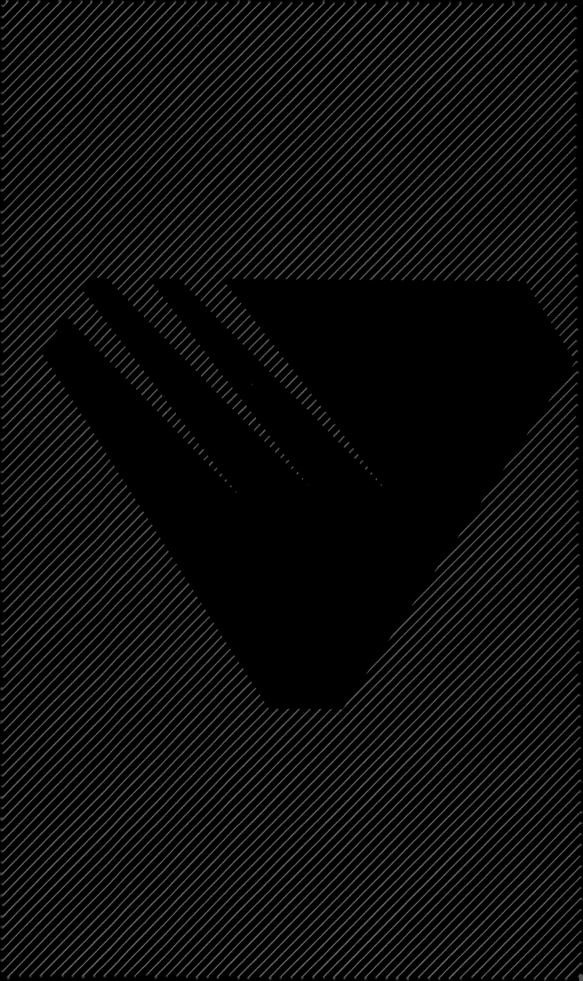

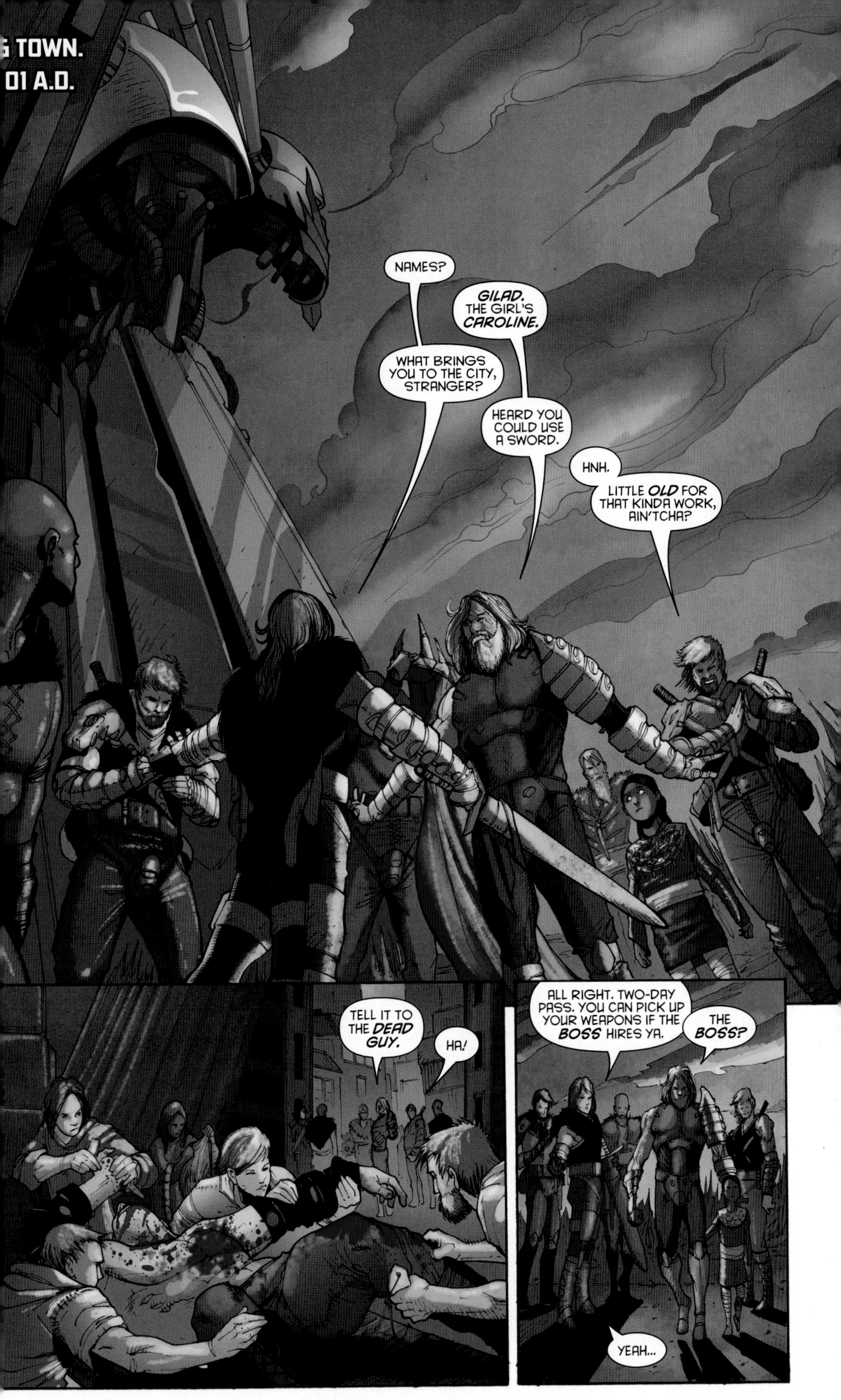

G TOWN.
01 A.D.
NAMES?
GILAD. THE GIRL'S CAROLINE.
WHAT BRINGS YOU TO THE CITY, STRANGER?
HEARD YOU COULD USE A SWORD.
HNH.
LITTLE OLD FOR THAT KINDA WORK, AIN'TCHA?
TELL IT TO THE DEAD GUY.
HA!
ALL RIGHT. TWO-DAY PASS. YOU CAN PICK UP YOUR WEAPONS IF THE BOSS HIRES YA.
THE BOSS?
YEAH...

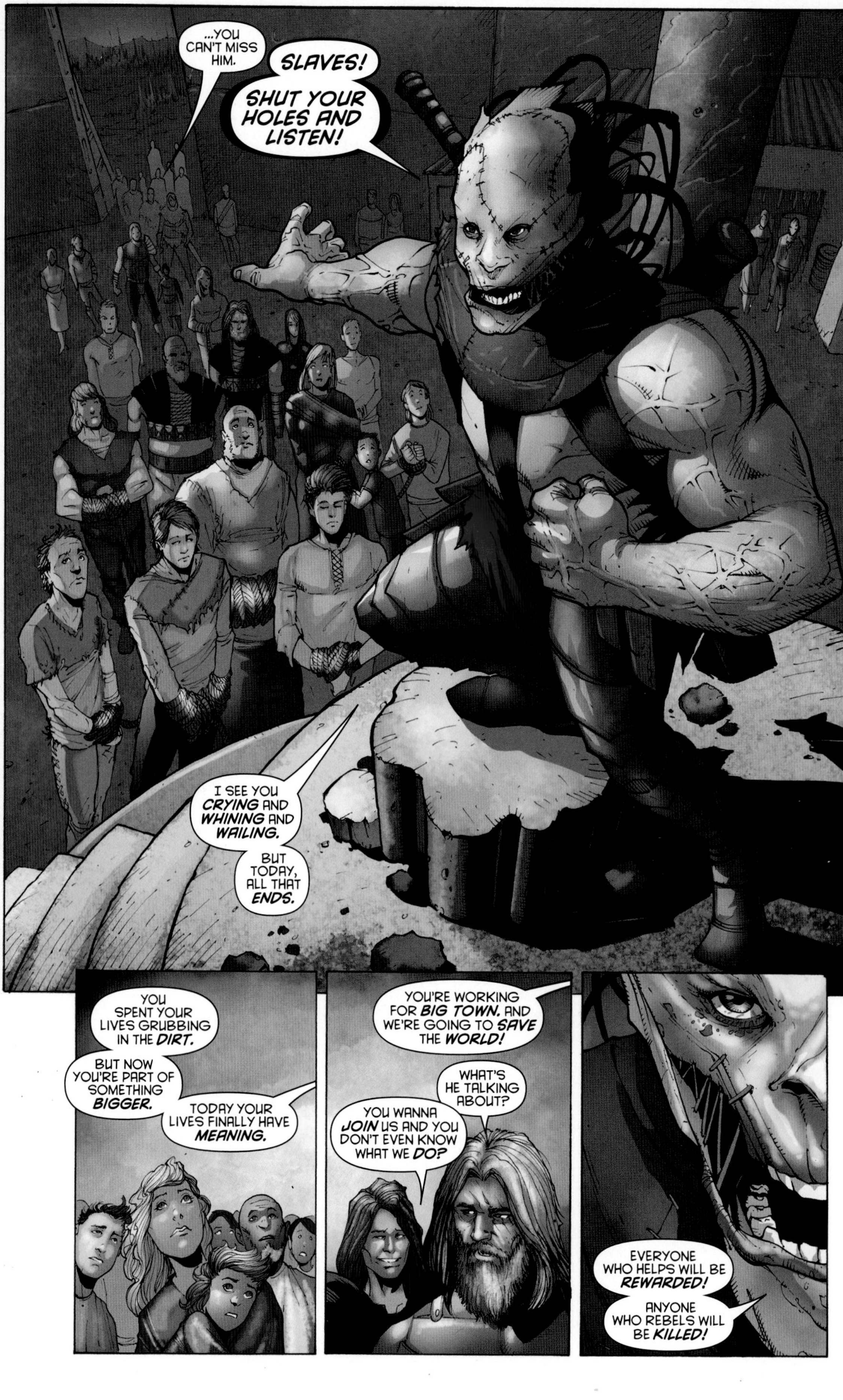
...YOU CAN'T MISS HIM.
SLAVES!
SHUT YOUR HOLES AND LISTEN!
I SEE YOU CRYING AND WHINING AND WAILING.
BUT TODAY, ALL THAT ENDS.
YOU SPENT YOUR LIVES GRUBBING IN THE DIRT.
BUT NOW YOU'RE PART OF SOMETHING BIGGER.
TODAY YOUR LIVES FINALLY HAVE MEANING.
YOU'RE WORKING FOR BIG TOWN. AND WE'RE GOING TO SAVE THE WORLD!
WHAT'S HE TALKING ABOUT?
YOU WANNA JOIN US AND YOU DON'T EVEN KNOW WHAT WE DO?
EVERYONE WHO HELPS WILL BE REWARDED!
ANYONE WHO REBELS WILL BE KILLED!

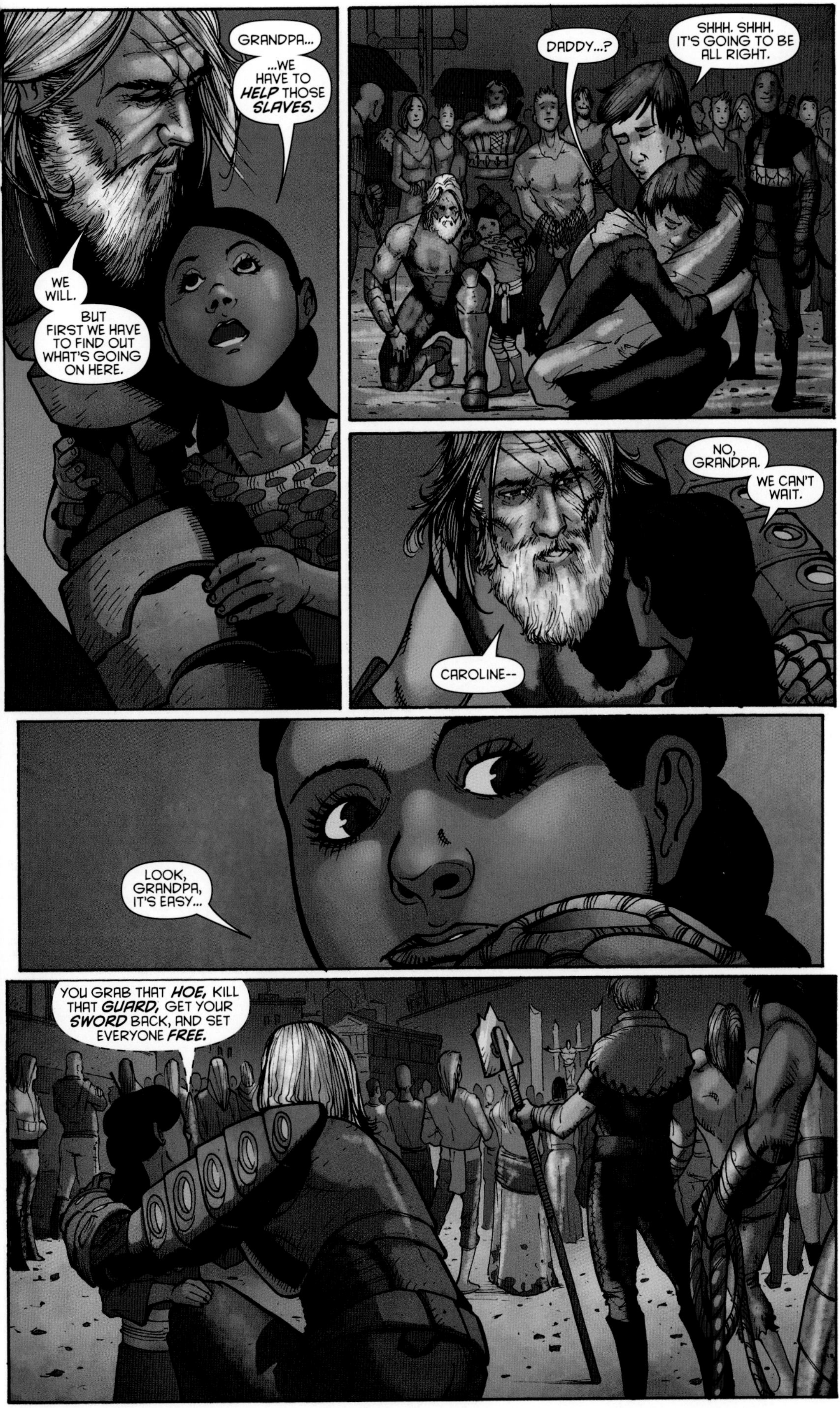
GRANDPA...
...WE HAVE TO HELP THOSE SLAVES.
WE WILL.
BUT FIRST WE HAVE TO FIND OUT WHAT'S GOING ON HERE.
DADDY...?
SHHH. SHHH. IT'S GOING TO BE ALL RIGHT.
NO, GRANDPA.
WE CAN'T WAIT.
CAROLINE--
LOOK, GRANDPA, IT'S EASY...
YOU GRAB THAT HOE, KILL THAT GUARD, GET YOUR SWORD BACK, AND SET EVERYONE FREE.

EASY, HUH?

YEAH.

YOU'RE FORGETTING ABOUT THE *ROBOTS.*

IF I DO ANYTHING, THEY'LL *ATTACK.*

AND IF THEY CUT LOOSE WITH THOSE BLADES, HOW MANY OF THESE *SLAVES* DO YOU THINK WILL *DIE?*

BUT IF WE WAIT...WHO KNOWS WHAT'LL HAPPEN?

TOUGH ONE, ISN'T IT?

I PLAYED THIS KIND OF GAME FOR *CENTURIES.* AND I STILL DON'T KNOW THE RIGHT ANSWER.

SO... WHATEVER YOU SAY, CAROLINE.

ALL RIGHT! INTO THE PITS!

DADDY!

HUSH, NOW, RUSSELL. IT'S GONNA BE OKAY...

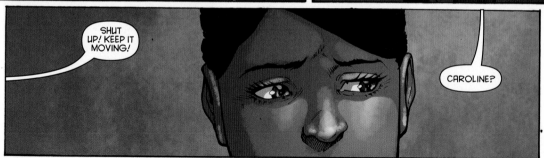

SHUT UP! KEEP IT MOVING!

CAROLINE?

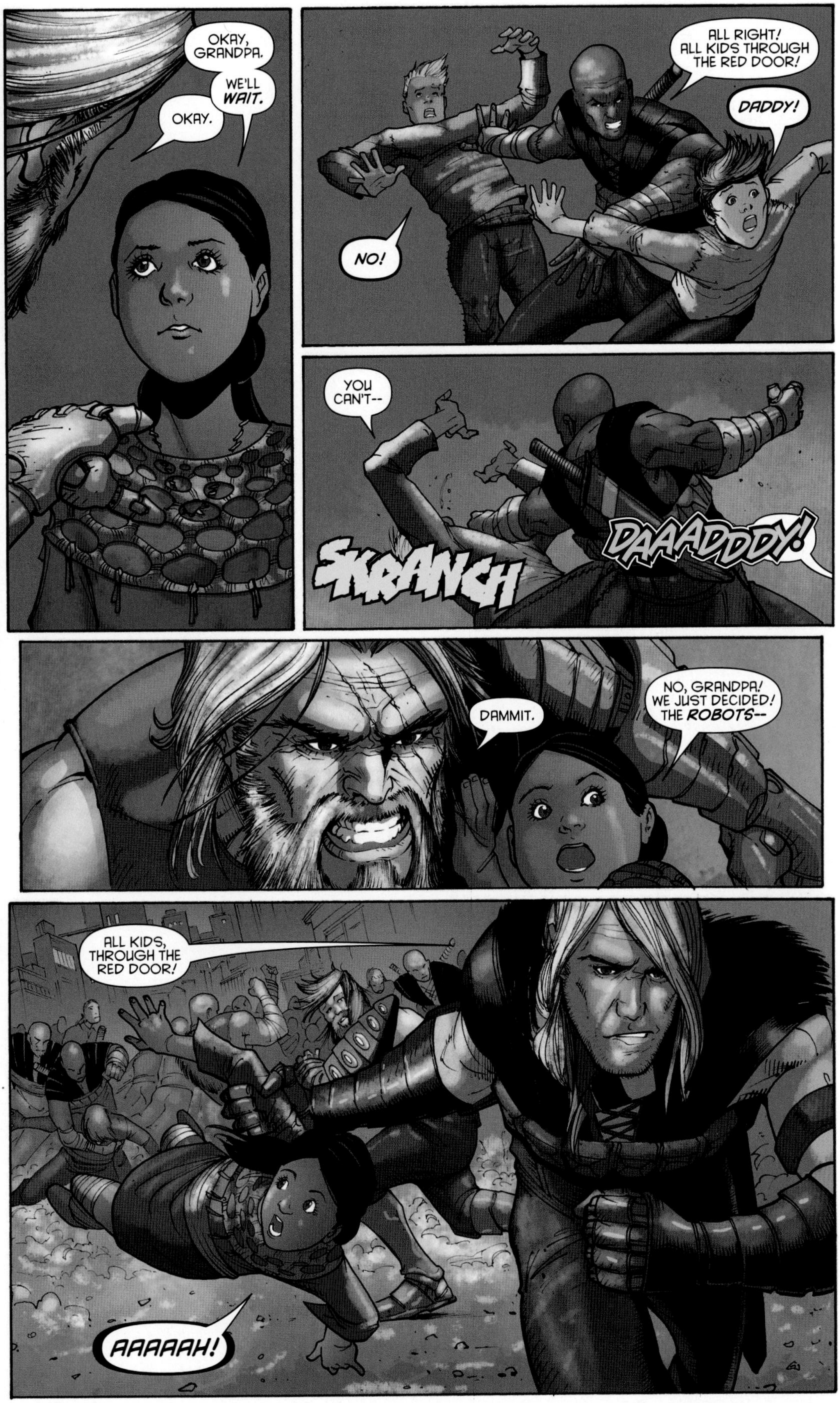
OKAY, GRANDPA.
WE'LL *WAIT.*
OKAY.
ALL RIGHT! ALL KIDS THROUGH THE RED DOOR!
DADDY!
NO!
YOU CAN'T--
SKRANCH
DAAADDDY!
DAMMIT.
NO, GRANDPA! WE JUST DECIDED! THE *ROBOTS*--
ALL KIDS, THROUGH THE RED DOOR!
AAAAAH!

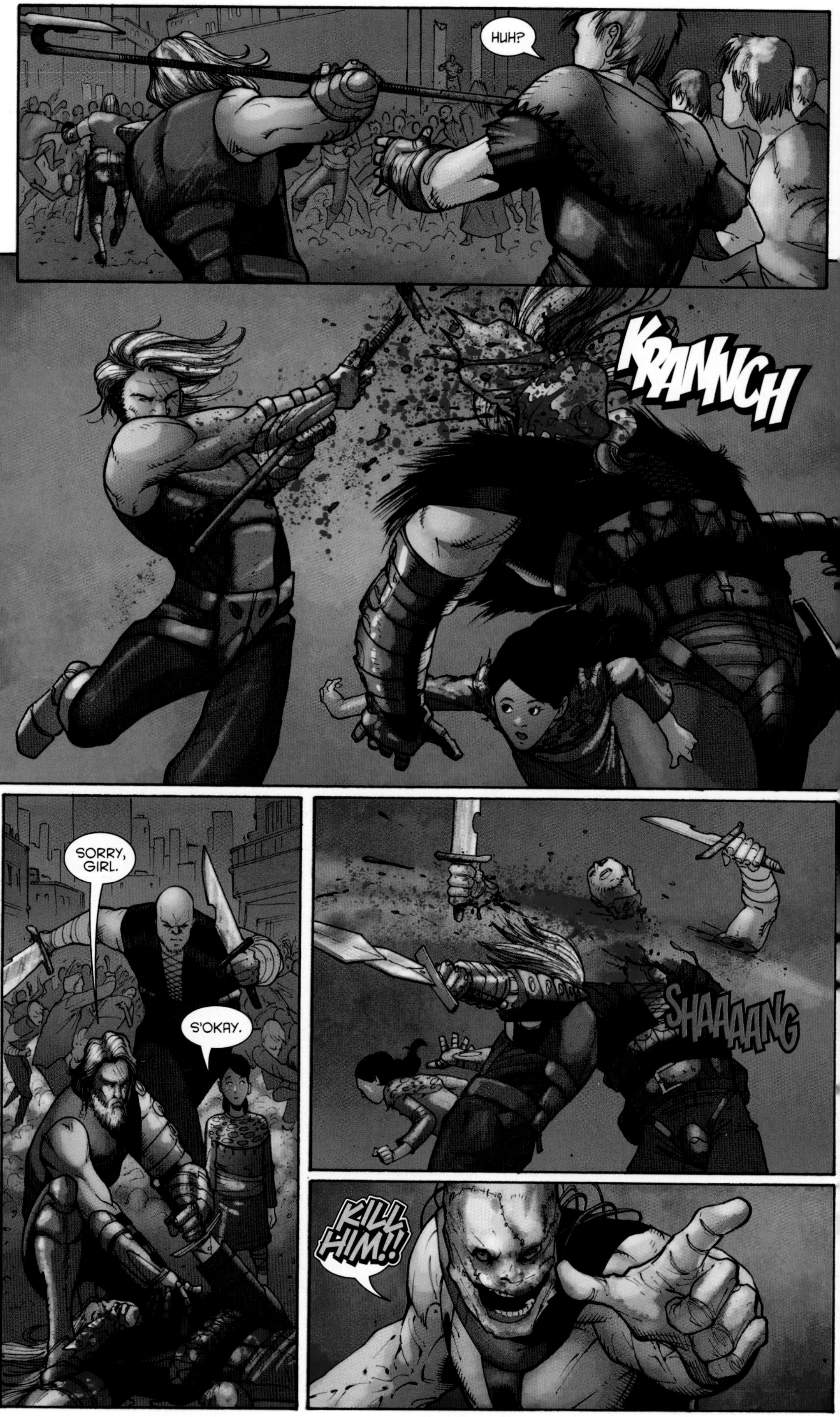
HUH?
KRANNCH
SORRY, GIRL.
S'OKAY.
SHAAAANG
KILL HIM!!

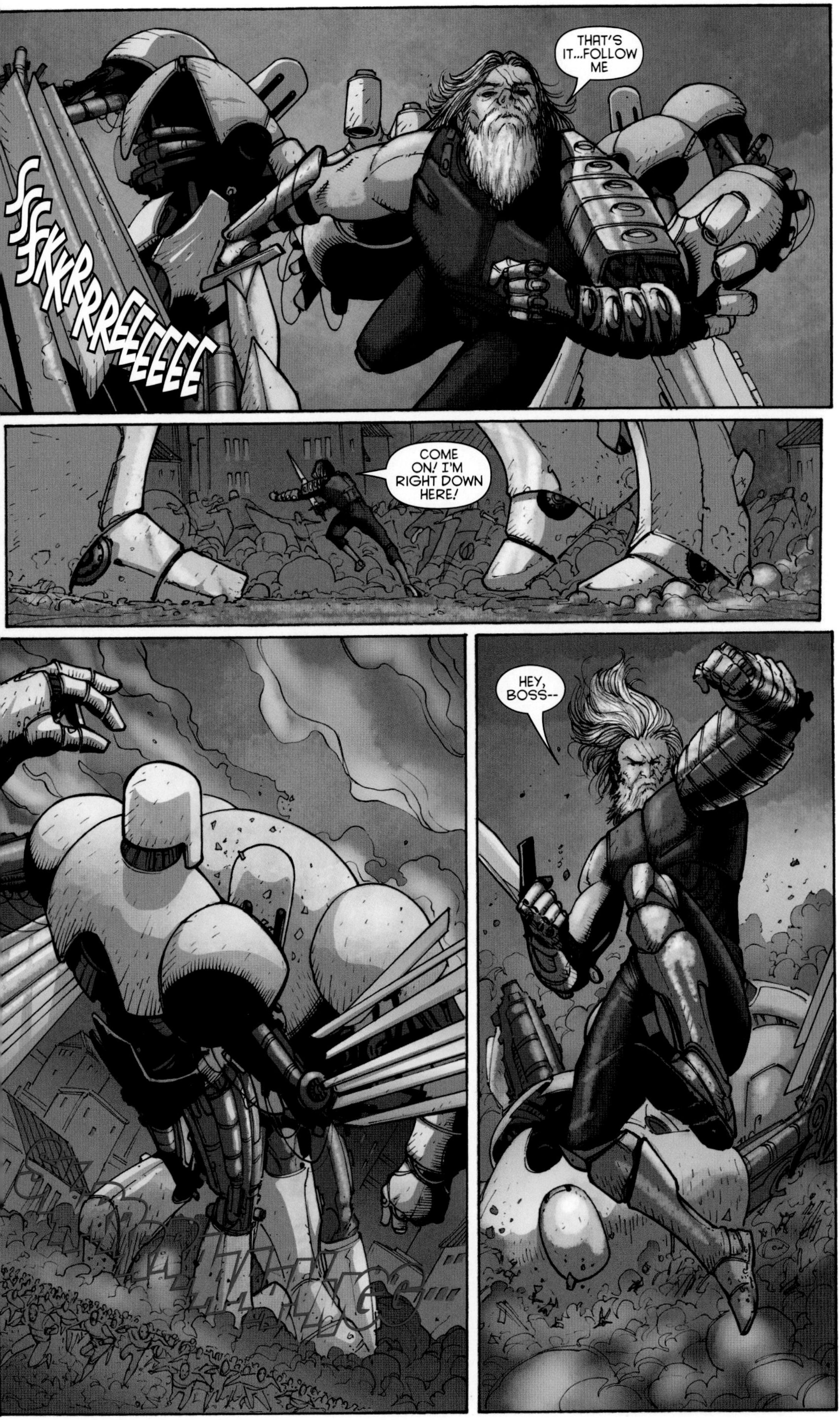
THAT'S IT...FOLLOW ME
SSSKKRRREEEEEEE
COME ON! I'M RIGHT DOWN HERE!
HEY, BOSS--

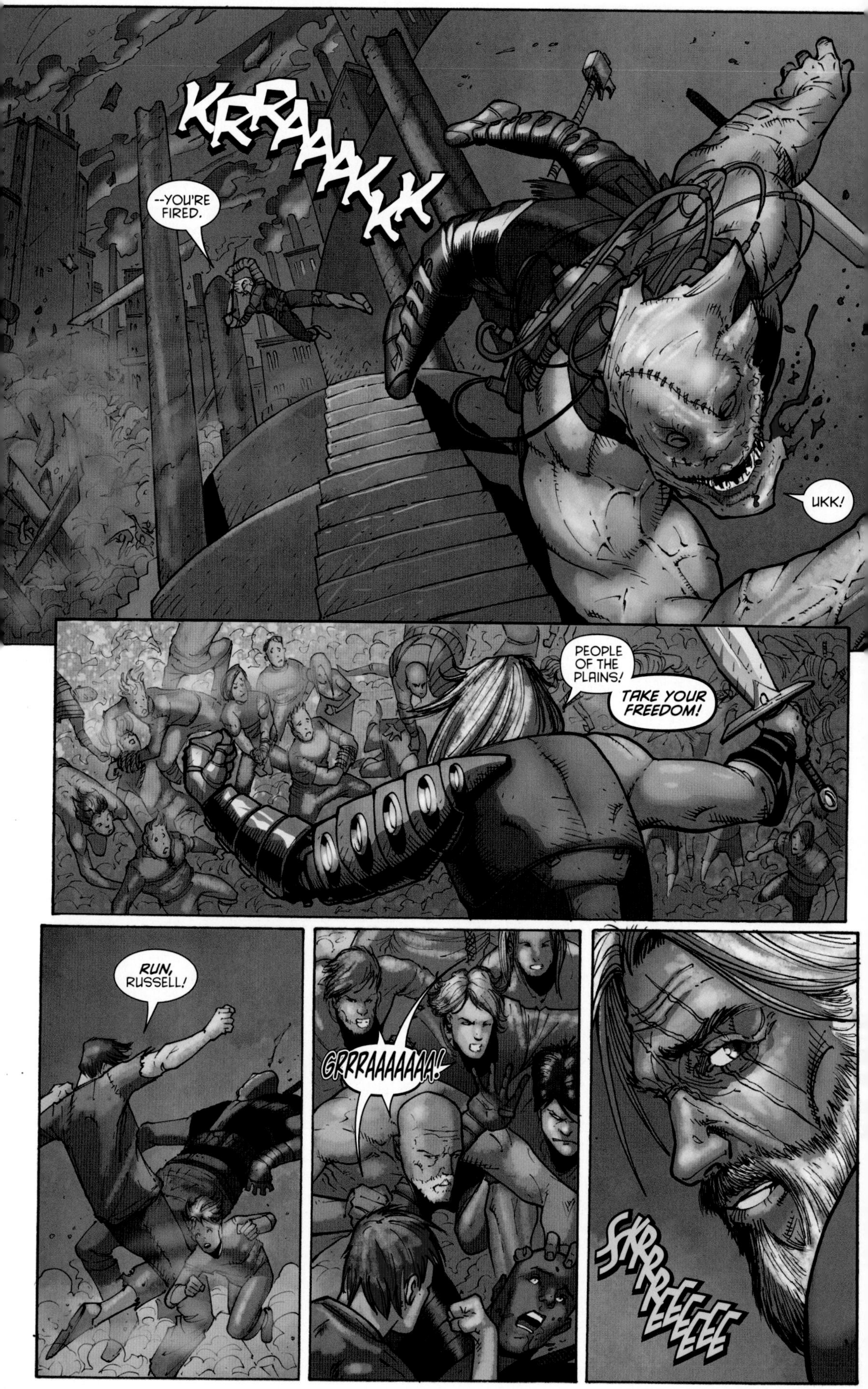

KRRAAAKKK
--YOU'RE FIRED.
UKK!
PEOPLE OF THE PLAINS!
TAKE YOUR FREEDOM!
RUN, RUSSELL!
GRRRAAAAAAA!
SKRREEEEEE

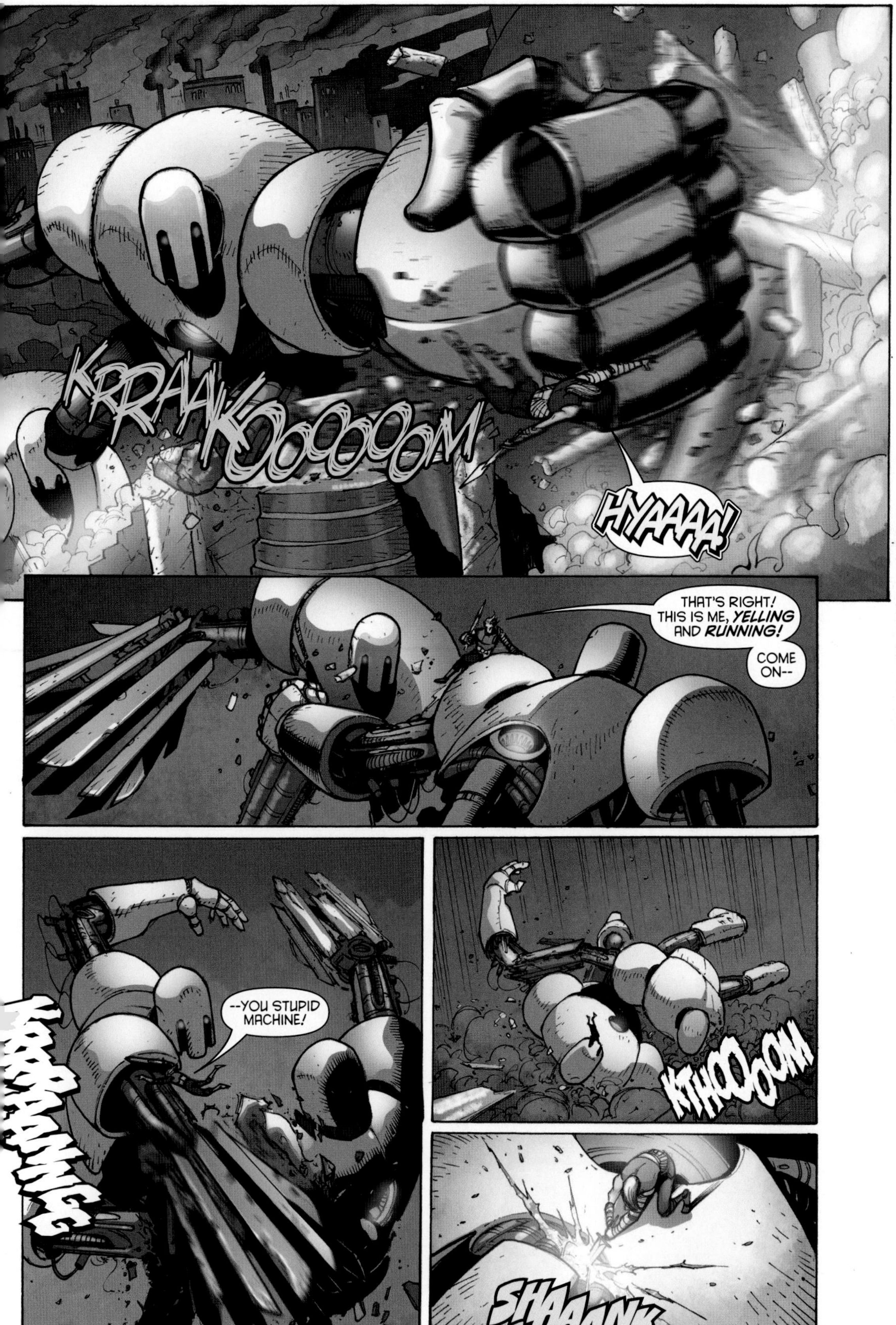
KRRAAKOOOOOOOM
HYAAAA!
THAT'S RIGHT! THIS IS ME, *YELLING* AND *RUNNING!*
COME ON--
--YOU STUPID MACHINE!
KRRRANNG
KTHOOOOOM
SHAAAANK

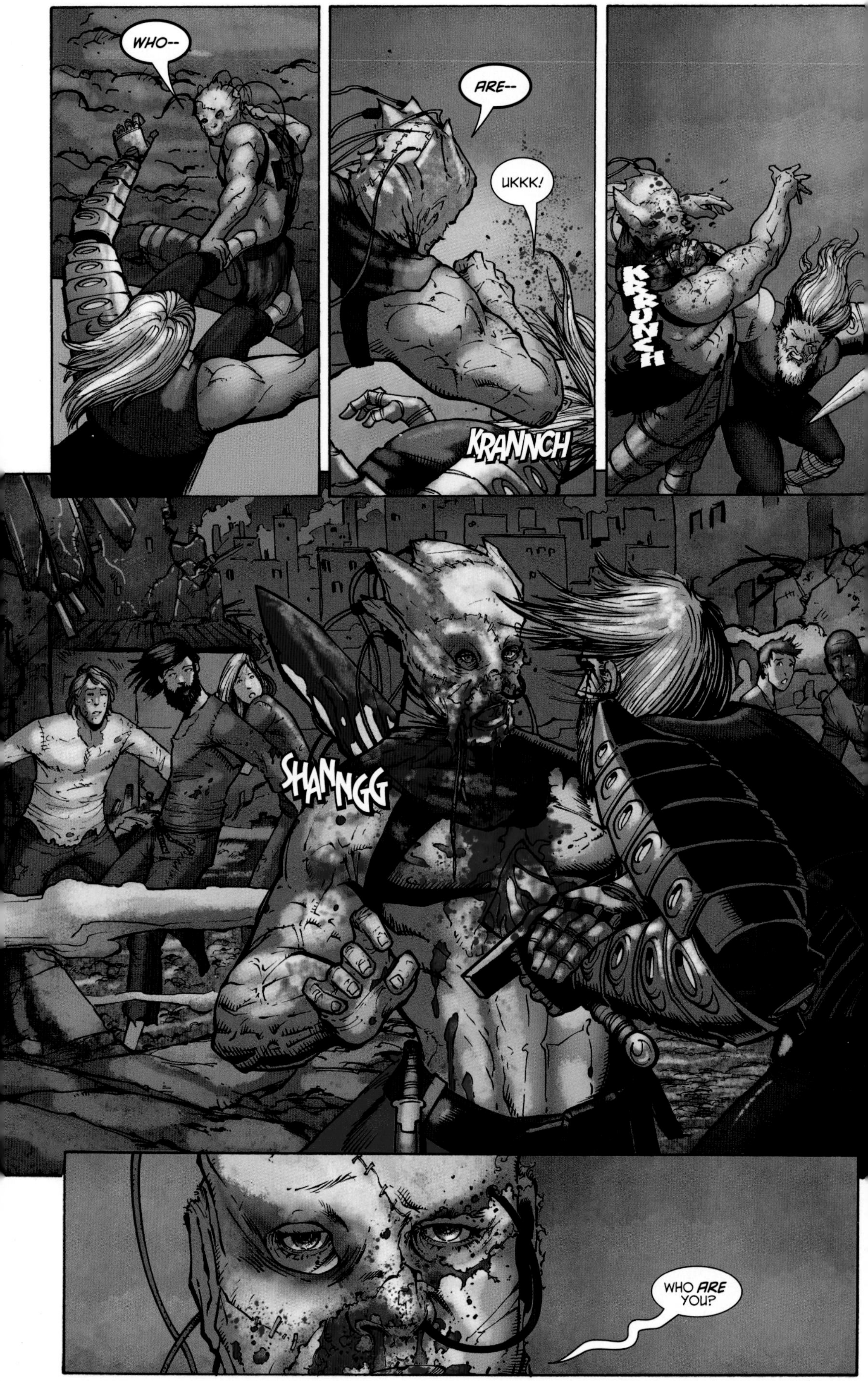
WHO--
ARE--
UKKK!
KRANNCH
KRRUNCH
SHANNGG
WHO ARE YOU?

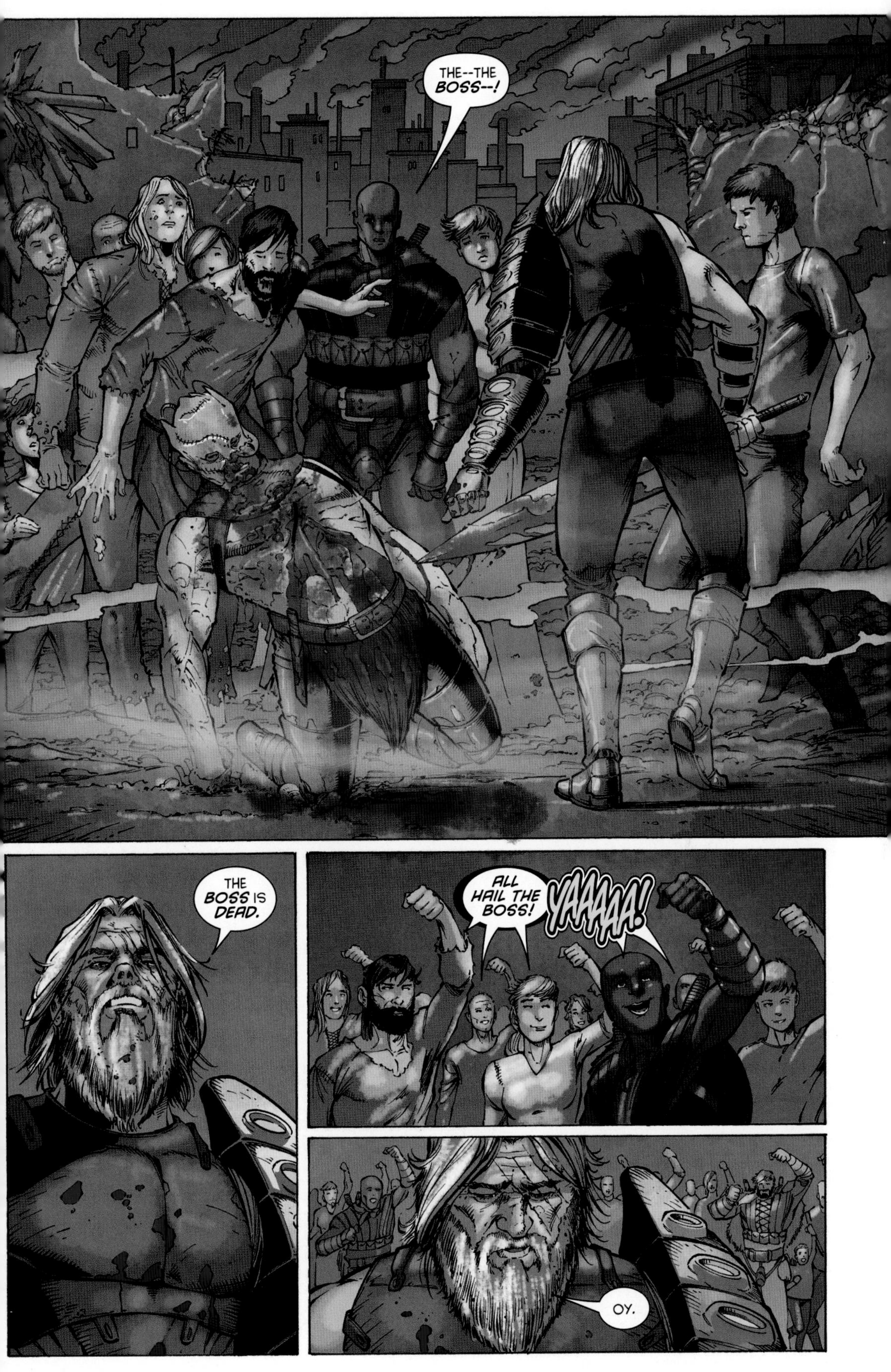
THE--THE BOSS--!
THE BOSS IS DEAD.
ALL HAIL THE BOSS!
YAAAAA!
OY.

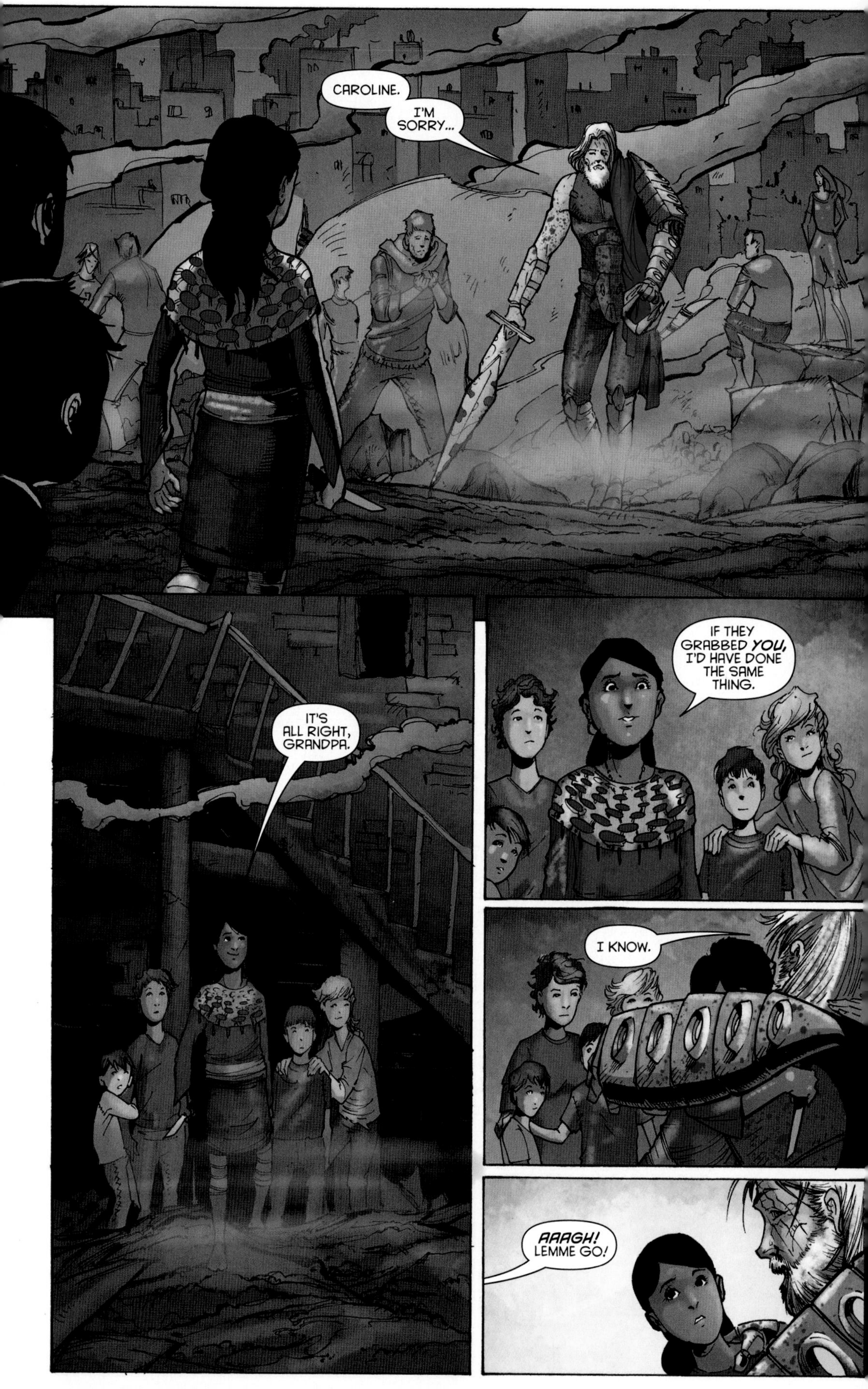
CAROLINE.
I'M SORRY...
IT'S ALL RIGHT, GRANDPA.
IF THEY GRABBED *YOU,* I'D HAVE DONE THE SAME THING.
I KNOW.
AAAGH! LEMME GO!

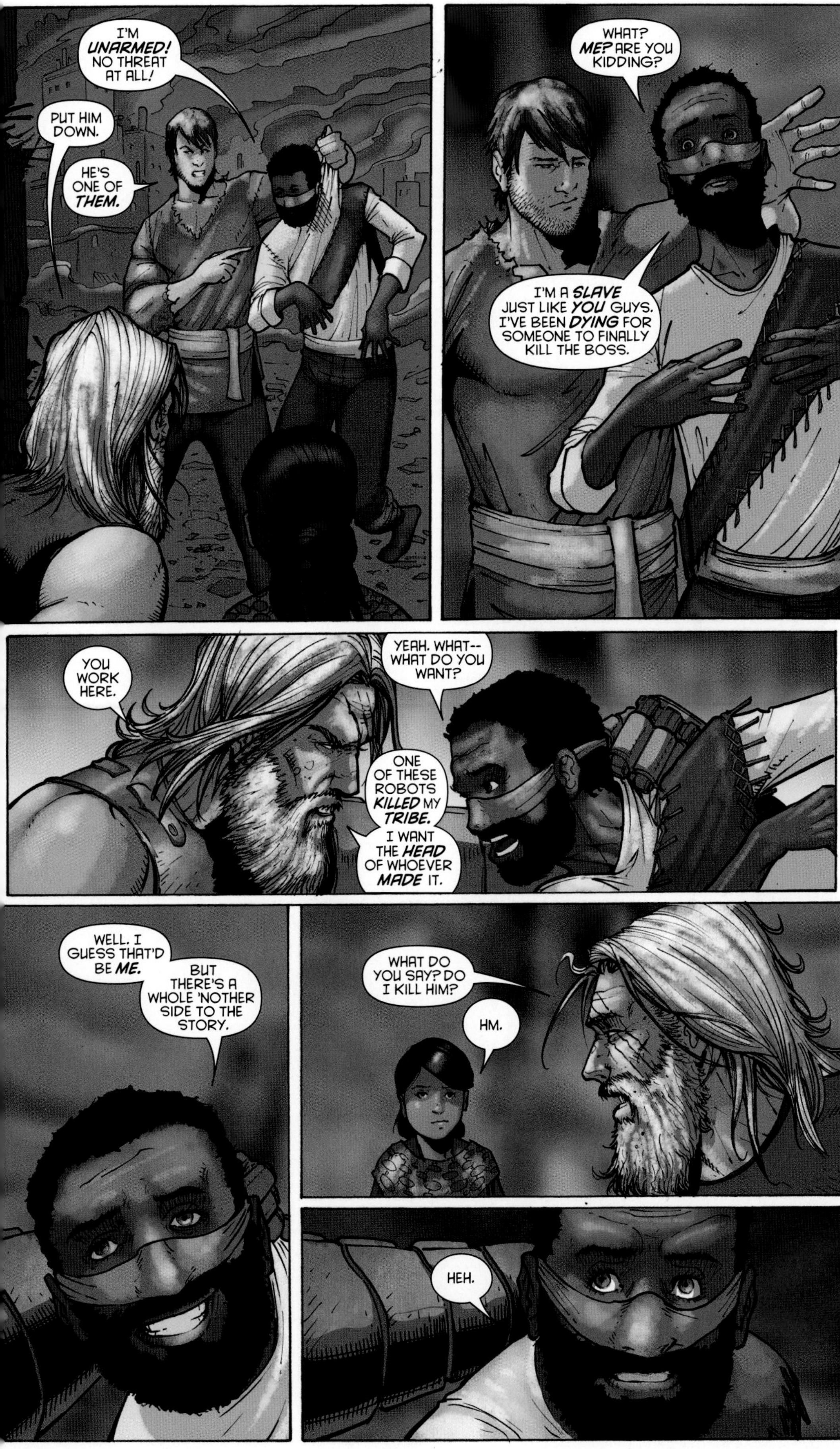
I'M UNARMED! NO THREAT AT ALL!
PUT HIM DOWN.
HE'S ONE OF THEM.
WHAT? ME? ARE YOU KIDDING?
I'M A SLAVE JUST LIKE YOU GUYS. I'VE BEEN DYING FOR SOMEONE TO FINALLY KILL THE BOSS.
YOU WORK HERE.
YEAH. WHAT-- WHAT DO YOU WANT?
ONE OF THESE ROBOTS KILLED MY TRIBE.
I WANT THE HEAD OF WHOEVER MADE IT.
WELL. I GUESS THAT'D BE ME.
BUT THERE'S A WHOLE 'NOTHER SIDE TO THE STORY.
WHAT DO YOU SAY? DO I KILL HIM?
HM.
HEH.

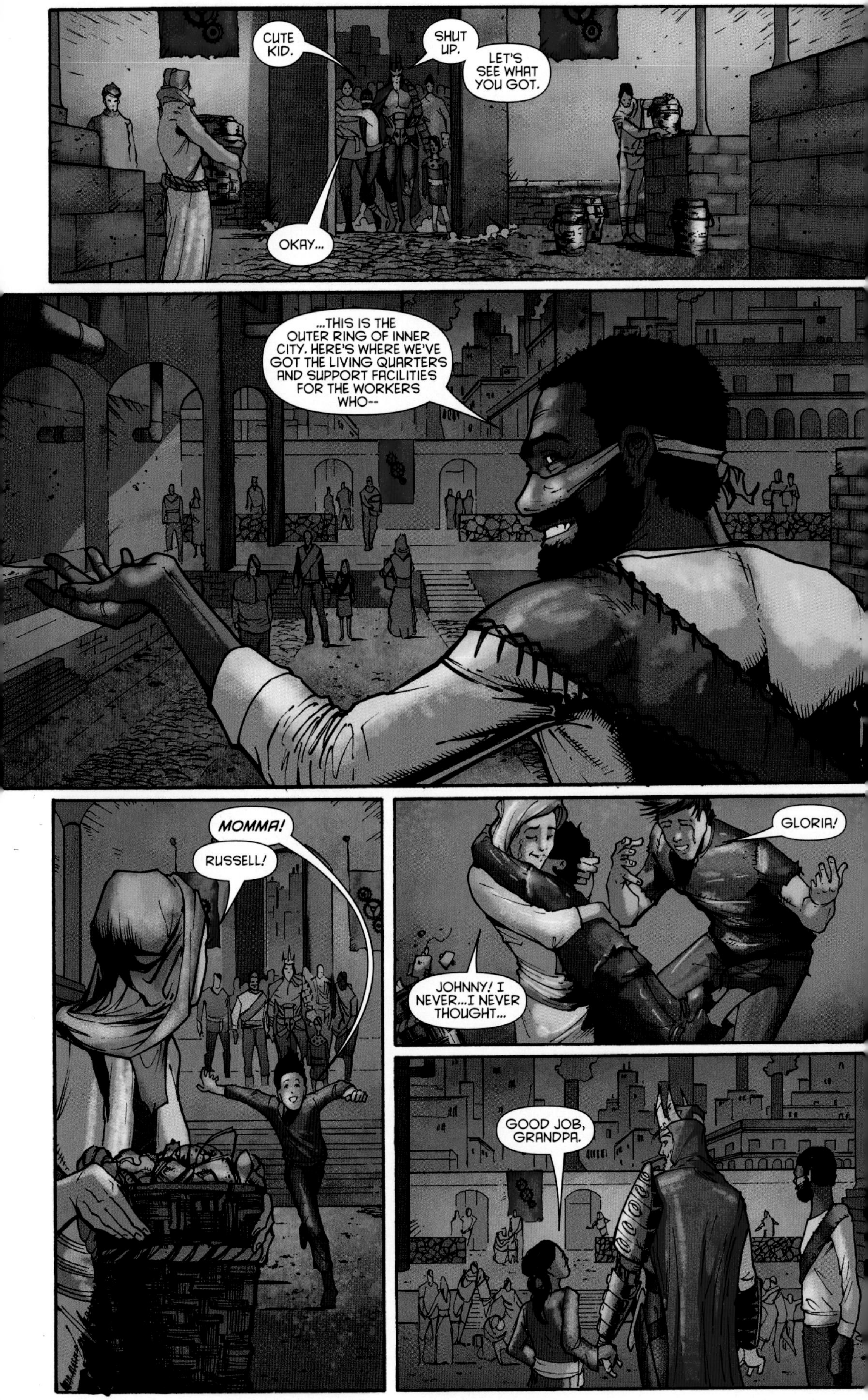
CUTE KID.
SHUT UP.
LET'S SEE WHAT YOU GOT.
OKAY...
...THIS IS THE OUTER RING OF INNER CITY. HERE'S WHERE WE'VE GOT THE LIVING QUARTERS AND SUPPORT FACILITIES FOR THE WORKERS WHO--
MOMMA!
RUSSELL!
GLORIA!
JOHNNY! I NEVER...I NEVER THOUGHT...
GOOD JOB, GRANDPA.

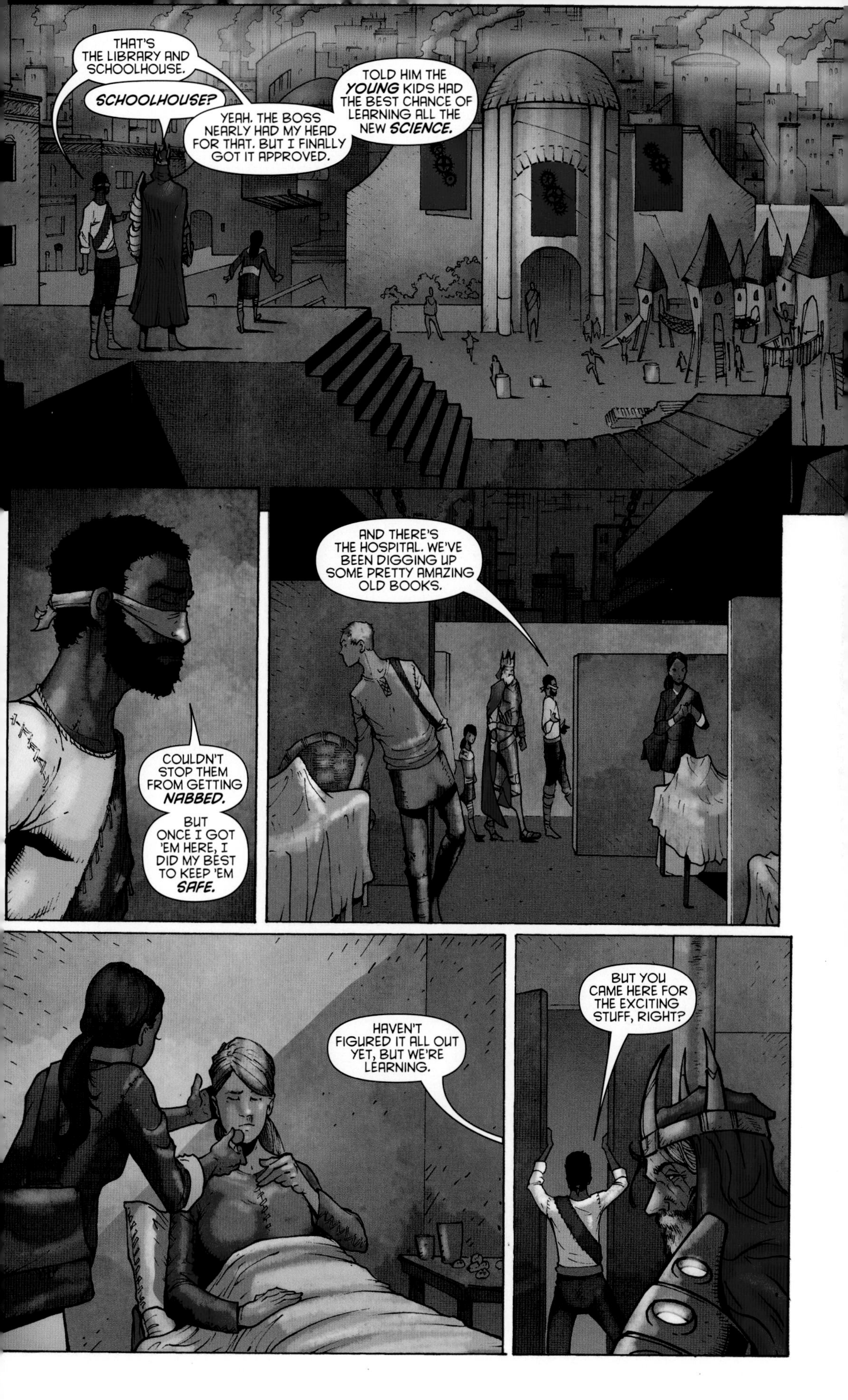
THAT'S THE LIBRARY AND SCHOOLHOUSE.
SCHOOLHOUSE?
YEAH. THE BOSS NEARLY HAD MY HEAD FOR THAT. BUT I FINALLY GOT IT APPROVED.
TOLD HIM THE YOUNG KIDS HAD THE BEST CHANCE OF LEARNING ALL THE NEW SCIENCE.
COULDN'T STOP THEM FROM GETTING NABBED.
BUT ONCE I GOT 'EM HERE, I DID MY BEST TO KEEP 'EM SAFE.
AND THERE'S THE HOSPITAL. WE'VE BEEN DIGGING UP SOME PRETTY AMAZING OLD BOOKS.
HAVEN'T FIGURED IT ALL OUT YET, BUT WE'RE LEARNING.
BUT YOU CAME HERE FOR THE EXCITING STUFF, RIGHT?

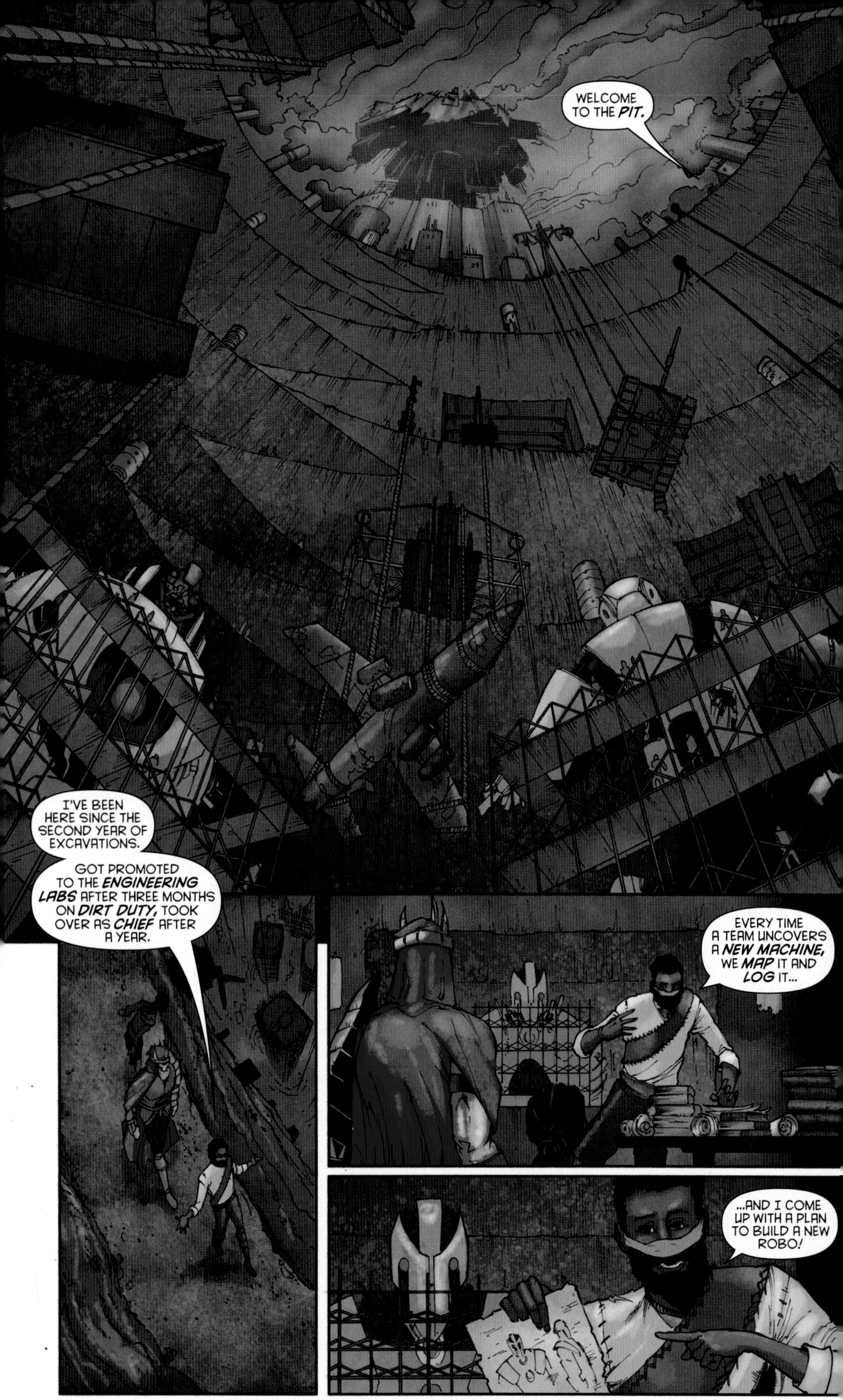

WELCOME TO THE *PIT.*
I'VE BEEN HERE SINCE THE SECOND YEAR OF EXCAVATIONS.
GOT PROMOTED TO THE ***ENGINEERING LABS*** AFTER THREE MONTHS ON ***DIRT DUTY,*** TOOK OVER AS ***CHIEF*** AFTER A YEAR.
EVERY TIME A TEAM UNCOVERS A ***NEW MACHINE,*** WE ***MAP*** IT AND ***LOG*** IT...
...AND I COME UP WITH A PLAN TO BUILD A NEW ROBO!

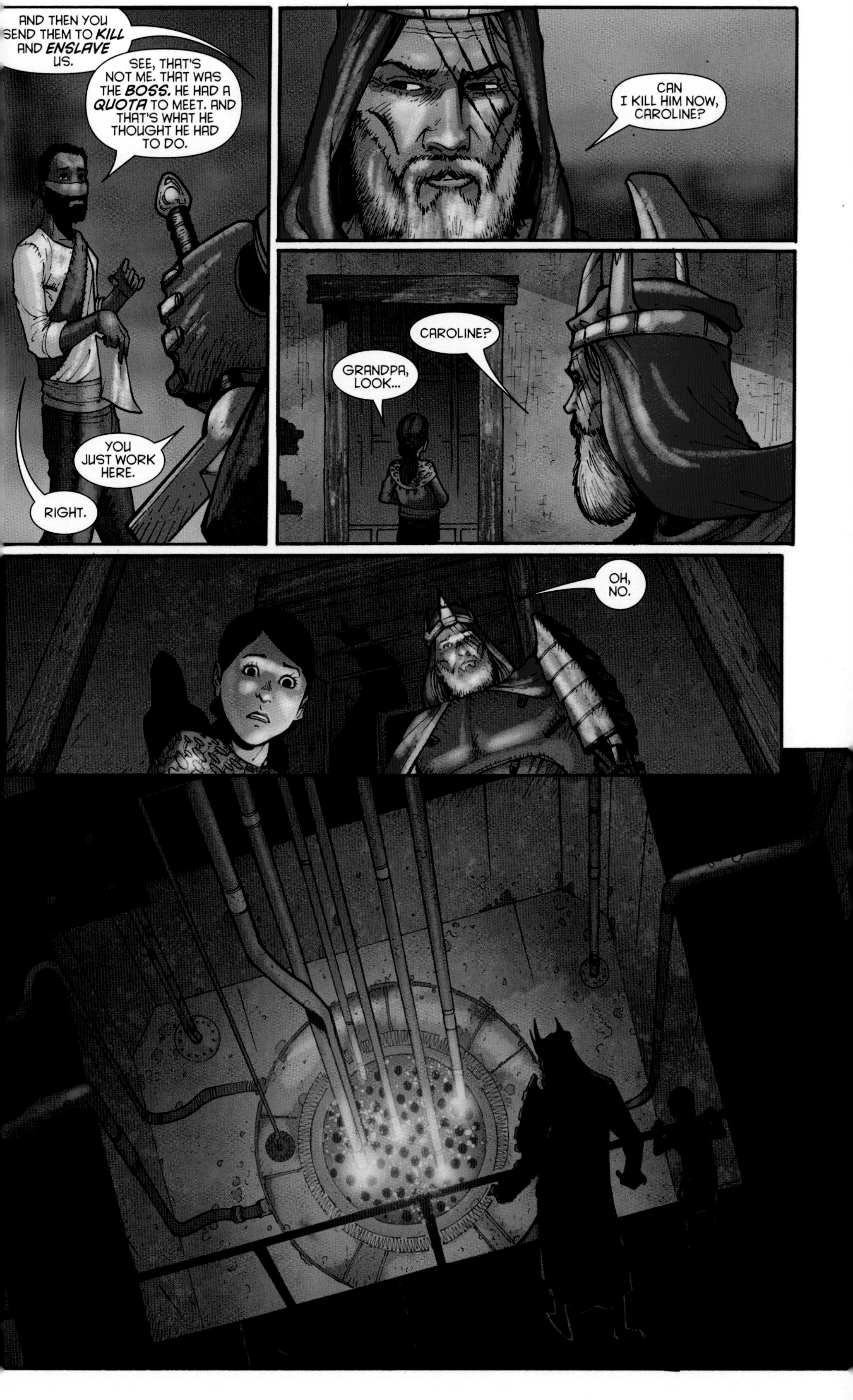
AND THEN YOU SEND THEM TO *KILL* AND *ENSLAVE* US.
SEE, THAT'S NOT ME. THAT WAS THE *BOSS.* HE HAD A *QUOTA* TO MEET. AND THAT'S WHAT HE THOUGHT HE HAD TO DO.
YOU JUST WORK HERE.
RIGHT.
CAN I KILL HIM NOW, CAROLINE?
CAROLINE?
GRANDPA, LOOK...
OH, NO.

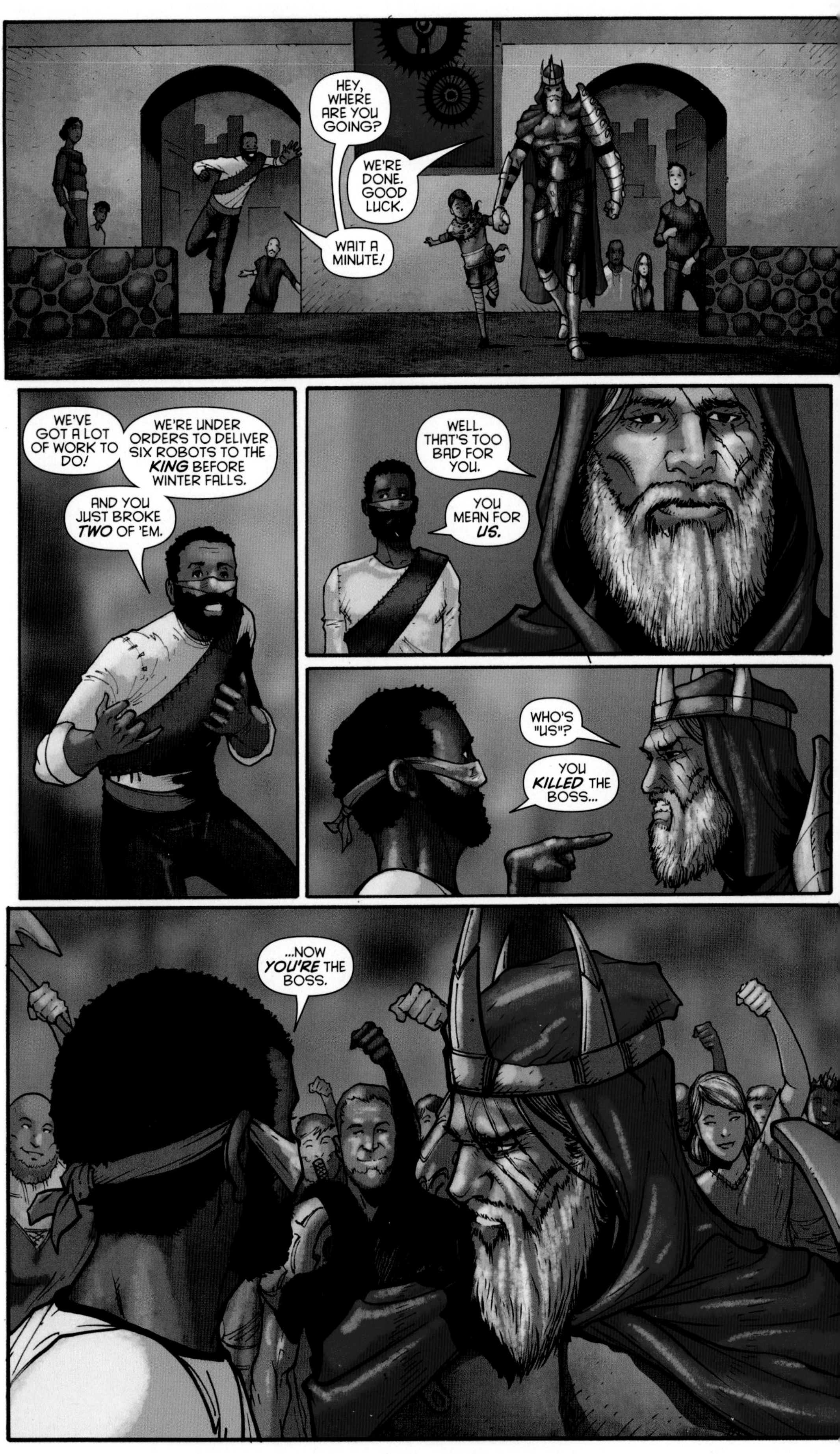
HEY, WHERE ARE YOU GOING?
WE'RE DONE. GOOD LUCK.
WAIT A MINUTE!
WE'VE GOT A LOT OF WORK TO DO!
WE'RE UNDER ORDERS TO DELIVER SIX ROBOTS TO THE *KING* BEFORE WINTER FALLS.
AND YOU JUST BROKE *TWO* OF 'EM.
WELL. THAT'S TOO BAD FOR YOU.
YOU MEAN FOR *US.*
WHO'S "US"?
YOU *KILLED* THE BOSS...
...NOW *YOU'RE* THE BOSS.

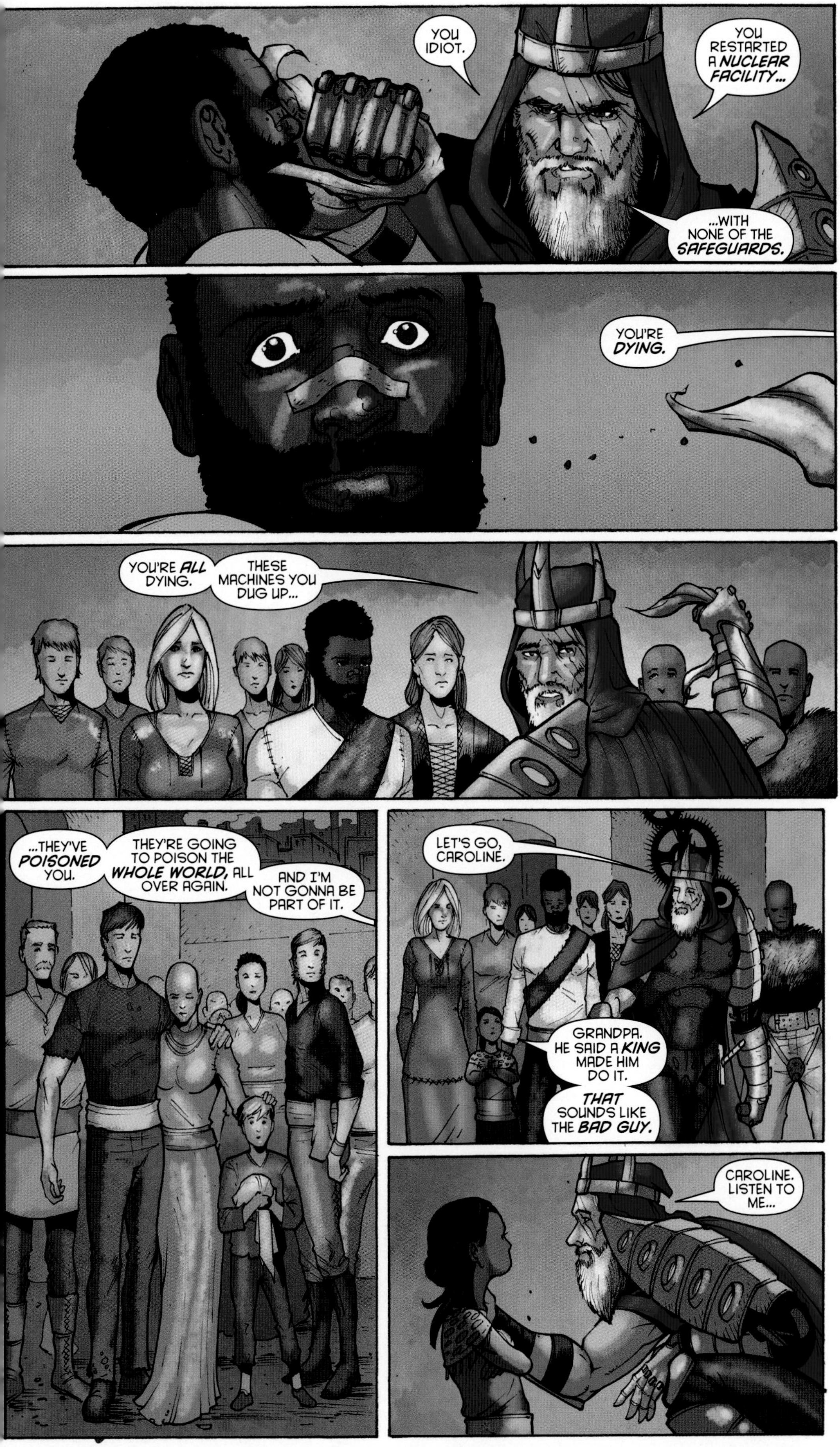

YOU IDIOT.
YOU RESTARTED A *NUCLEAR FACILITY...*
...WITH NONE OF THE *SAFEGUARDS.*
YOU'RE *DYING.*
YOU'RE *ALL* DYING.
THESE MACHINES YOU DUG UP...
...THEY'VE *POISONED* YOU.
THEY'RE GOING TO POISON THE *WHOLE WORLD,* ALL OVER AGAIN.
AND I'M NOT GONNA BE PART OF IT.
LET'S GO, CAROLINE.
GRANDPA. HE SAID A *KING* MADE HIM DO IT.
THAT SOUNDS LIKE THE *BAD GUY.*
CAROLINE. LISTEN TO ME...

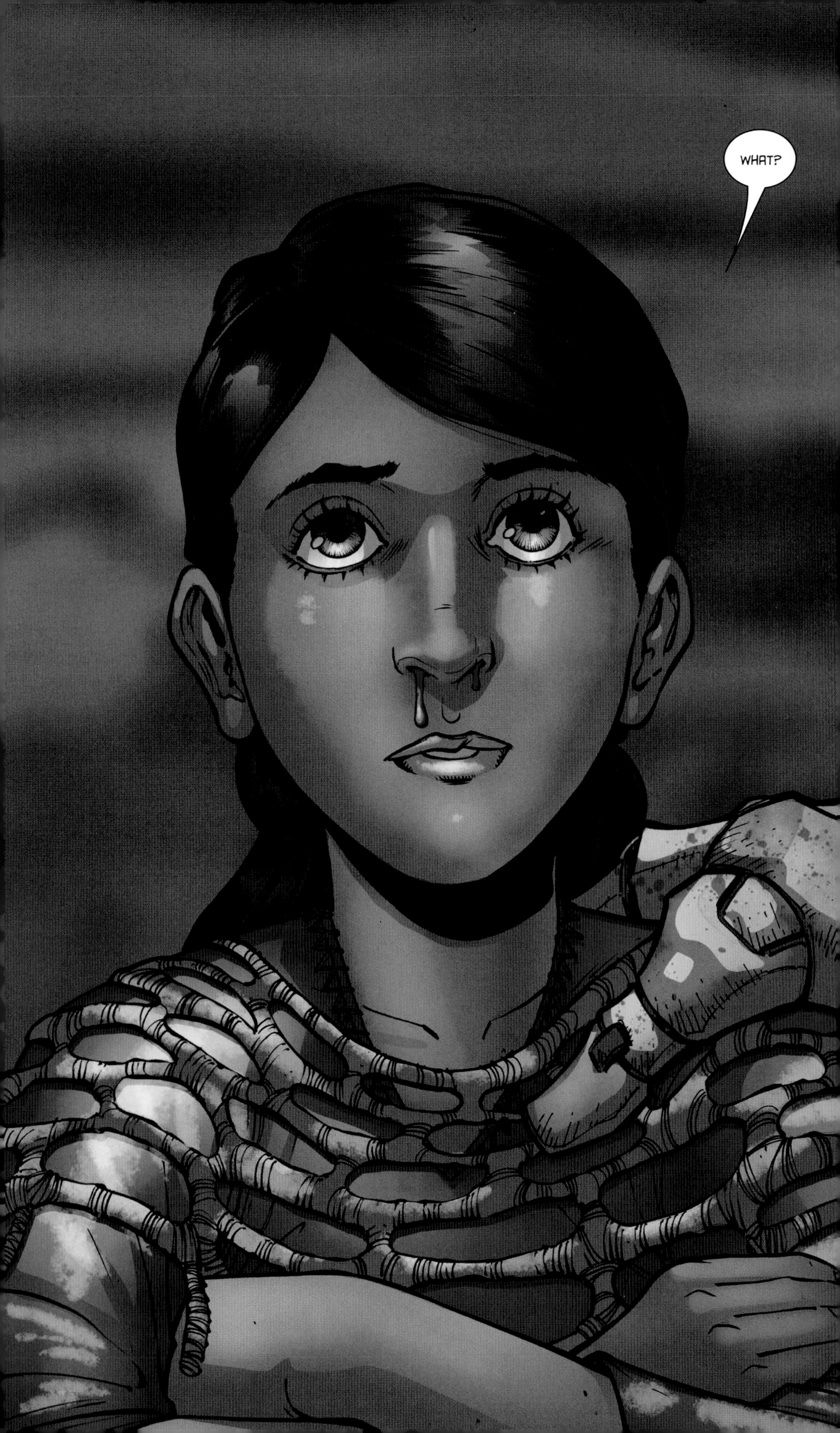
WHAT?

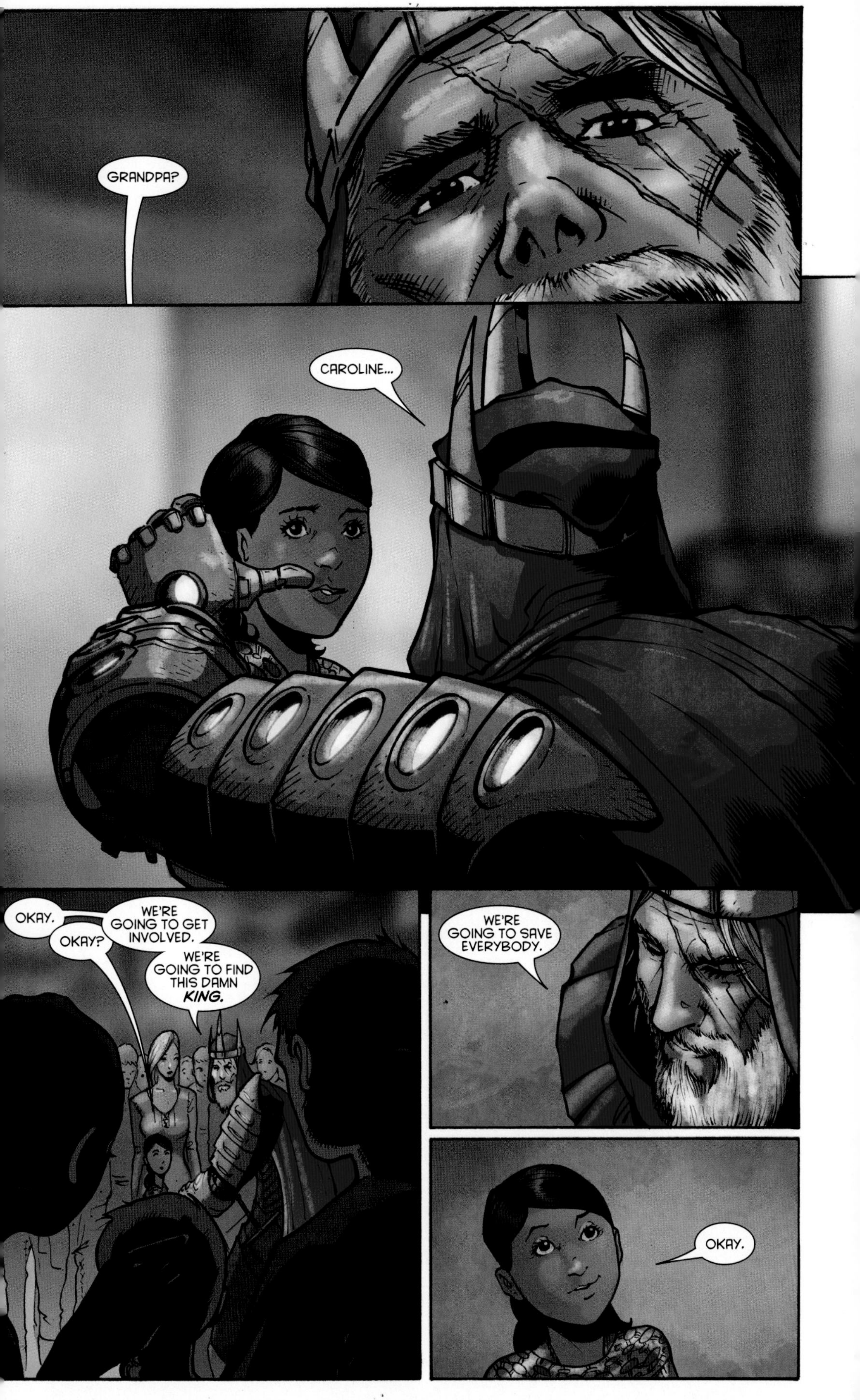
GRANDPA?
CAROLINE...
OKAY.
WE'RE GOING TO GET INVOLVED.
OKAY?
WE'RE GOING TO FIND THIS DAMN KING.
WE'RE GOING TO SAVE EVERYBODY.
OKAY.

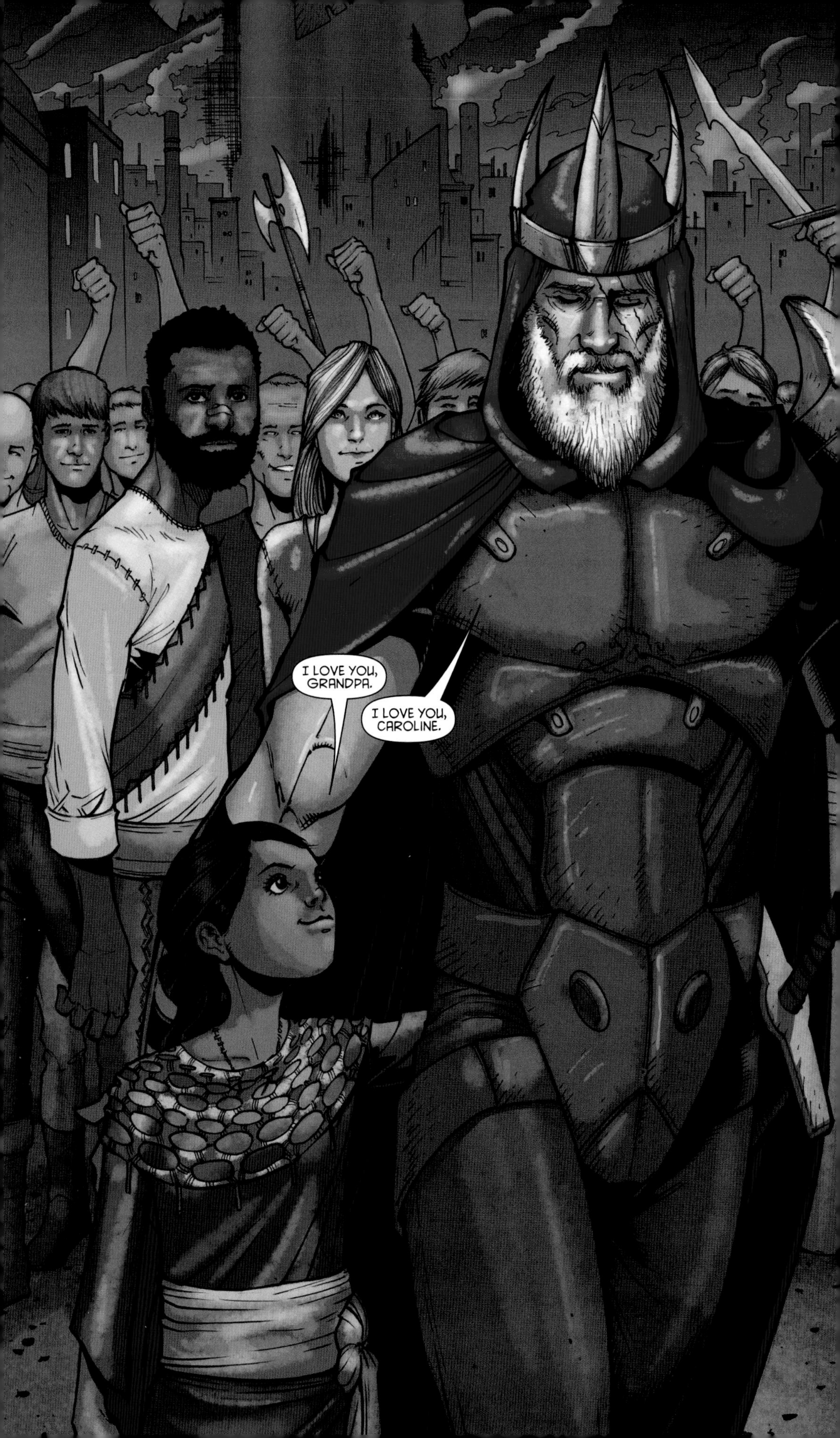
I LOVE YOU, GRANDPA.
I LOVE YOU, CAROLINE.

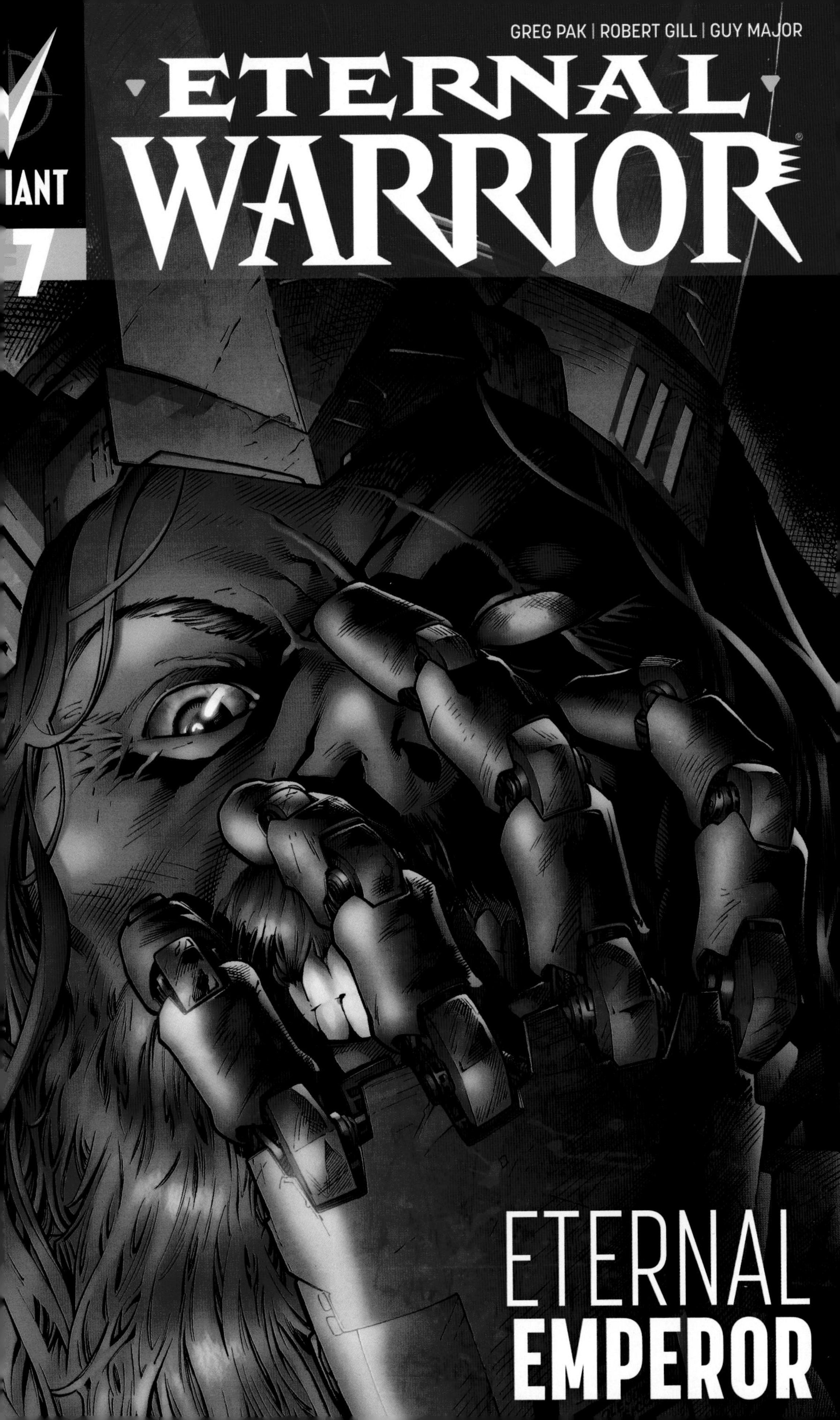
GREG PAK | ROBERT GILL | GUY MAJOR
ETERNAL WARRIOR
7
ETERNAL EMPEROR

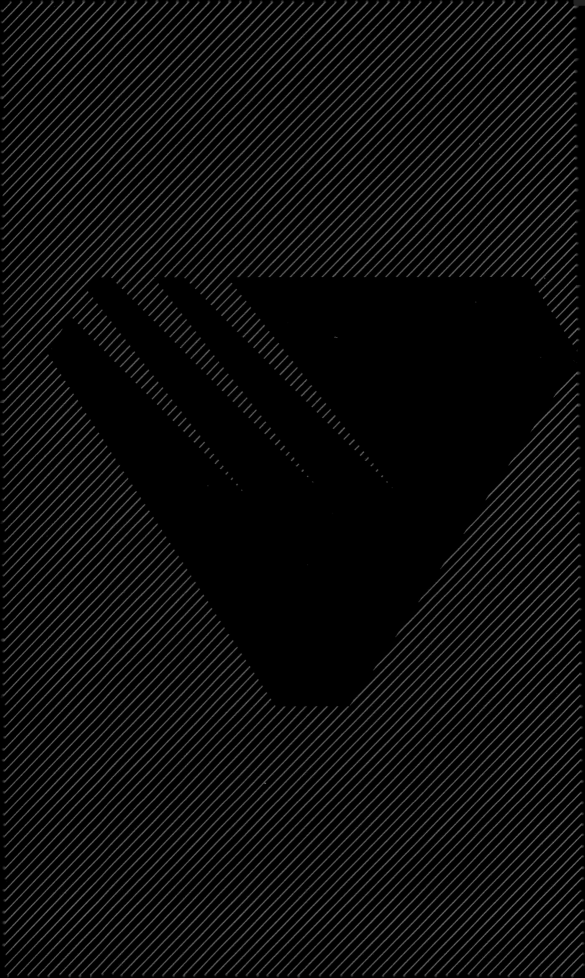

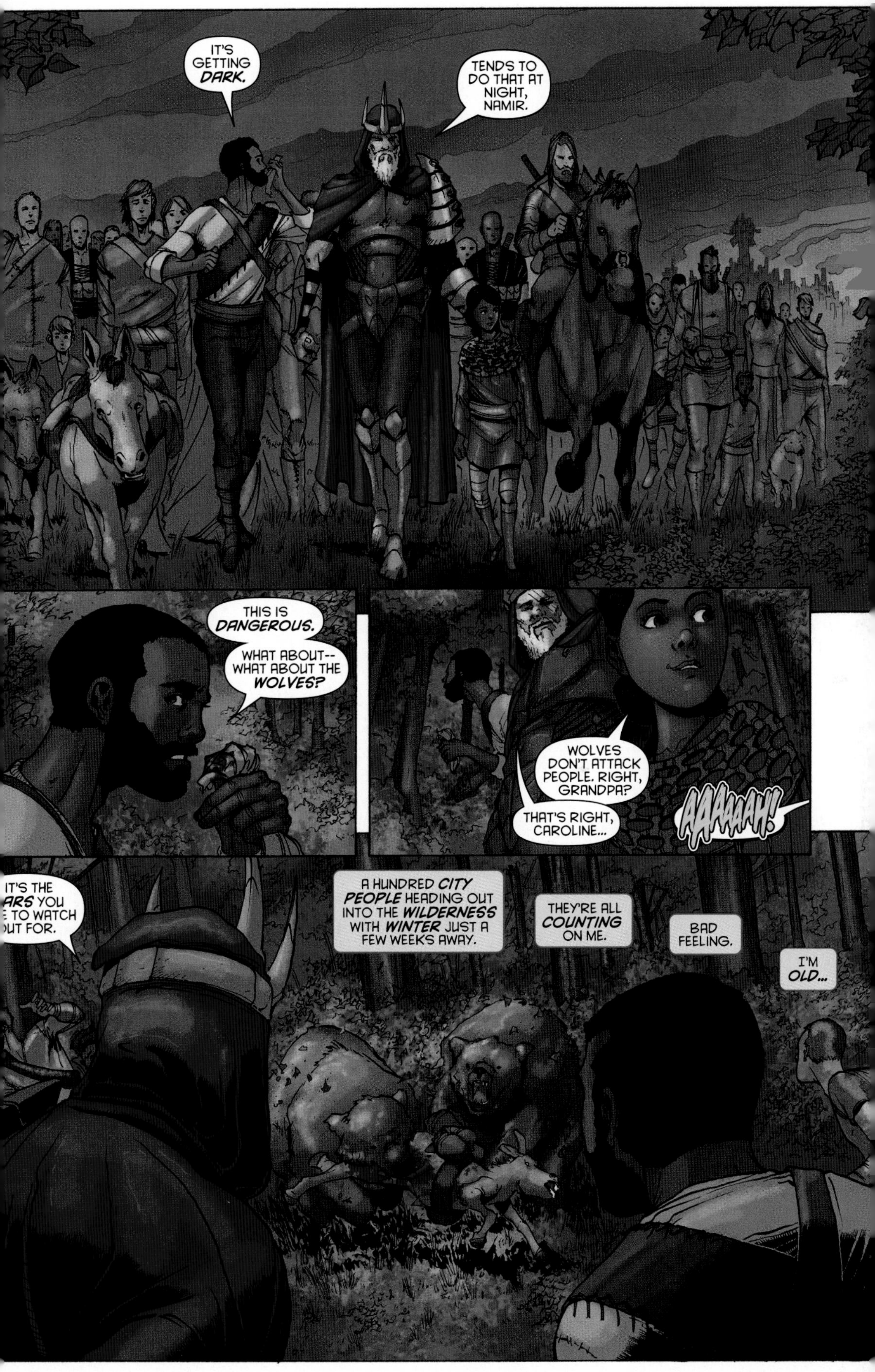
IT'S GETTING DARK.
TENDS TO DO THAT AT NIGHT, NAMIR.
THIS IS DANGEROUS.
WHAT ABOUT-- WHAT ABOUT THE WOLVES?
WOLVES DON'T ATTACK PEOPLE. RIGHT, GRANDPA?
THAT'S RIGHT, CAROLINE...
AAAAAAH!
IT'S THE
ARS YOU
E TO WATCH
UT FOR.
A HUNDRED CITY PEOPLE HEADING OUT INTO THE WILDERNESS WITH WINTER JUST A FEW WEEKS AWAY.
THEY'RE ALL COUNTING ON ME.
BAD FEELING.
I'M OLD...

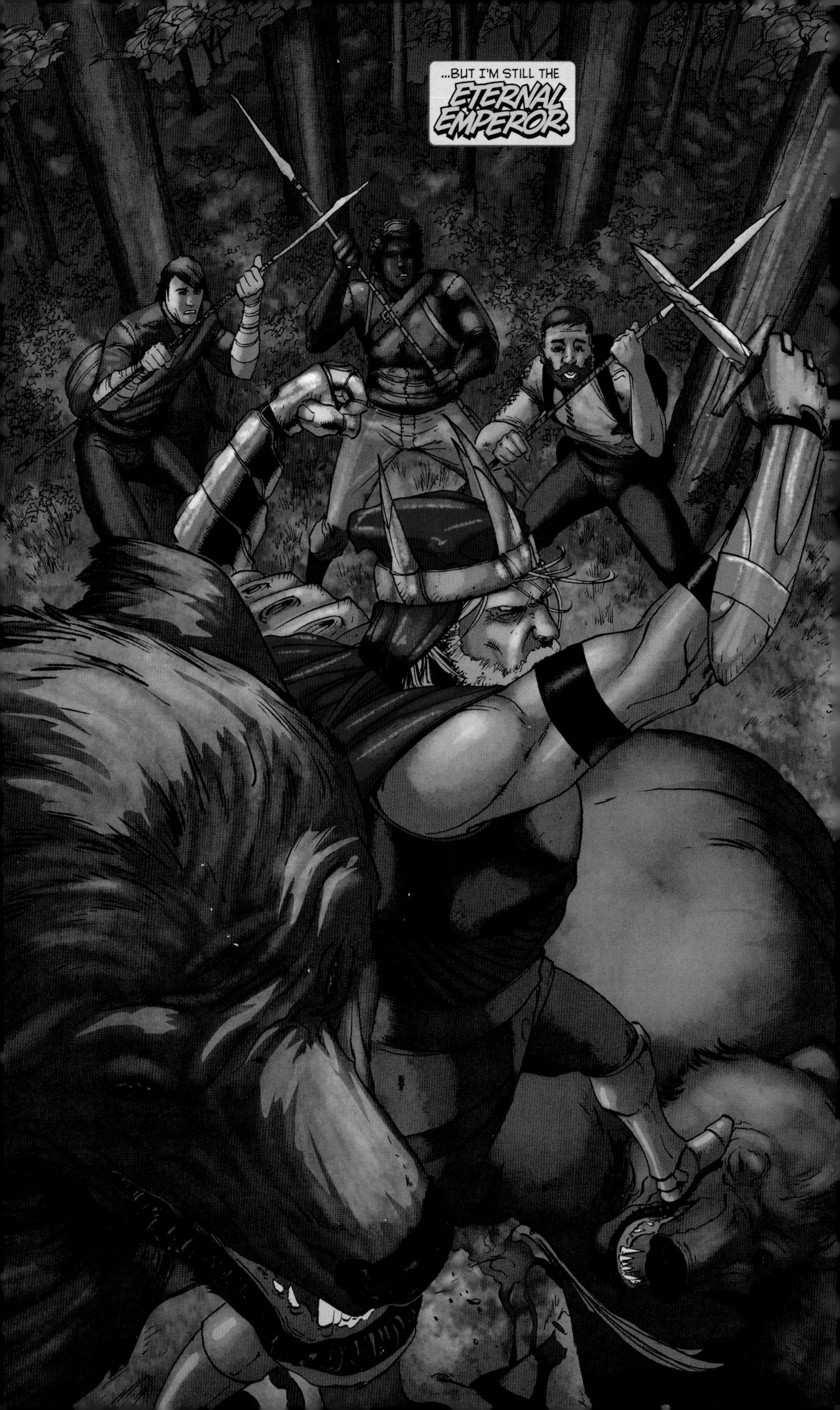
...BUT I'M STILL THE
ETERNAL EMPEROR.

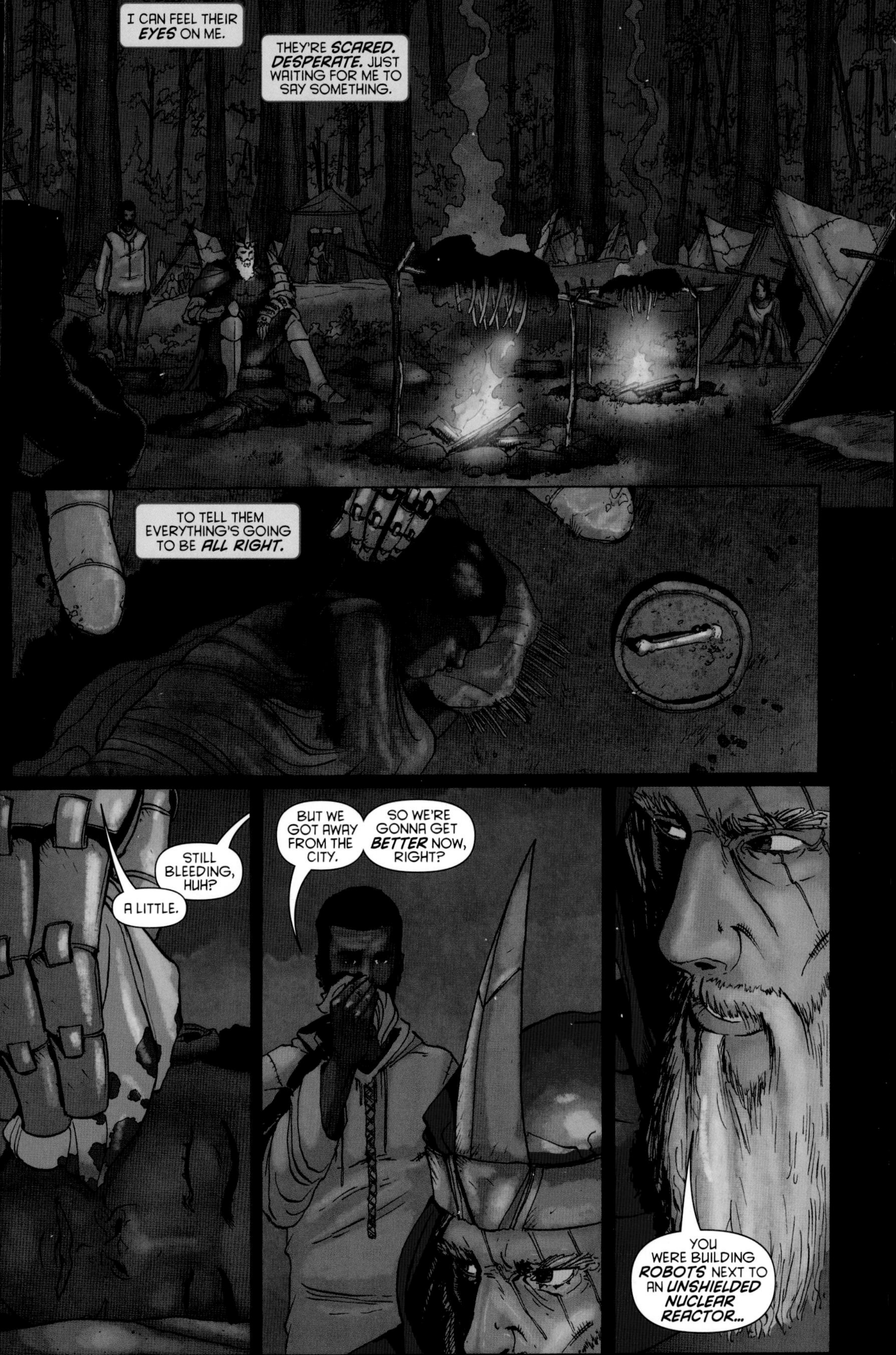

I CAN FEEL THEIR EYES ON ME.
THEY'RE SCARED. DESPERATE. JUST WAITING FOR ME TO SAY SOMETHING.
TO TELL THEM EVERYTHING'S GOING TO BE ALL RIGHT.
STILL BLEEDING, HUH?
A LITTLE.
BUT WE GOT AWAY FROM THE CITY.
SO WE'RE GONNA GET BETTER NOW, RIGHT?
YOU WERE BUILDING ROBOTS NEXT TO AN UNSHIELDED NUCLEAR REACTOR...

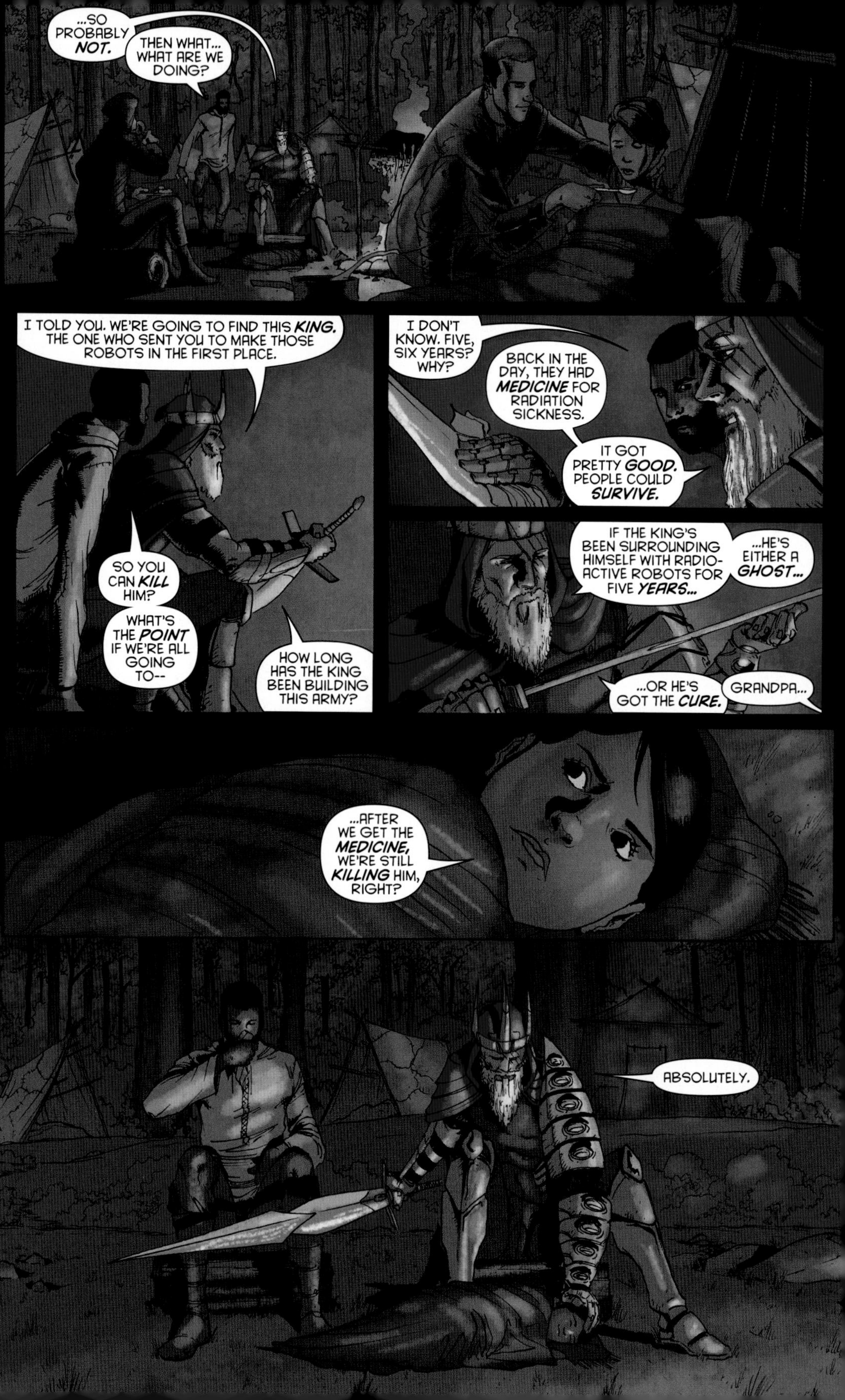
...SO PROBABLY *NOT.*
THEN WHAT... WHAT ARE WE DOING?
I TOLD YOU. WE'RE GOING TO FIND THIS *KING.* THE ONE WHO SENT YOU TO MAKE THOSE ROBOTS IN THE FIRST PLACE.
SO YOU CAN *KILL* HIM?
WHAT'S THE *POINT* IF WE'RE ALL GOING TO--
HOW LONG HAS THE KING BEEN BUILDING THIS ARMY?
I DON'T KNOW. FIVE, SIX YEARS? WHY?
BACK IN THE DAY, THEY HAD *MEDICINE* FOR RADIATION SICKNESS.
IT GOT PRETTY *GOOD.* PEOPLE COULD *SURVIVE.*
IF THE KING'S BEEN SURROUNDING HIMSELF WITH RADIO-ACTIVE ROBOTS FOR FIVE *YEARS...*
...HE'S EITHER A *GHOST...*
...OR HE'S GOT THE *CURE.*
GRANDPA...
...AFTER WE GET THE *MEDICINE,* WE'RE STILL *KILLING* HIM, RIGHT?
ABSOLUTELY.

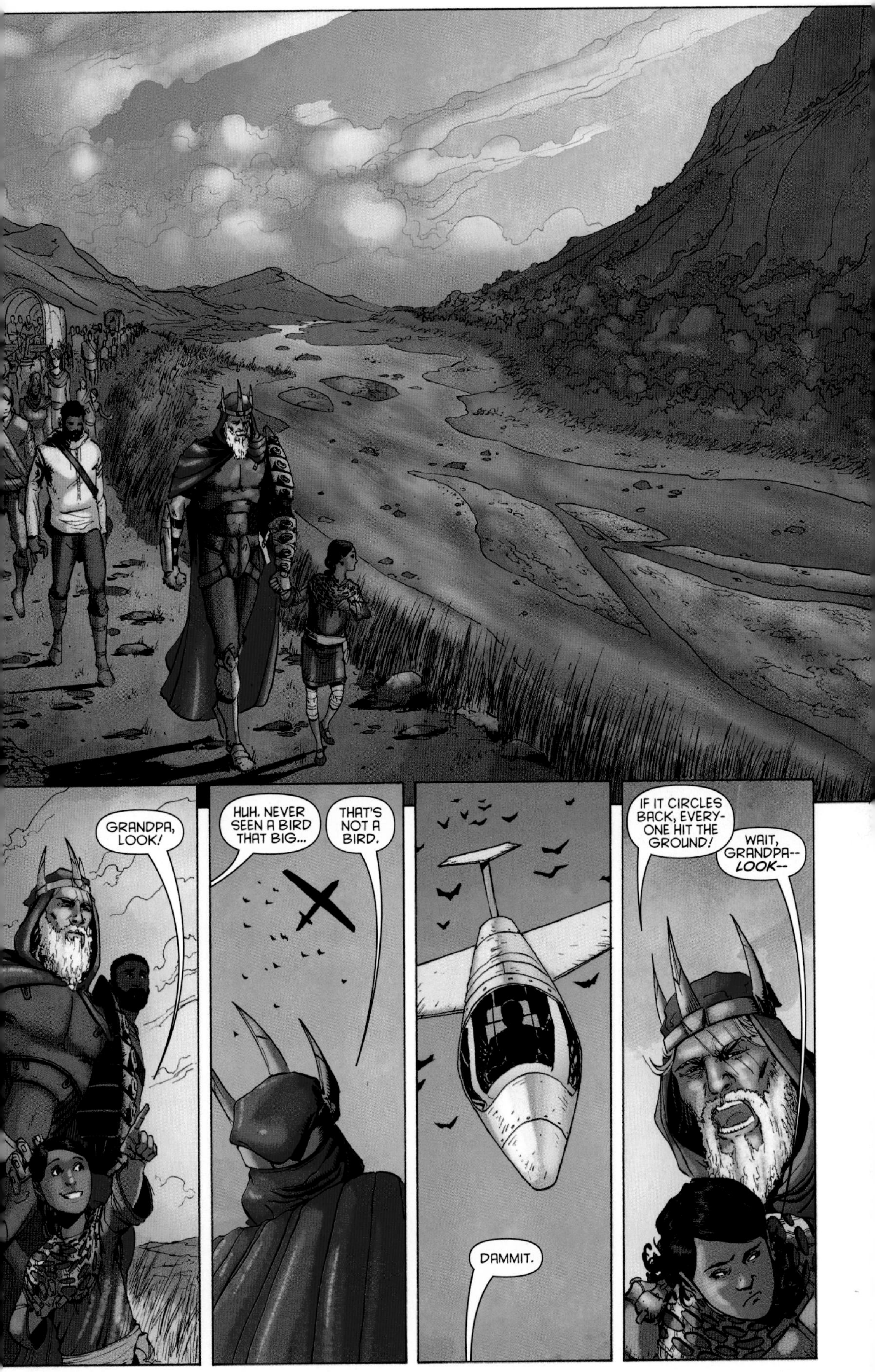
GRANDPA, LOOK!
HUH. NEVER SEEN A BIRD THAT BIG...
THAT'S NOT A BIRD.
DAMMIT.
IF IT CIRCLES BACK, EVERY-ONE HIT THE GROUND!
WAIT, GRANDPA-- LOOK--

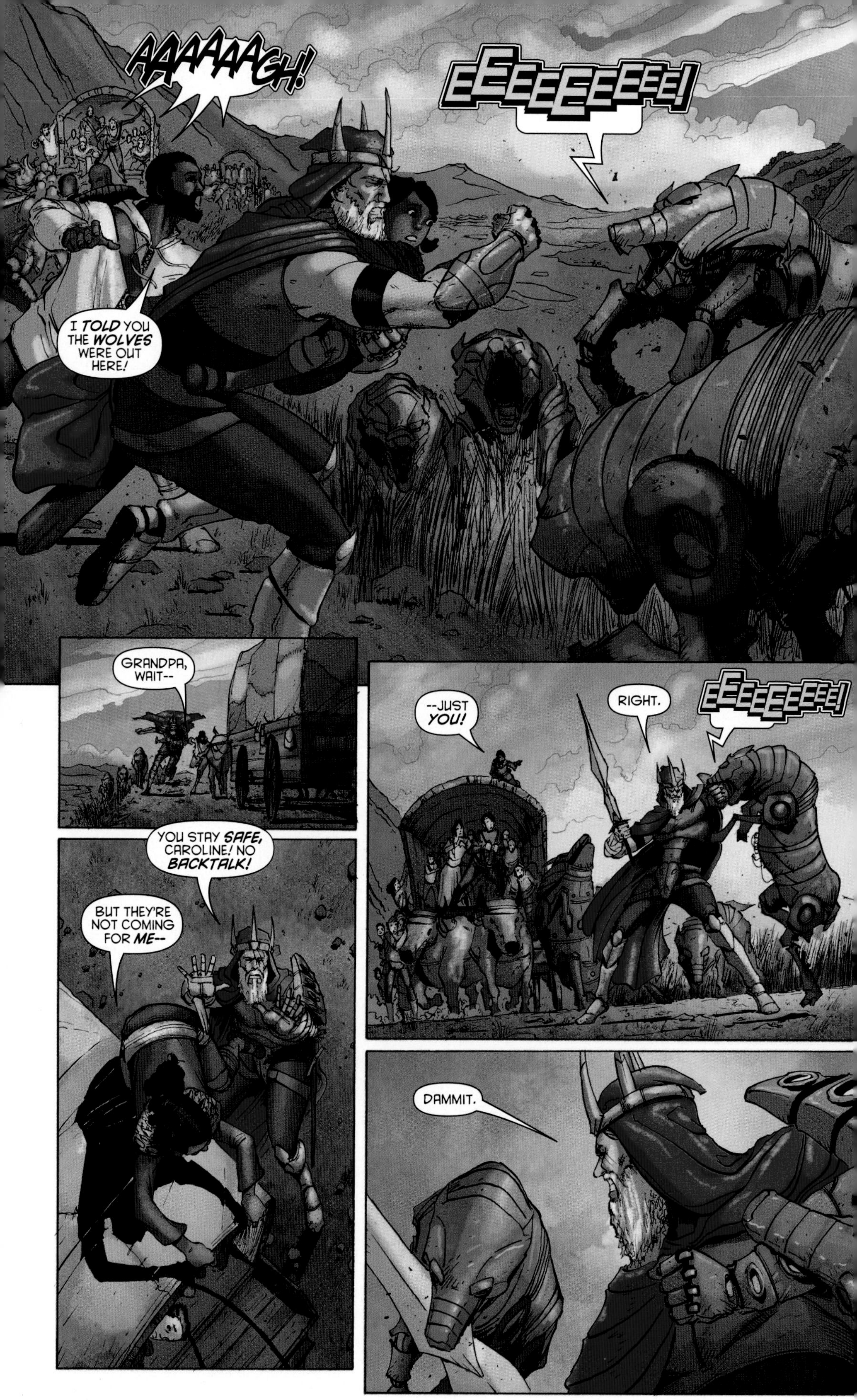
AAAAAAGH!
EEEEEEEEEE!
I TOLD YOU THE WOLVES WERE OUT HERE!
GRANDPA, WAIT--
--JUST YOU!
RIGHT.
EEEEEEEEE!
YOU STAY SAFE, CAROLINE! NO BACKTALK!
BUT THEY'RE NOT COMING FOR ME--
DAMMIT.

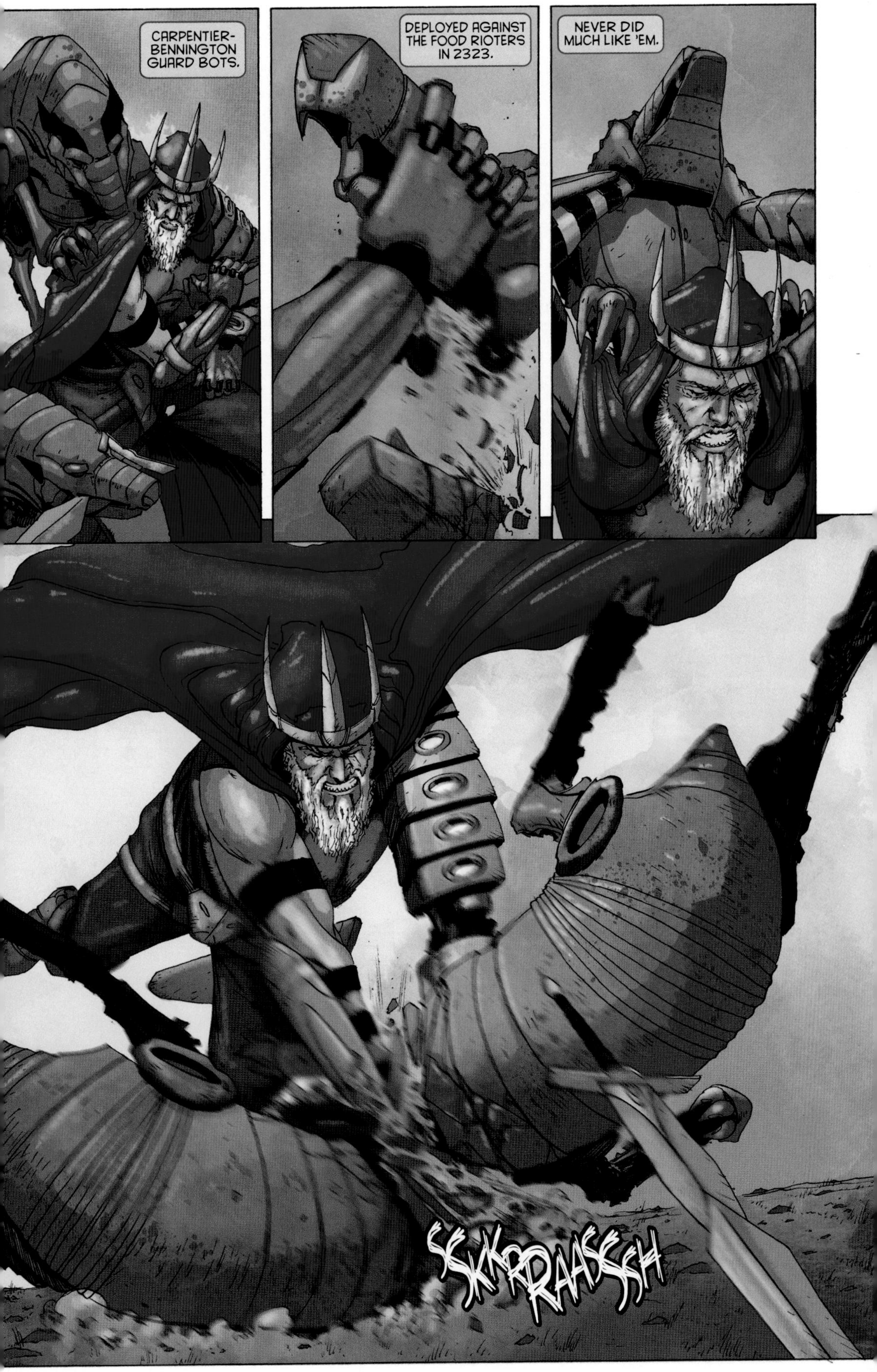
CARPENTIER-BENNINGTON GUARD BOTS.
DEPLOYED AGAINST THE FOOD RIOTERS IN 2323.
NEVER DID MUCH LIKE 'EM.
SKKRRAASSH

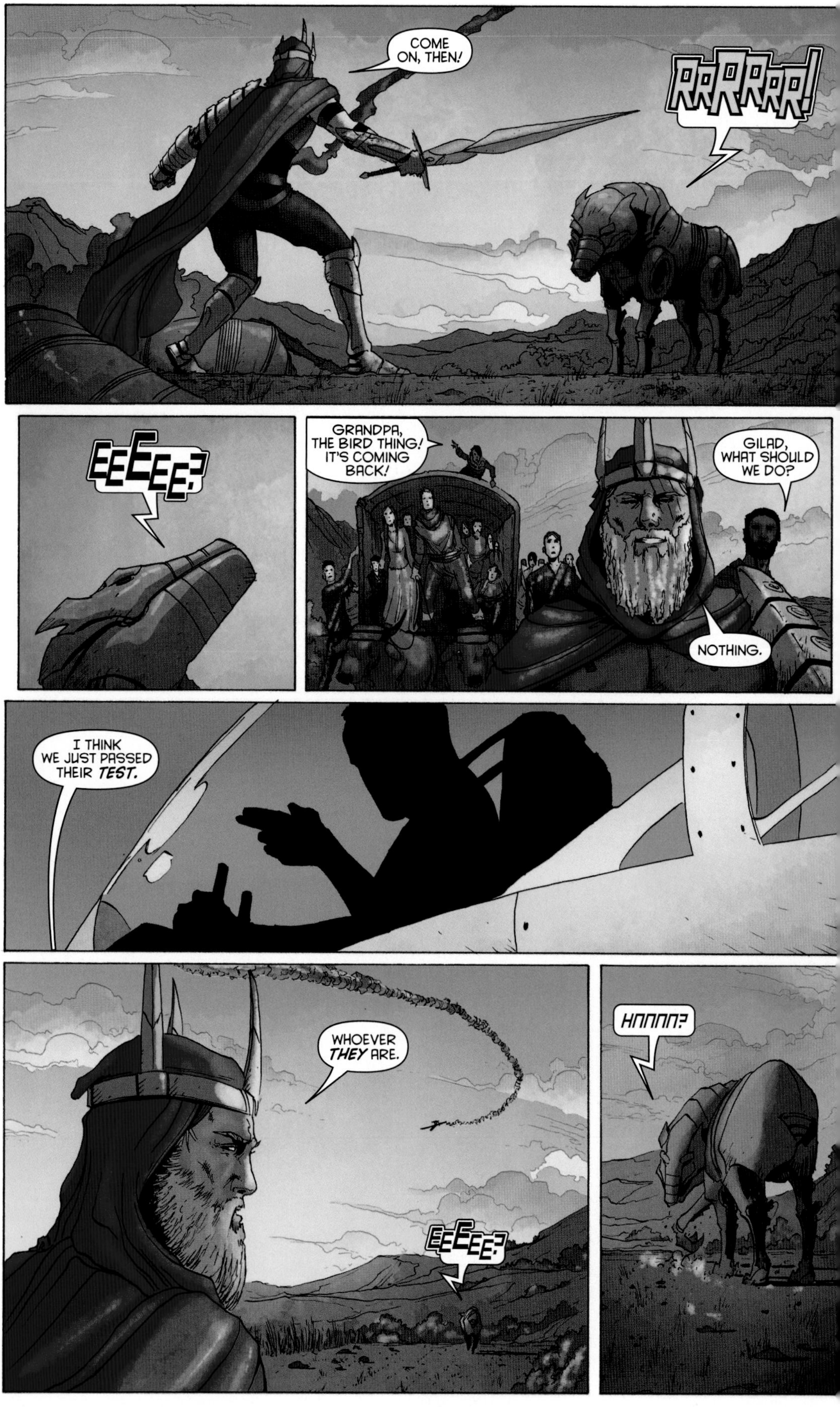
COME ON, THEN!
RRRRRR!
EEEEE?
GRANDPA, THE BIRD THING! IT'S COMING BACK!
GILAD, WHAT SHOULD WE DO?
NOTHING.
I THINK WE JUST PASSED THEIR TEST.
WHOEVER THEY ARE.
EEEEE?
HNNNN?

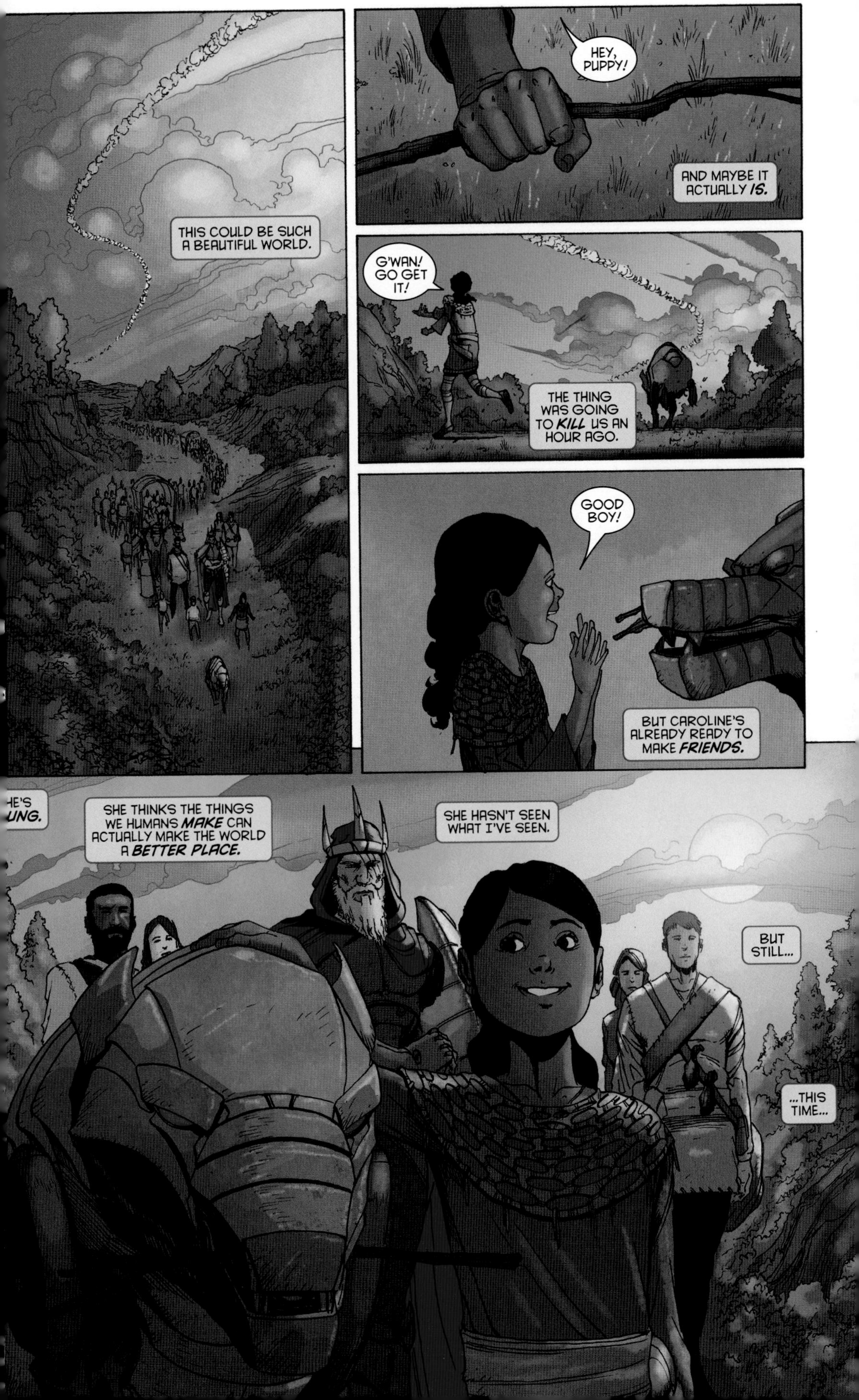
THIS COULD BE SUCH A BEAUTIFUL WORLD.
HEY, PUPPY!
AND MAYBE IT ACTUALLY *IS.*
G'WAN! GO GET IT!
THE THING WAS GOING TO *KILL* US AN HOUR AGO.
GOOD BOY!
BUT CAROLINE'S ALREADY READY TO MAKE *FRIENDS.*
HE'S UNG.
SHE THINKS THE THINGS WE HUMANS *MAKE* CAN ACTUALLY MAKE THE WORLD A *BETTER PLACE.*
SHE HASN'T SEEN WHAT I'VE SEEN.
BUT STILL...
...THIS TIME...

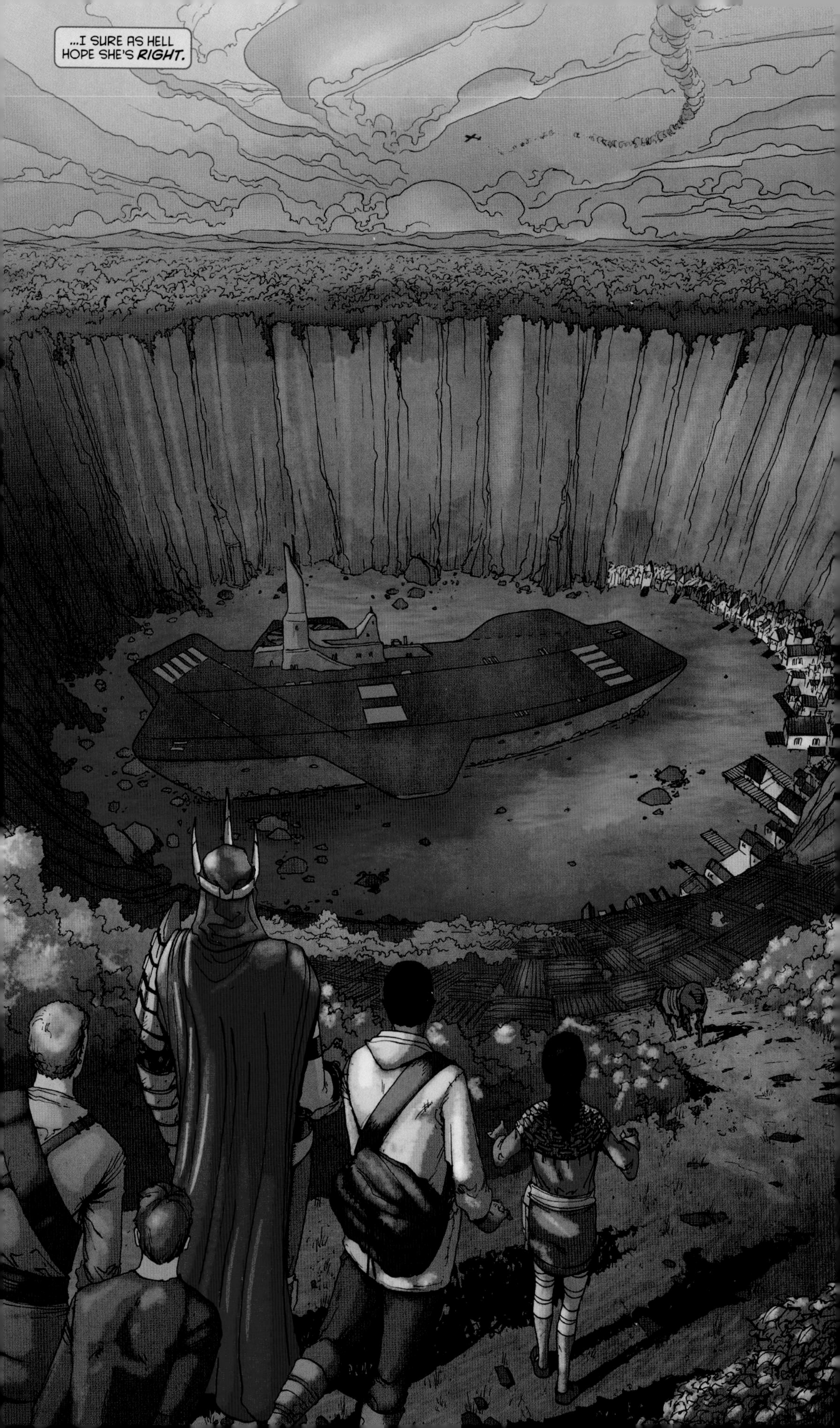
...I SURE AS HELL HOPE SHE'S *RIGHT.*

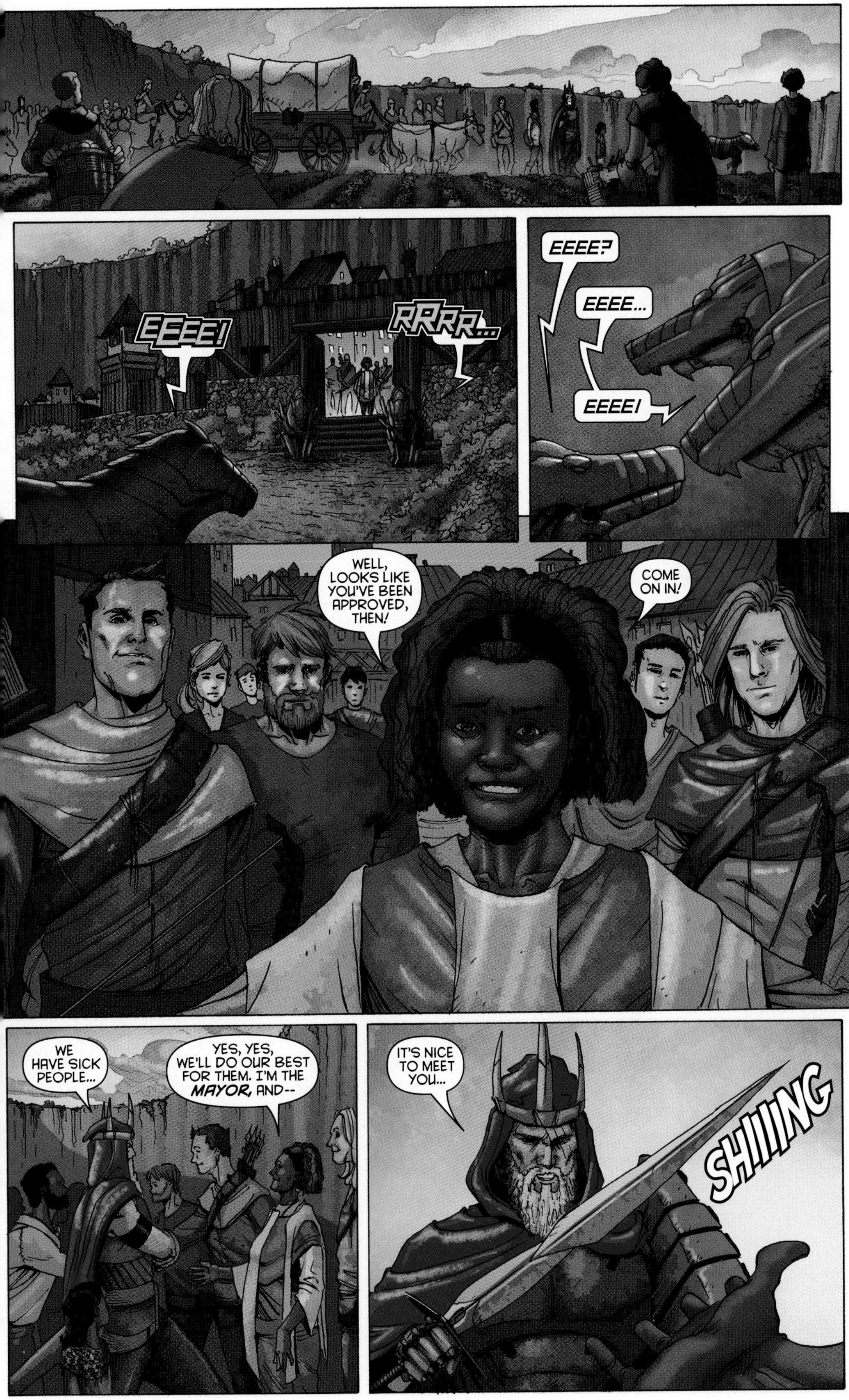
EEEE!
RRRR...
EEEE?
EEEE...
EEEE!
WELL, LOOKS LIKE YOU'VE BEEN APPROVED, THEN!
COME ON IN!
WE HAVE SICK PEOPLE...
YES, YES, WE'LL DO OUR BEST FOR THEM. I'M THE *MAYOR,* AND--
IT'S NICE TO MEET YOU...
SHIIING

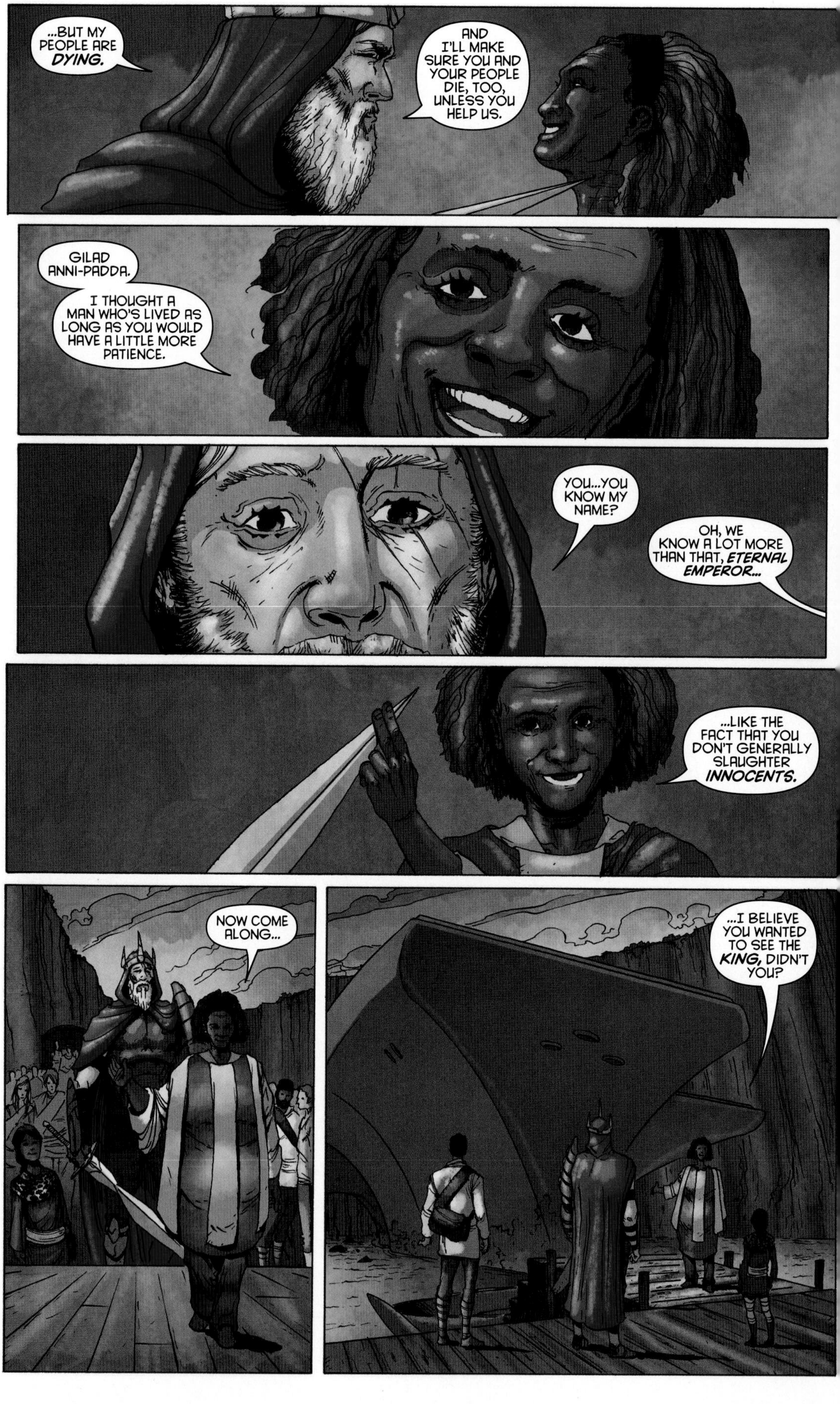
...BUT MY PEOPLE ARE *DYING.*
AND I'LL MAKE SURE YOU AND YOUR PEOPLE DIE, TOO, UNLESS YOU HELP US.
GILAD ANNI-PADDA.
I THOUGHT A MAN WHO'S LIVED AS LONG AS YOU WOULD HAVE A LITTLE MORE PATIENCE.
YOU...YOU KNOW MY NAME?
OH, WE KNOW A LOT MORE THAN THAT, *ETERNAL EMPEROR...*
...LIKE THE FACT THAT YOU DON'T GENERALLY SLAUGHTER *INNOCENTS.*
NOW COME ALONG...
...I BELIEVE YOU WANTED TO SEE THE *KING,* DIDN'T YOU?

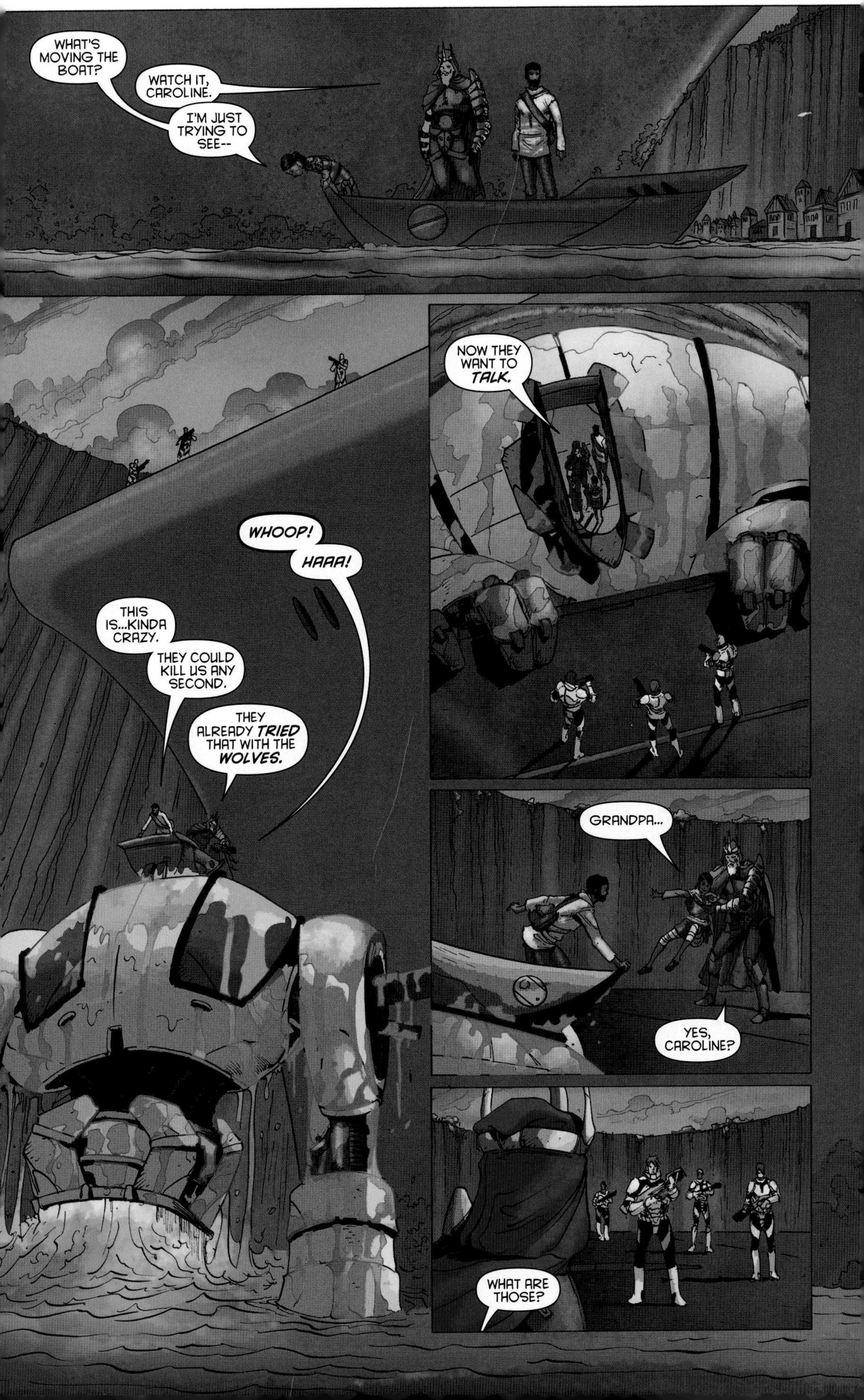
WHAT'S MOVING THE BOAT?
WATCH IT, CAROLINE.
I'M JUST TRYING TO SEE--
WHOOP!
HAAA!
THIS IS...KINDA CRAZY.
THEY COULD KILL US ANY SECOND.
THEY ALREADY TRIED THAT WITH THE WOLVES.
NOW THEY WANT TO TALK.
GRANDPA...
YES, CAROLINE?
WHAT ARE THOSE?

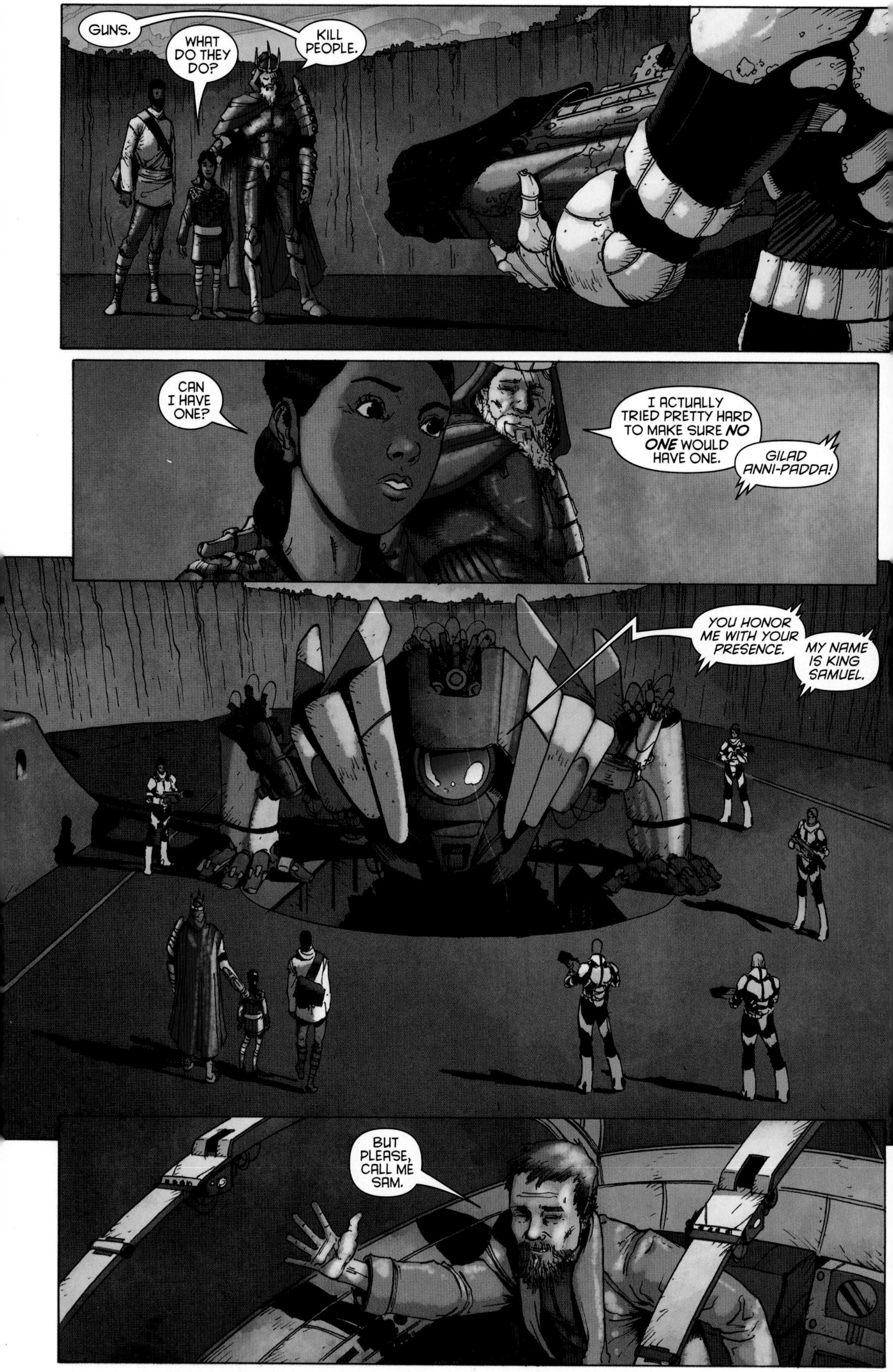
GUNS.
WHAT DO THEY DO?
KILL PEOPLE.
CAN I HAVE ONE?
I ACTUALLY TRIED PRETTY HARD TO MAKE SURE NO ONE WOULD HAVE ONE.
GILAD ANNI-PADDA!
YOU HONOR ME WITH YOUR PRESENCE.
MY NAME IS KING SAMUEL.
BUT PLEASE, CALL ME SAM.

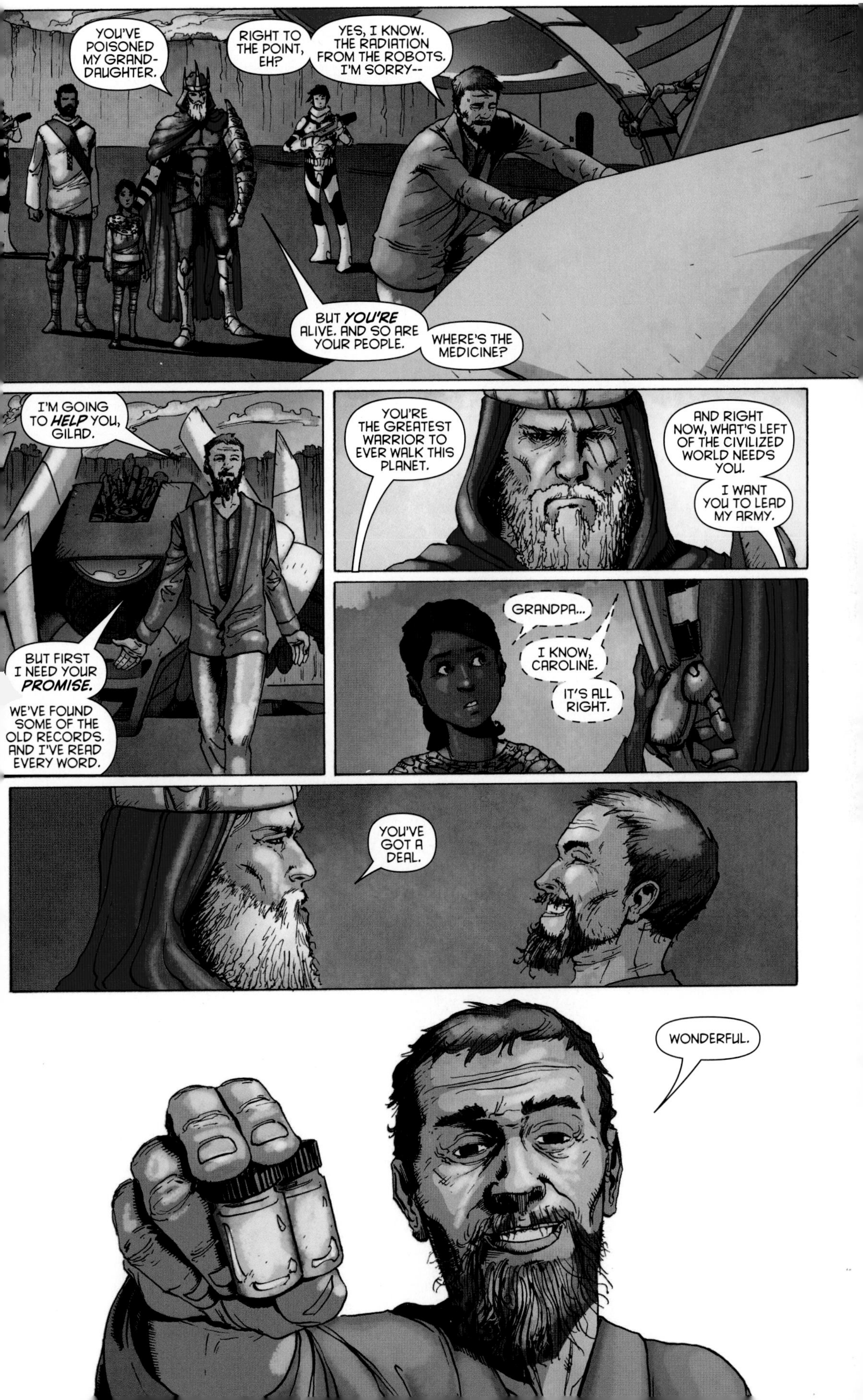
YOU'VE POISONED MY GRAND-DAUGHTER.
RIGHT TO THE POINT, EH?
YES, I KNOW. THE RADIATION FROM THE ROBOTS. I'M SORRY--
BUT YOU'RE ALIVE. AND SO ARE YOUR PEOPLE.
WHERE'S THE MEDICINE?
I'M GOING TO HELP YOU, GILAD.
BUT FIRST I NEED YOUR PROMISE.
WE'VE FOUND SOME OF THE OLD RECORDS. AND I'VE READ EVERY WORD.
YOU'RE THE GREATEST WARRIOR TO EVER WALK THIS PLANET.
AND RIGHT NOW, WHAT'S LEFT OF THE CIVILIZED WORLD NEEDS YOU.
I WANT YOU TO LEAD MY ARMY.
GRANDPA...
I KNOW, CAROLINE.
IT'S ALL RIGHT.
YOU'VE GOT A DEAL.
WONDERFUL.

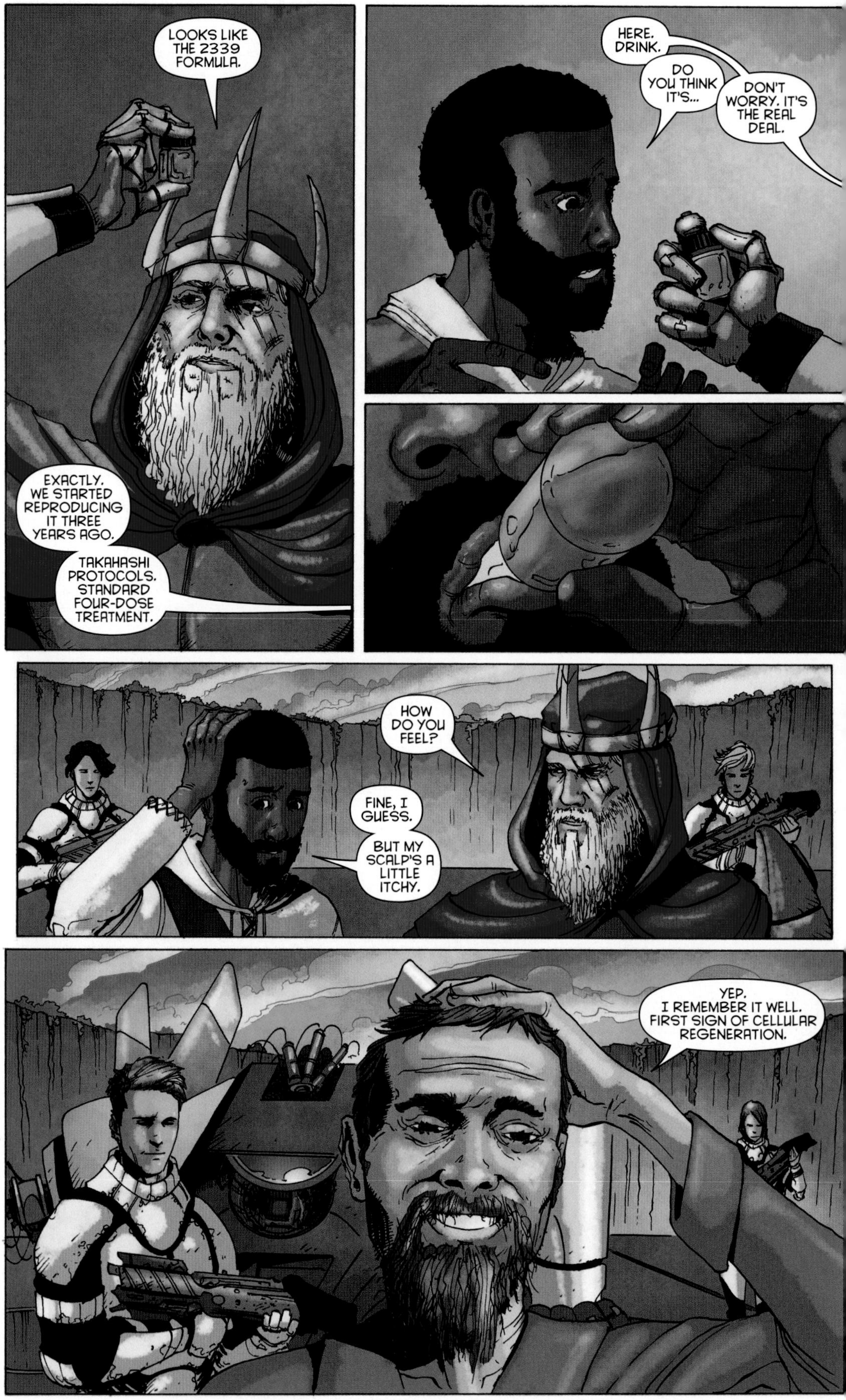
LOOKS LIKE THE 2339 FORMULA.
EXACTLY. WE STARTED REPRODUCING IT THREE YEARS AGO.
TAKAHASHI PROTOCOLS. STANDARD FOUR-DOSE TREATMENT.
HERE. DRINK.
DO YOU THINK IT'S...
DON'T WORRY. IT'S THE REAL DEAL.
HOW DO YOU FEEL?
FINE, I GUESS.
BUT MY SCALP'S A LITTLE ITCHY.
YEP. I REMEMBER IT WELL. FIRST SIGN OF CELLULAR REGENERATION.

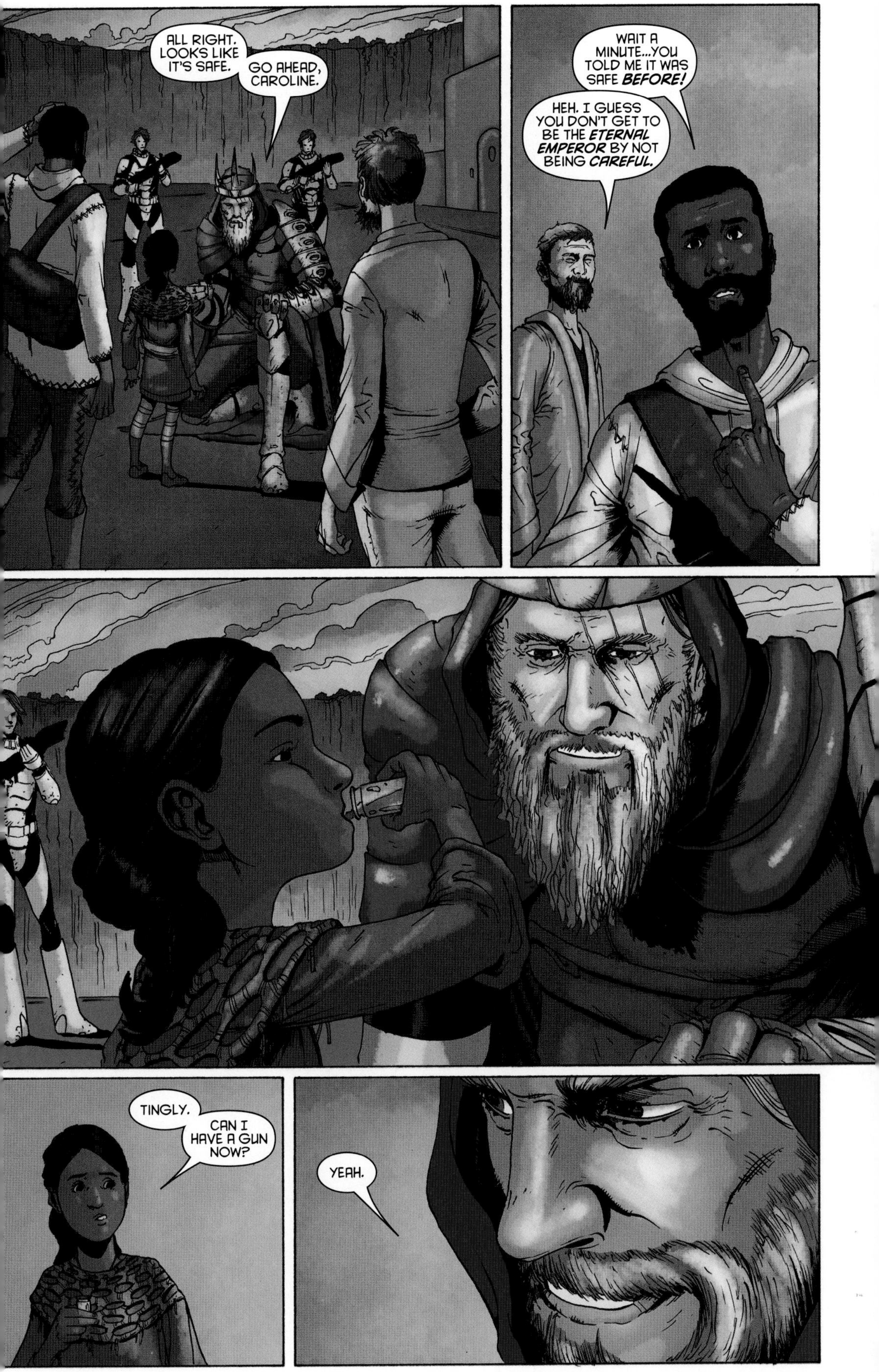
ALL RIGHT. LOOKS LIKE IT'S SAFE.
GO AHEAD, CAROLINE.
WAIT A MINUTE...YOU TOLD ME IT WAS SAFE **BEFORE!**
HEH. I GUESS YOU DON'T GET TO BE THE ***ETERNAL EMPEROR*** BY NOT BEING ***CAREFUL.***
TINGLY.
CAN I HAVE A GUN NOW?
YEAH.

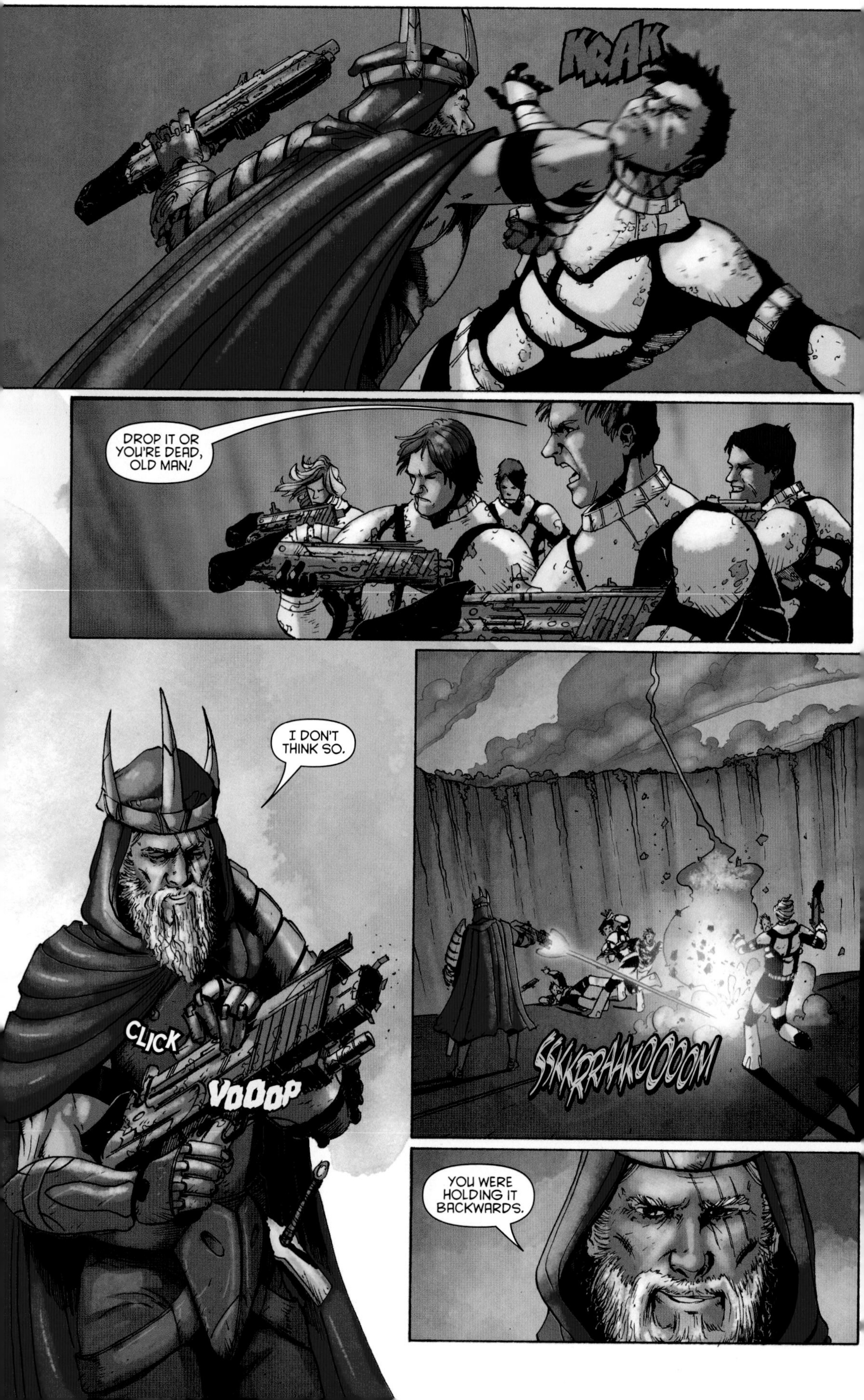
KRAK
DROP IT OR YOU'RE DEAD, OLD MAN!
I DON'T THINK SO.
CLICK
VOOOP
SSKKRRAAKOOOOOM
YOU WERE HOLDING IT BACKWARDS.

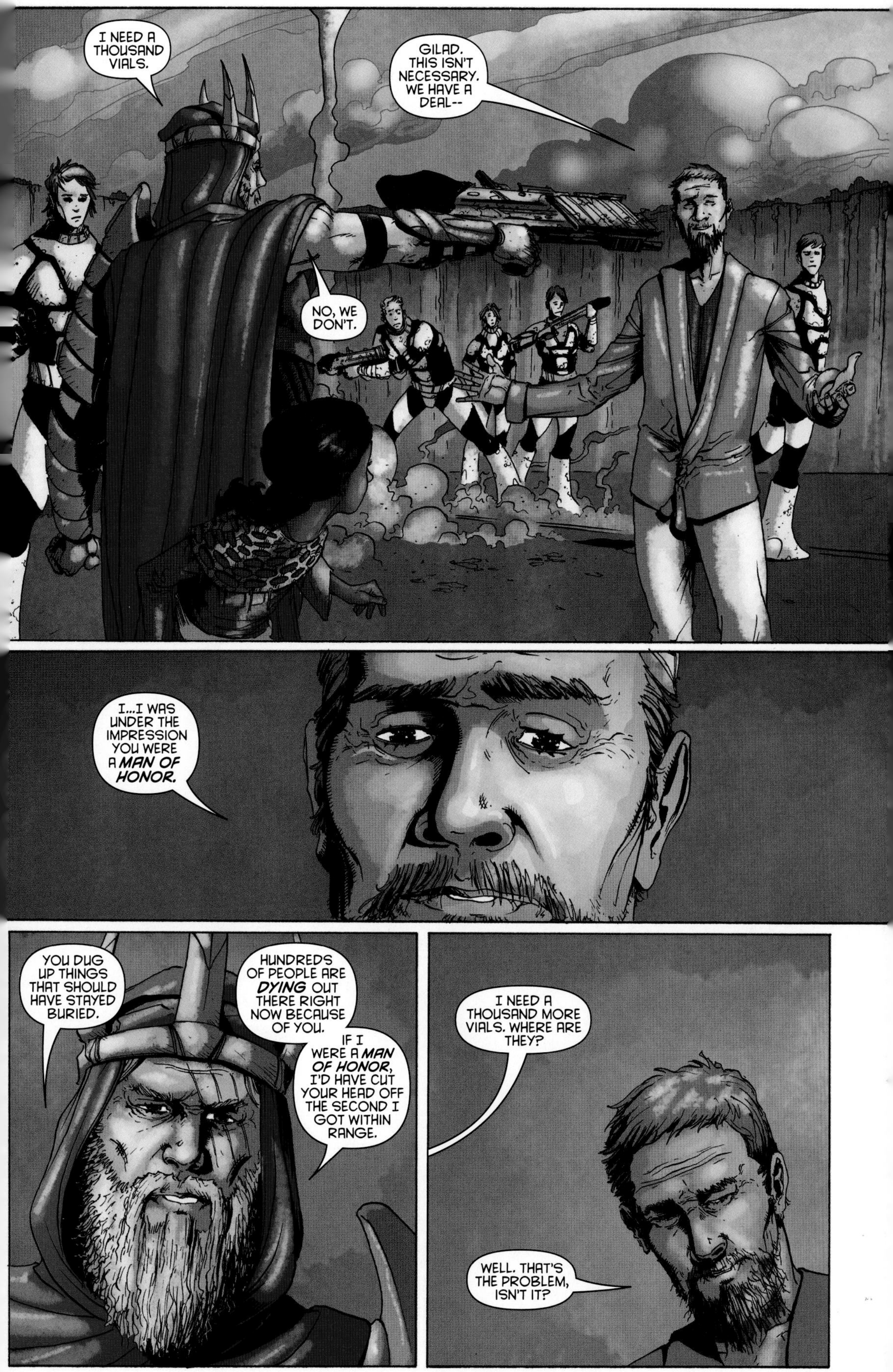
I NEED A THOUSAND VIALS.
GILAD. THIS ISN'T NECESSARY. WE HAVE A DEAL--
NO, WE DON'T.
I...I WAS UNDER THE IMPRESSION YOU WERE A MAN OF HONOR.
YOU DUG UP THINGS THAT SHOULD HAVE STAYED BURIED.
HUNDREDS OF PEOPLE ARE DYING OUT THERE RIGHT NOW BECAUSE OF YOU.
IF I WERE A MAN OF HONOR, I'D HAVE CUT YOUR HEAD OFF THE SECOND I GOT WITHIN RANGE.
I NEED A THOUSAND MORE VIALS. WHERE ARE THEY?
WELL. THAT'S THE PROBLEM, ISN'T IT?

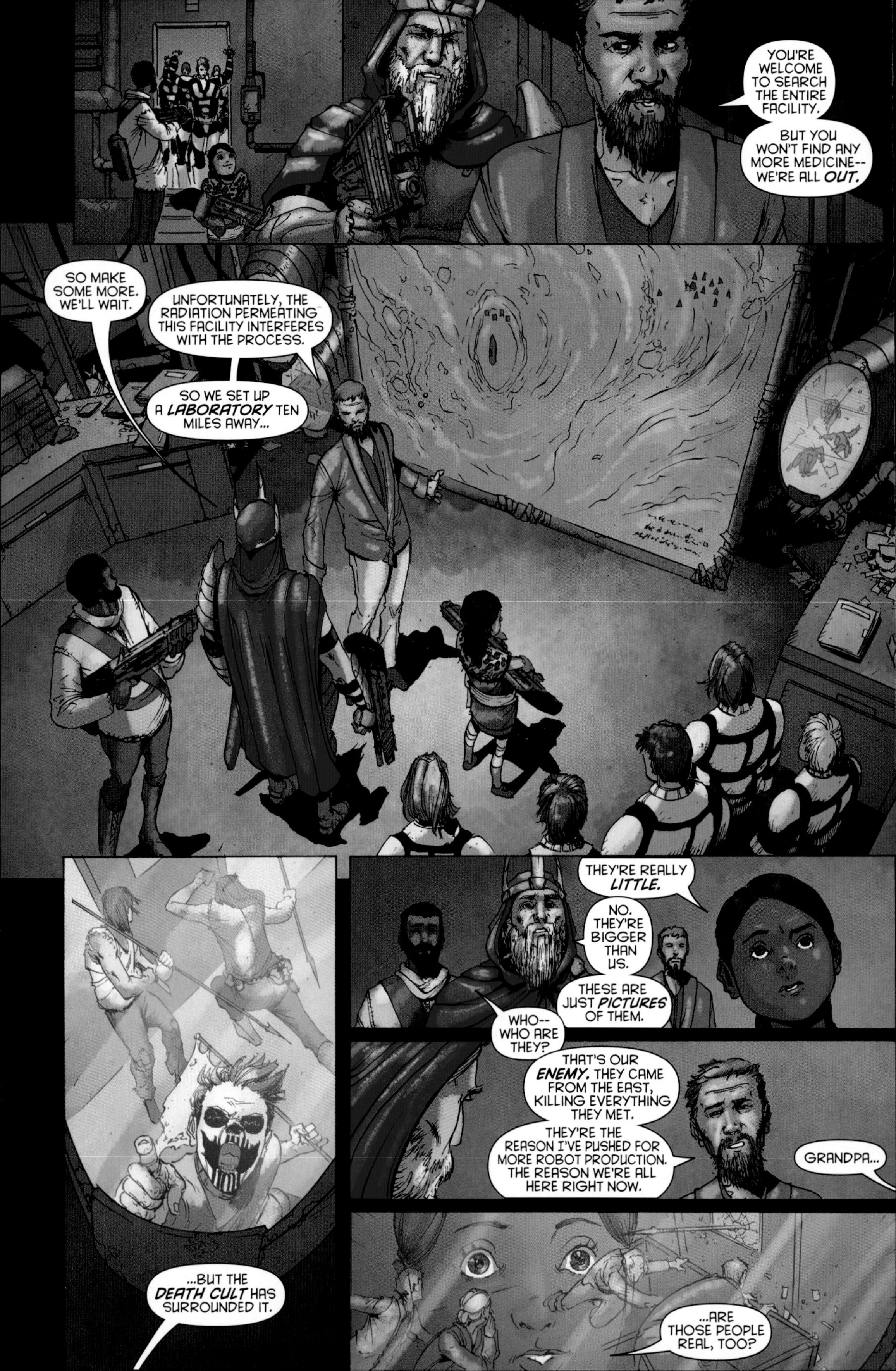
YOU'RE WELCOME TO SEARCH THE ENTIRE FACILITY.
BUT YOU WON'T FIND ANY MORE MEDICINE-- WE'RE ALL OUT.
SO MAKE SOME MORE. WE'LL WAIT.
UNFORTUNATELY, THE RADIATION PERMEATING THIS FACILITY INTERFERES WITH THE PROCESS.
SO WE SET UP A LABORATORY TEN MILES AWAY...
...BUT THE DEATH CULT HAS SURROUNDED IT.
THEY'RE REALLY LITTLE.
NO. THEY'RE BIGGER THAN US.
THESE ARE JUST PICTURES OF THEM.
WHO-- WHO ARE THEY?
THAT'S OUR ENEMY. THEY CAME FROM THE EAST, KILLING EVERYTHING THEY MET.
THEY'RE THE REASON I'VE PUSHED FOR MORE ROBOT PRODUCTION. THE REASON WE'RE ALL HERE RIGHT NOW.
GRANDPA...
...ARE THOSE PEOPLE REAL, TOO?

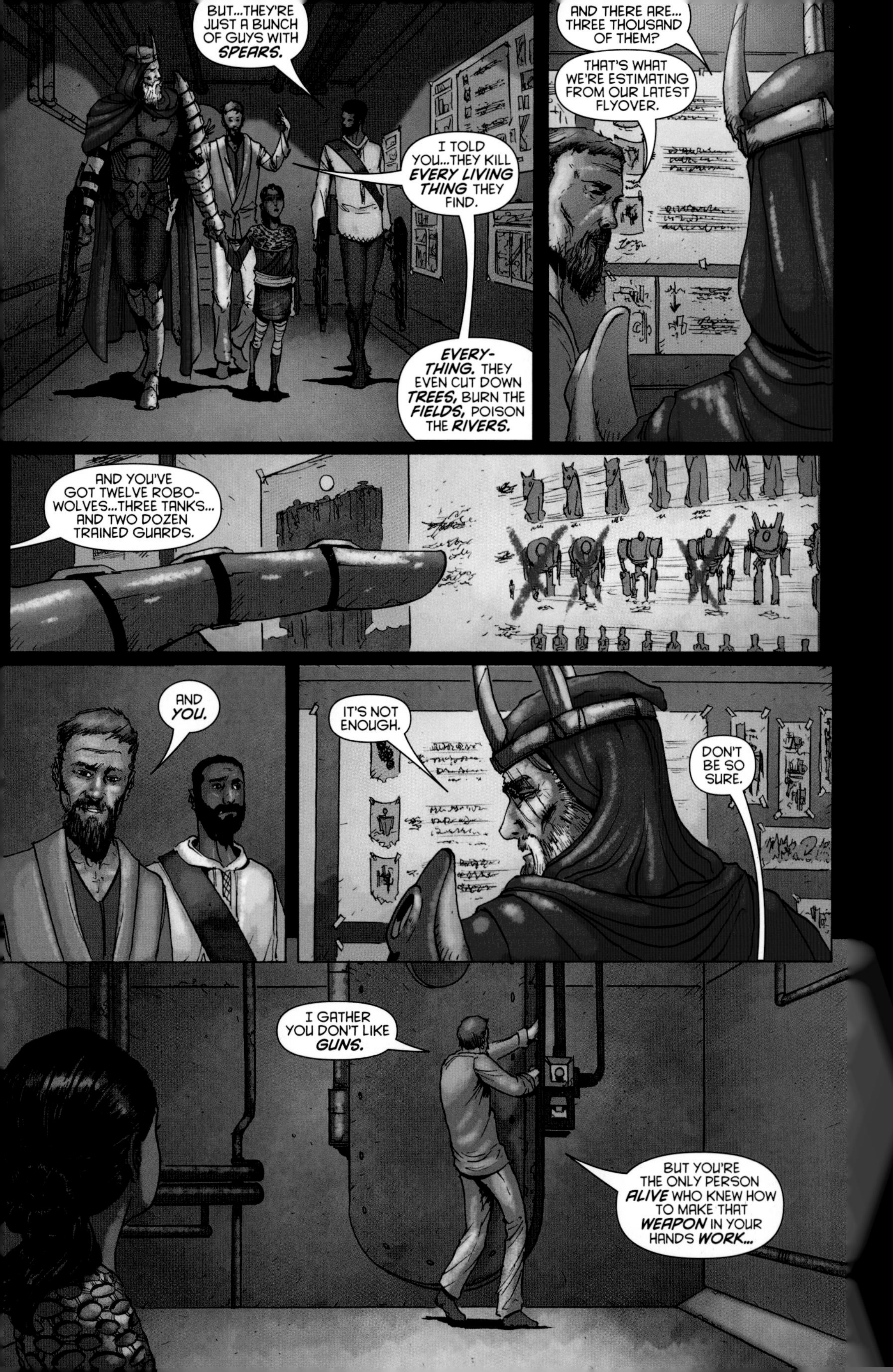

BUT...THEY'RE JUST A BUNCH OF GUYS WITH **SPEARS.**
I TOLD YOU...THEY KILL **EVERY LIVING THING** THEY FIND.
EVERY-THING. THEY EVEN CUT DOWN **TREES,** BURN THE **FIELDS,** POISON THE **RIVERS.**
AND THERE ARE... THREE THOUSAND OF THEM?
THAT'S WHAT WE'RE ESTIMATING FROM OUR LATEST FLYOVER.
AND YOU'VE GOT TWELVE ROBO-WOLVES...THREE TANKS... AND TWO DOZEN TRAINED GUARDS.
AND **YOU.**
IT'S NOT ENOUGH.
DON'T BE SO SURE.
I GATHER YOU DON'T LIKE **GUNS.**
BUT YOU'RE THE ONLY PERSON **ALIVE** WHO KNEW HOW TO MAKE THAT **WEAPON** IN YOUR HANDS **WORK...**

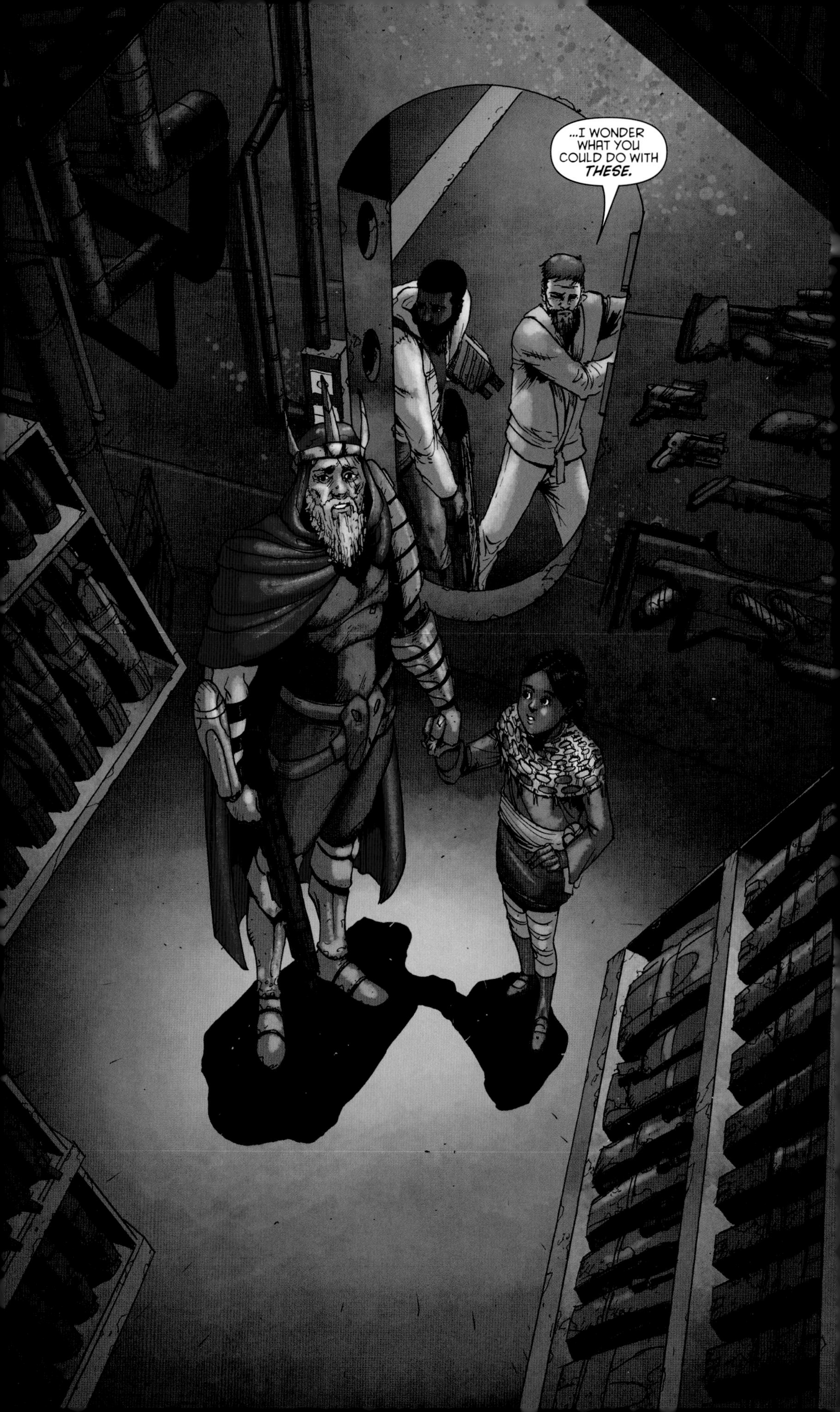
...I WONDER WHAT YOU COULD DO WITH THESE.

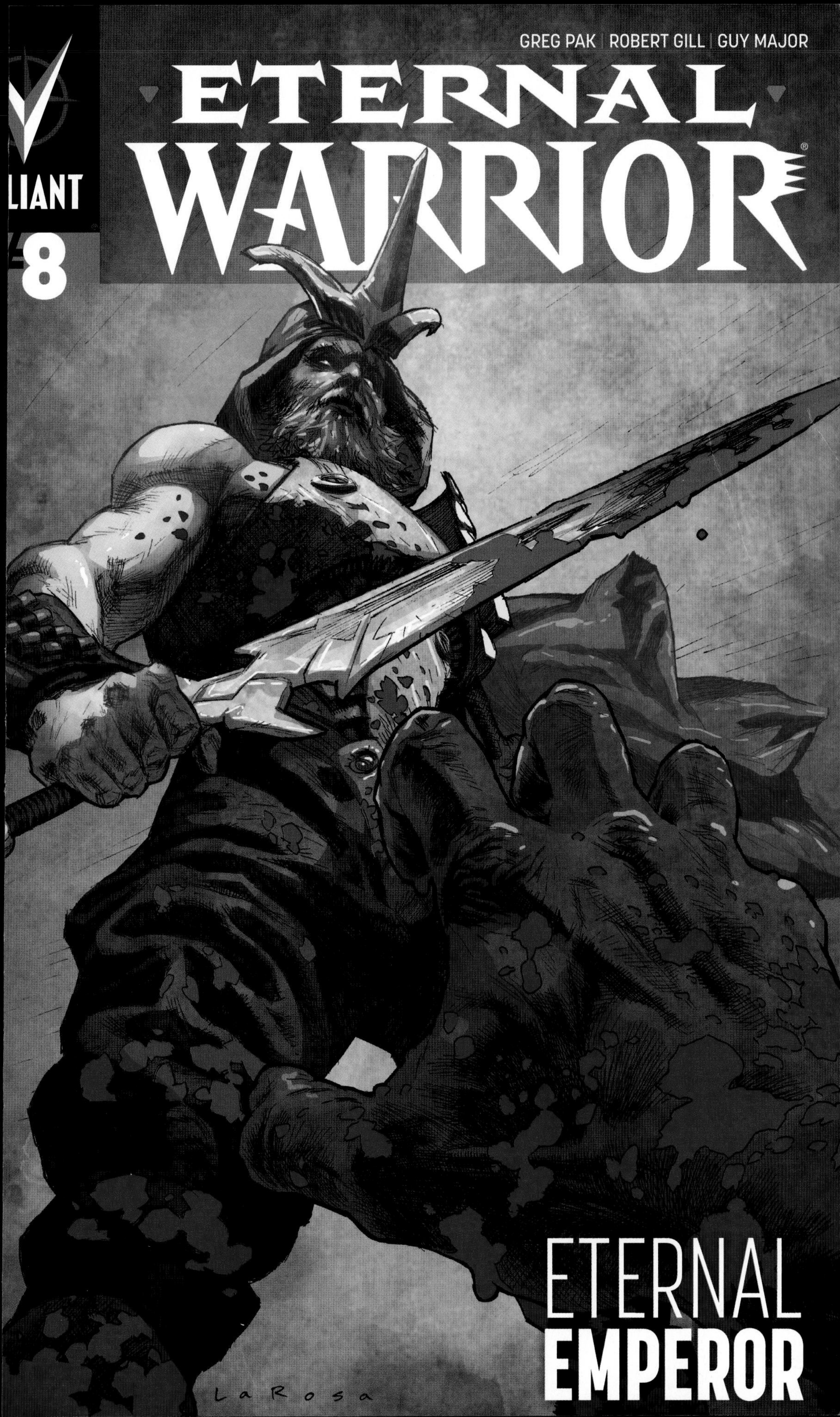

GREG PAK | ROBERT GILL | GUY MAJOR
ETERNAL WARRIOR
LIANT
8
ETERNAL EMPEROR
LaRosa

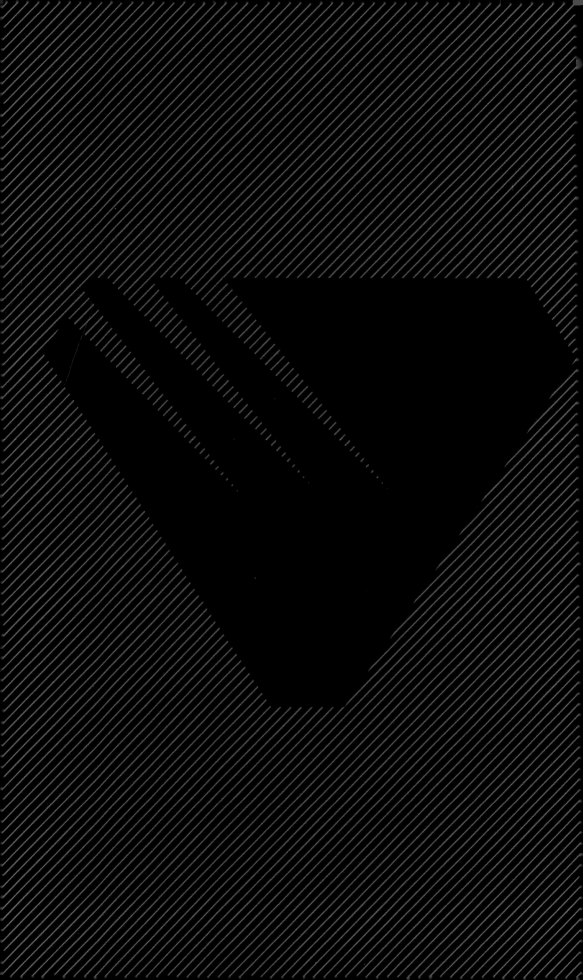

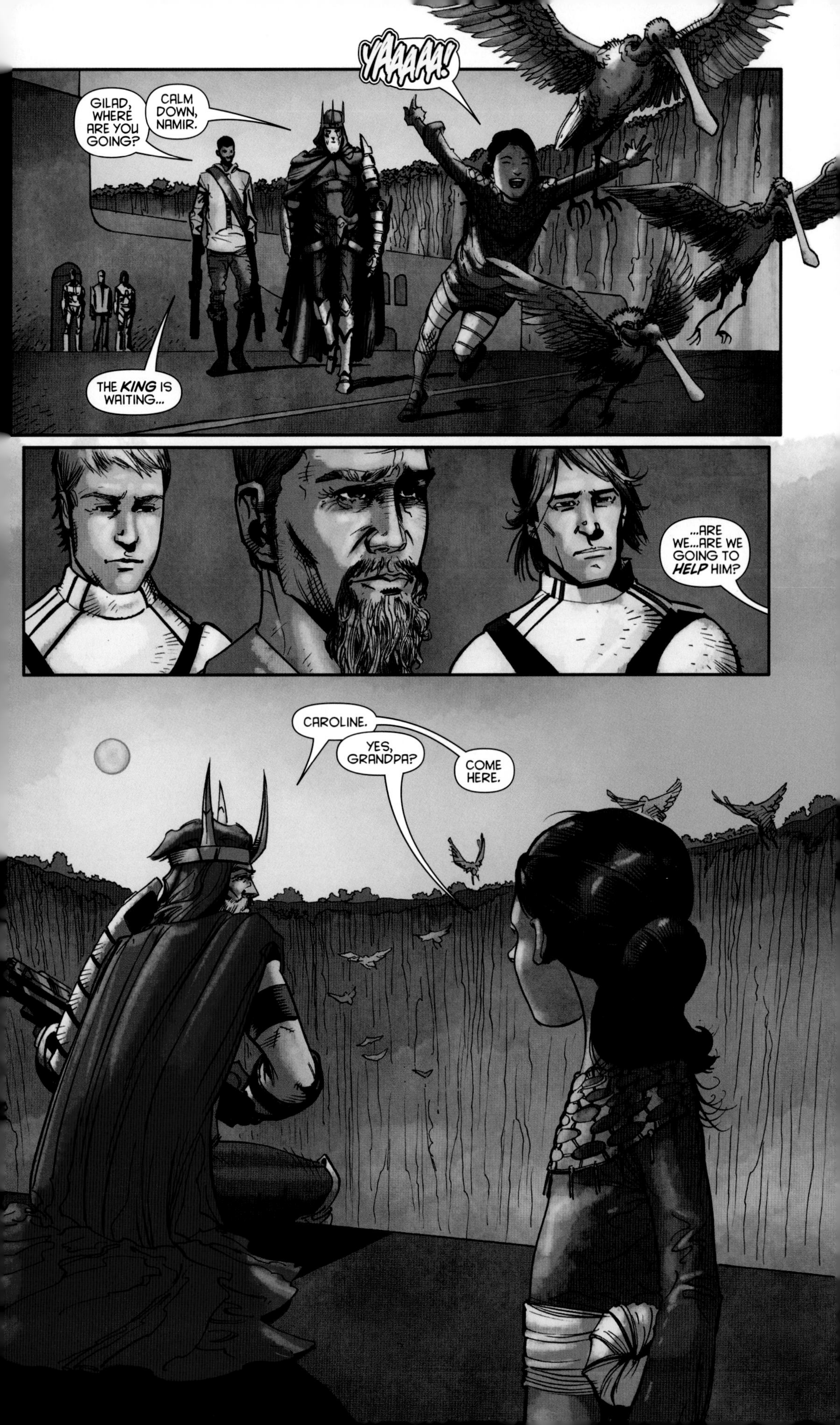
YAAAAA!
GILAD, WHERE ARE YOU GOING?
CALM DOWN, NAMIR.
THE KING IS WAITING...
...ARE WE...ARE WE GOING TO HELP HIM?
CAROLINE.
YES, GRANDPA?
COME HERE.

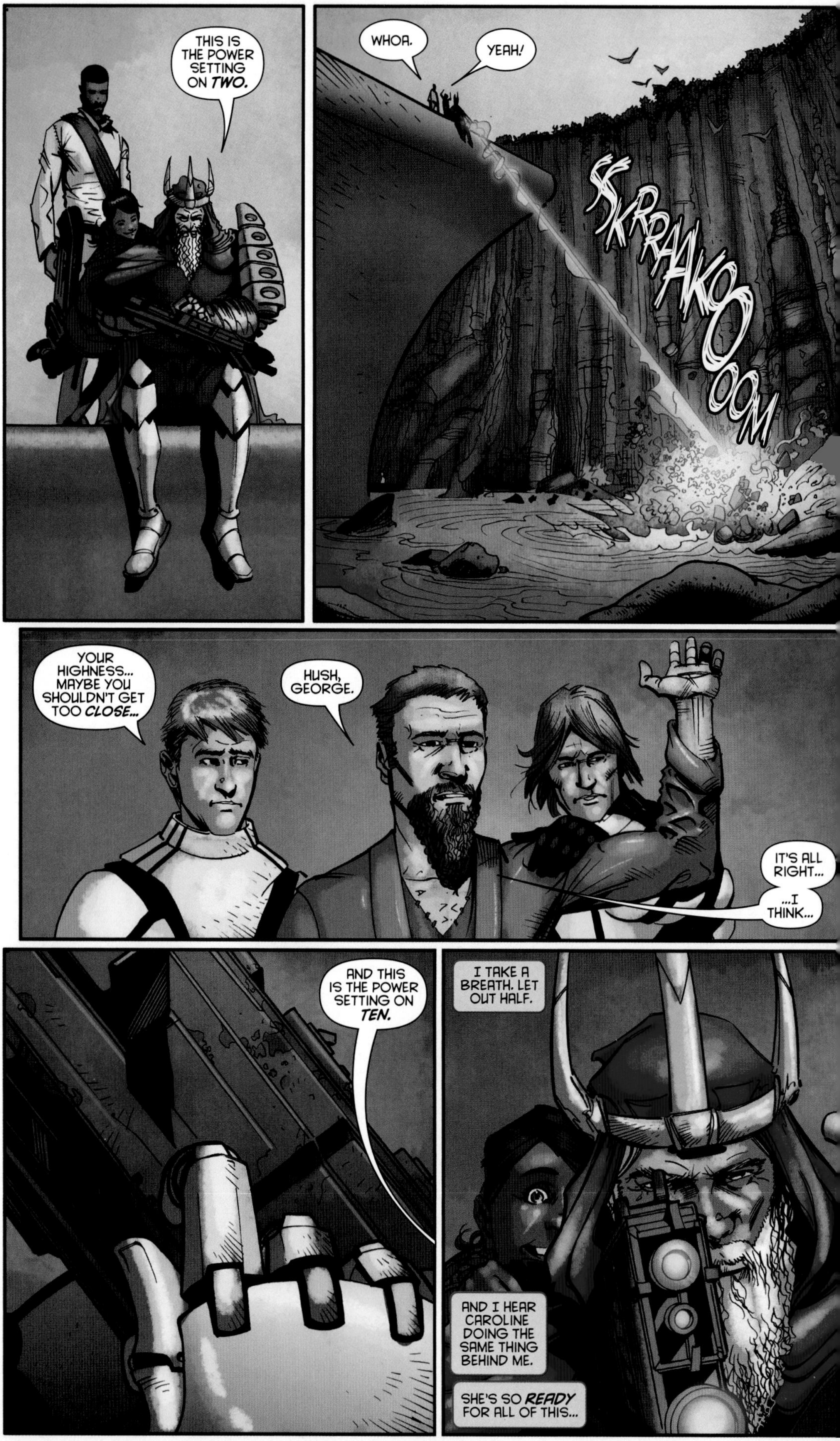
THIS IS THE POWER SETTING ON *TWO.*
WHOA.
YEAH!
SKRRAAKOOOOM
YOUR HIGHNESS... MAYBE YOU SHOULDN'T GET TOO *CLOSE...*
HUSH, GEORGE.
IT'S ALL RIGHT...
...I THINK...
AND THIS IS THE POWER SETTING ON *TEN.*
I TAKE A BREATH. LET OUT HALF.
AND I HEAR CAROLINE DOING THE SAME THING BEHIND ME.
SHE'S SO *READY* FOR ALL OF THIS...

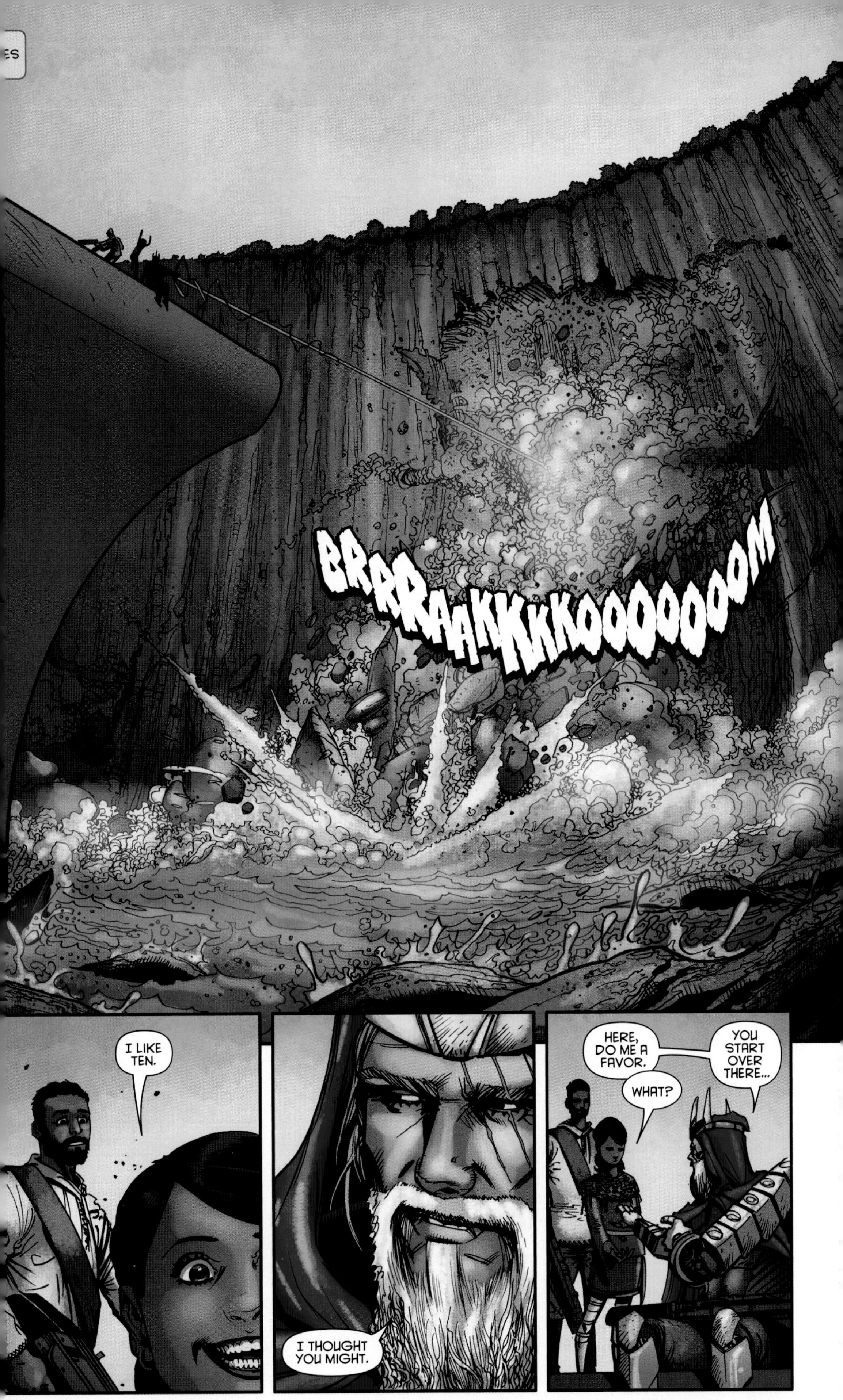

ES
BRRRAAKKKKOOOOOOOM
I LIKE TEN.
I THOUGHT YOU MIGHT.
HERE, DO ME A FAVOR.
WHAT?
YOU START OVER THERE...

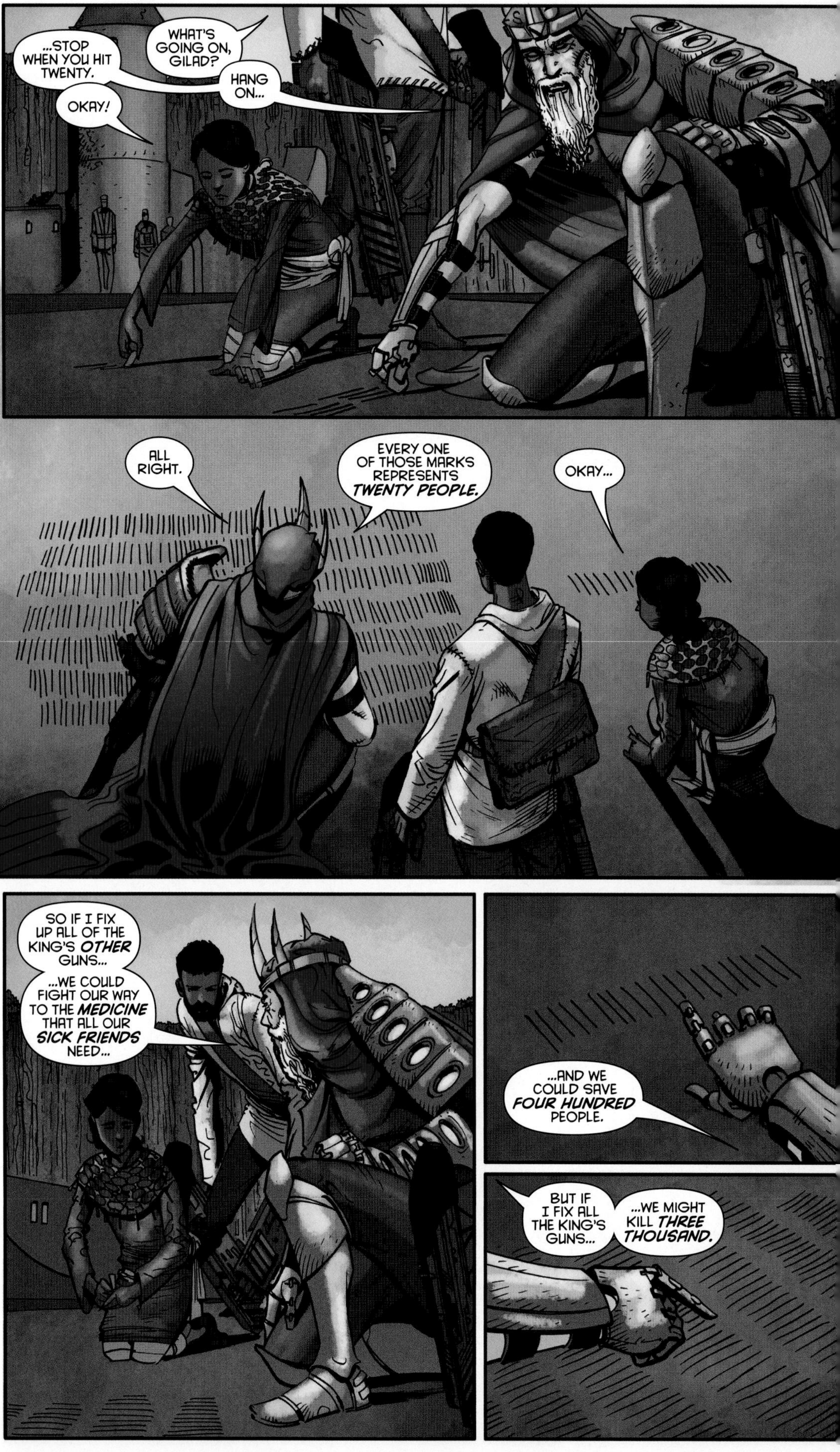

...STOP WHEN YOU HIT TWENTY.
WHAT'S GOING ON, GILAD?
OKAY!
HANG ON...
ALL RIGHT.
EVERY ONE OF THOSE MARKS REPRESENTS TWENTY PEOPLE.
OKAY...
SO IF I FIX UP ALL OF THE KING'S OTHER GUNS...
...WE COULD FIGHT OUR WAY TO THE MEDICINE THAT ALL OUR SICK FRIENDS NEED...
...AND WE COULD SAVE FOUR HUNDRED PEOPLE.
BUT IF I FIX ALL THE KING'S GUNS...
...WE MIGHT KILL THREE THOUSAND.

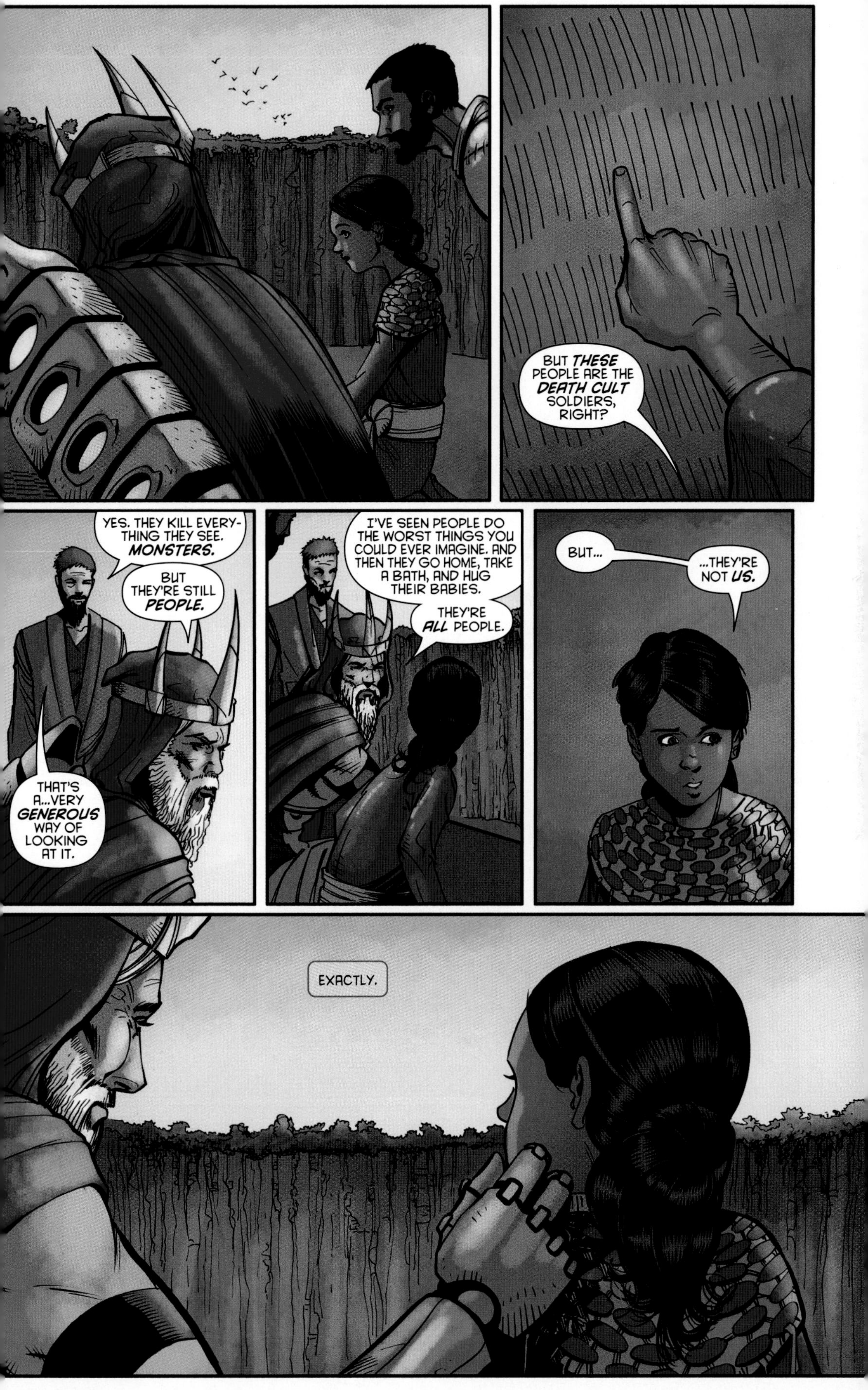
BUT THESE PEOPLE ARE THE DEATH CULT SOLDIERS, RIGHT?
YES. THEY KILL EVERY-THING THEY SEE. MONSTERS.
BUT THEY'RE STILL PEOPLE.
THAT'S A...VERY GENEROUS WAY OF LOOKING AT IT.
I'VE SEEN PEOPLE DO THE WORST THINGS YOU COULD EVER IMAGINE. AND THEN THEY GO HOME, TAKE A BATH, AND HUG THEIR BABIES.
THEY'RE ALL PEOPLE.
BUT...
...THEY'RE NOT US.
EXACTLY.

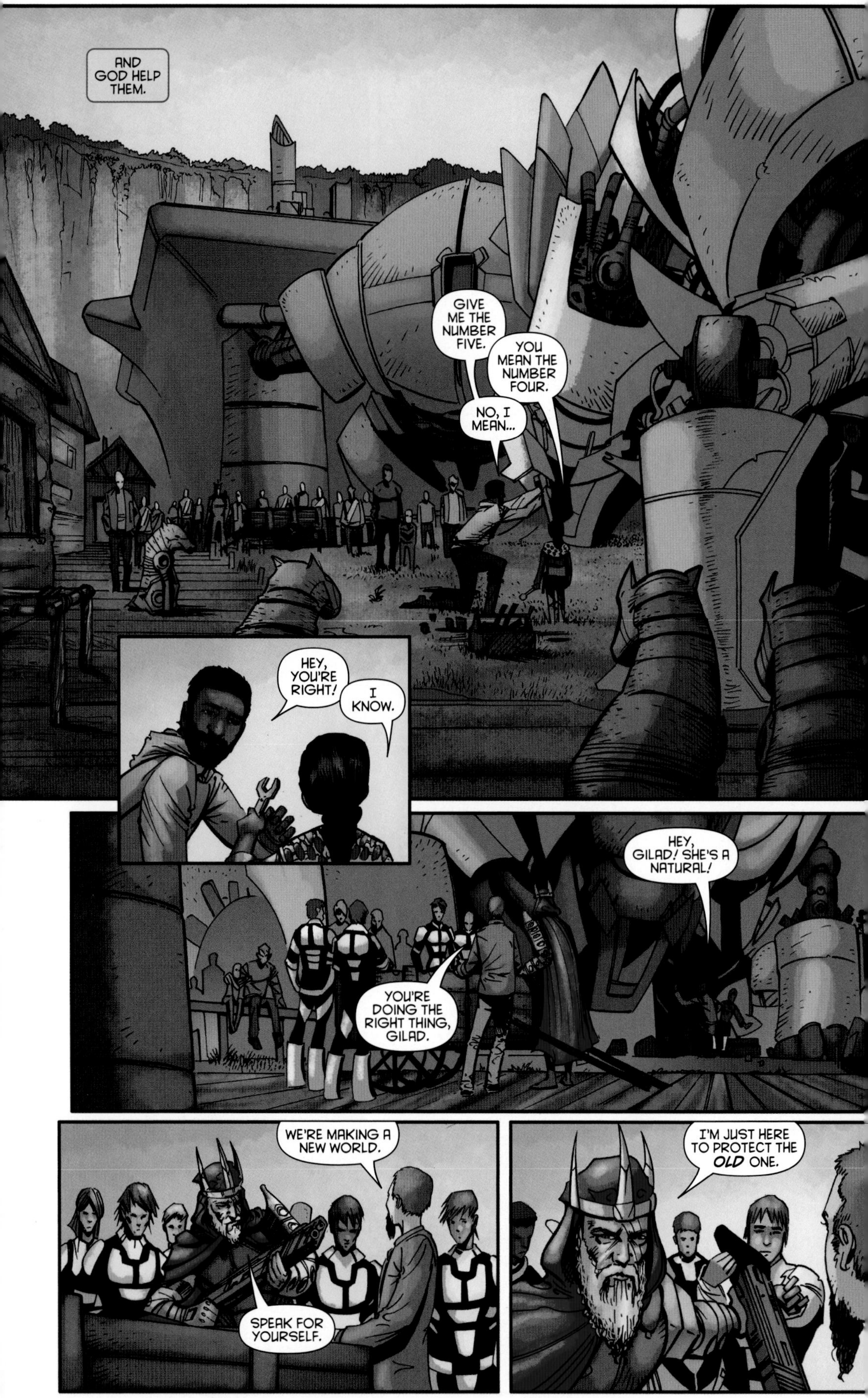
AND GOD HELP THEM.
GIVE ME THE NUMBER FIVE.
YOU MEAN THE NUMBER FOUR.
NO, I MEAN...
HEY, YOU'RE RIGHT!
I KNOW.
HEY, GILAD! SHE'S A NATURAL!
YOU'RE DOING THE RIGHT THING, GILAD.
WE'RE MAKING A NEW WORLD.
SPEAK FOR YOURSELF.
I'M JUST HERE TO PROTECT THE *OLD* ONE.

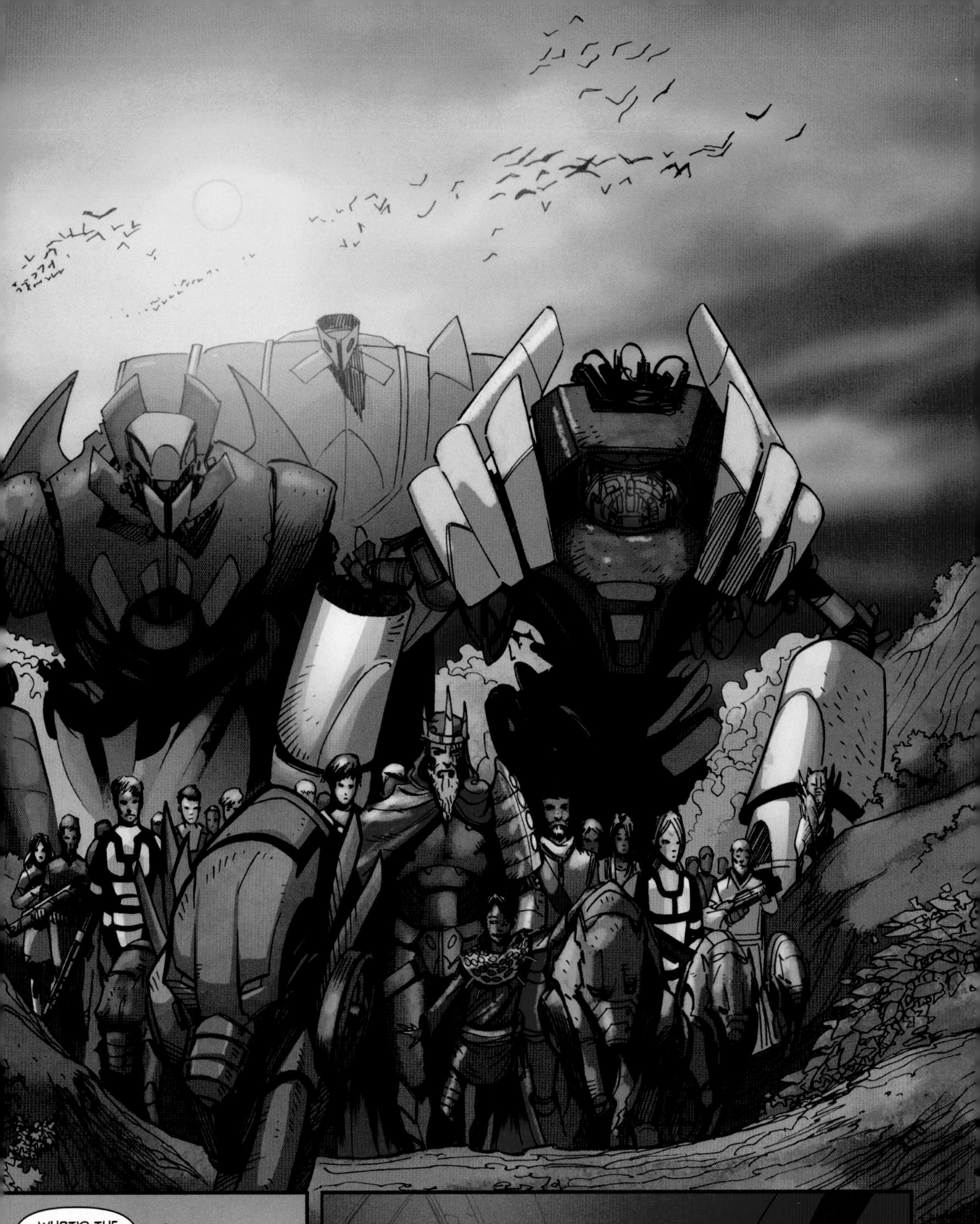

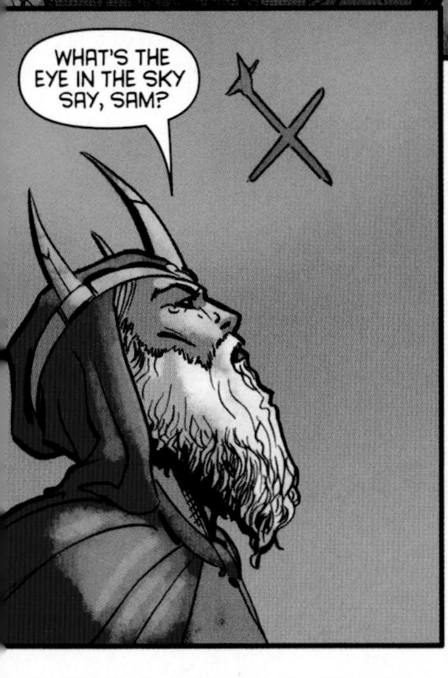
WHAT'S THE EYE IN THE SKY SAY, SAM?

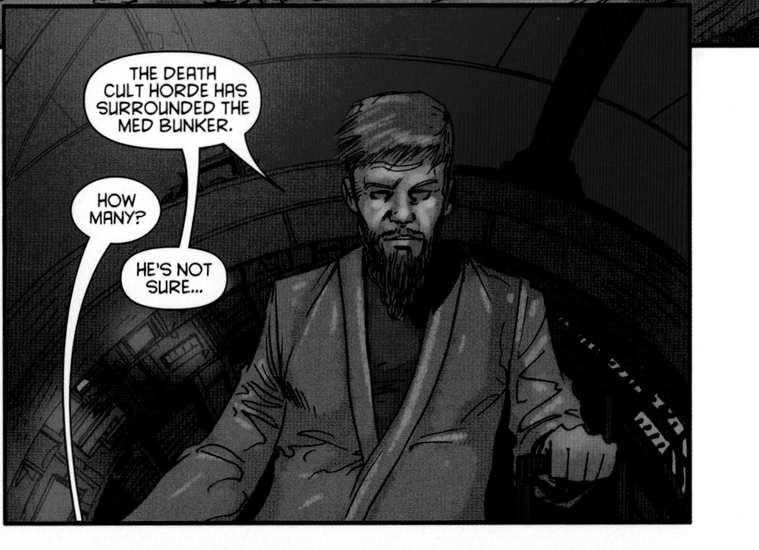
THE DEATH CULT HORDE HAS SURROUNDED THE MED BUNKER.
HOW MANY?
HE'S NOT SURE...

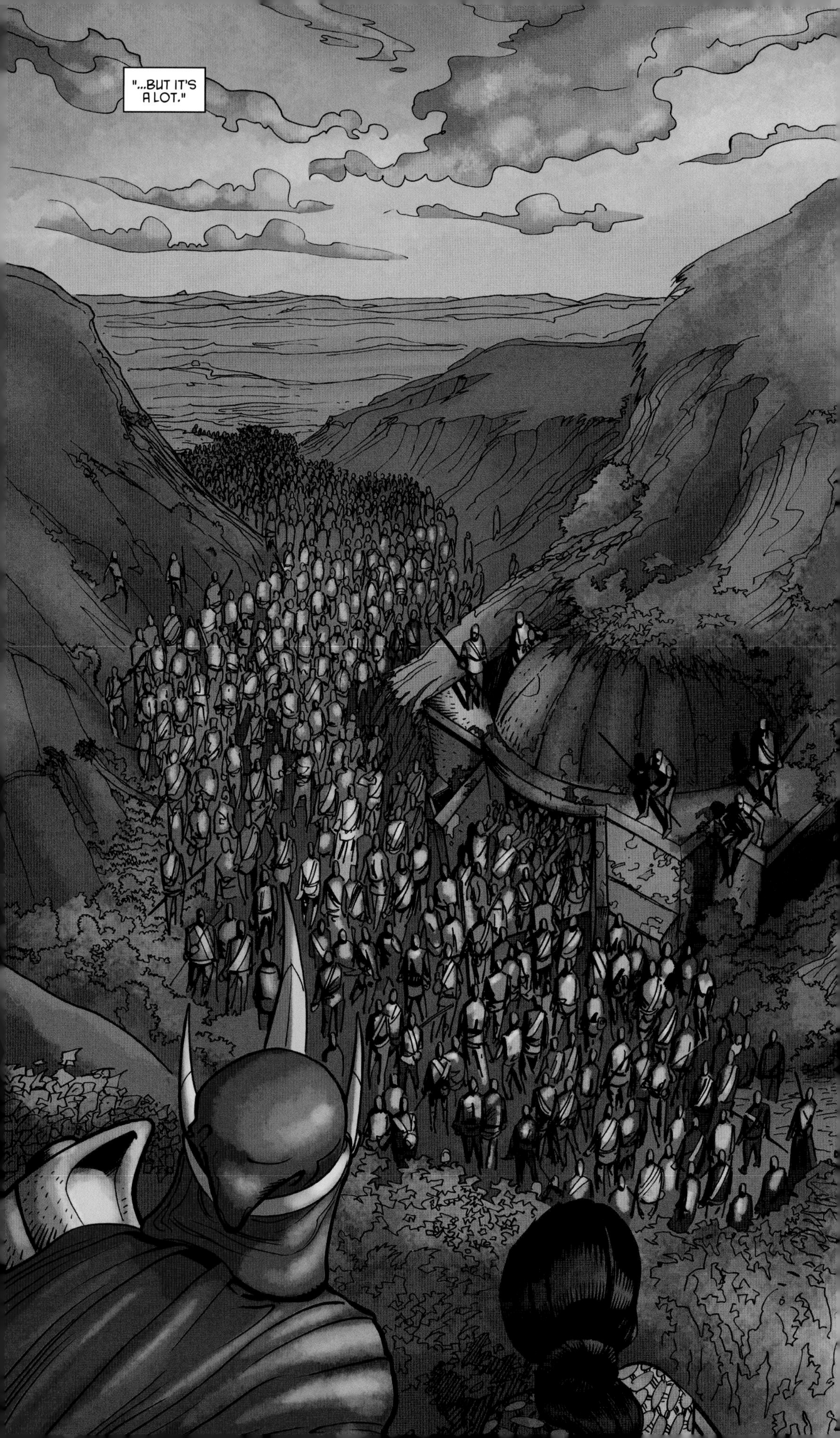
"...BUT IT'S A LOT."

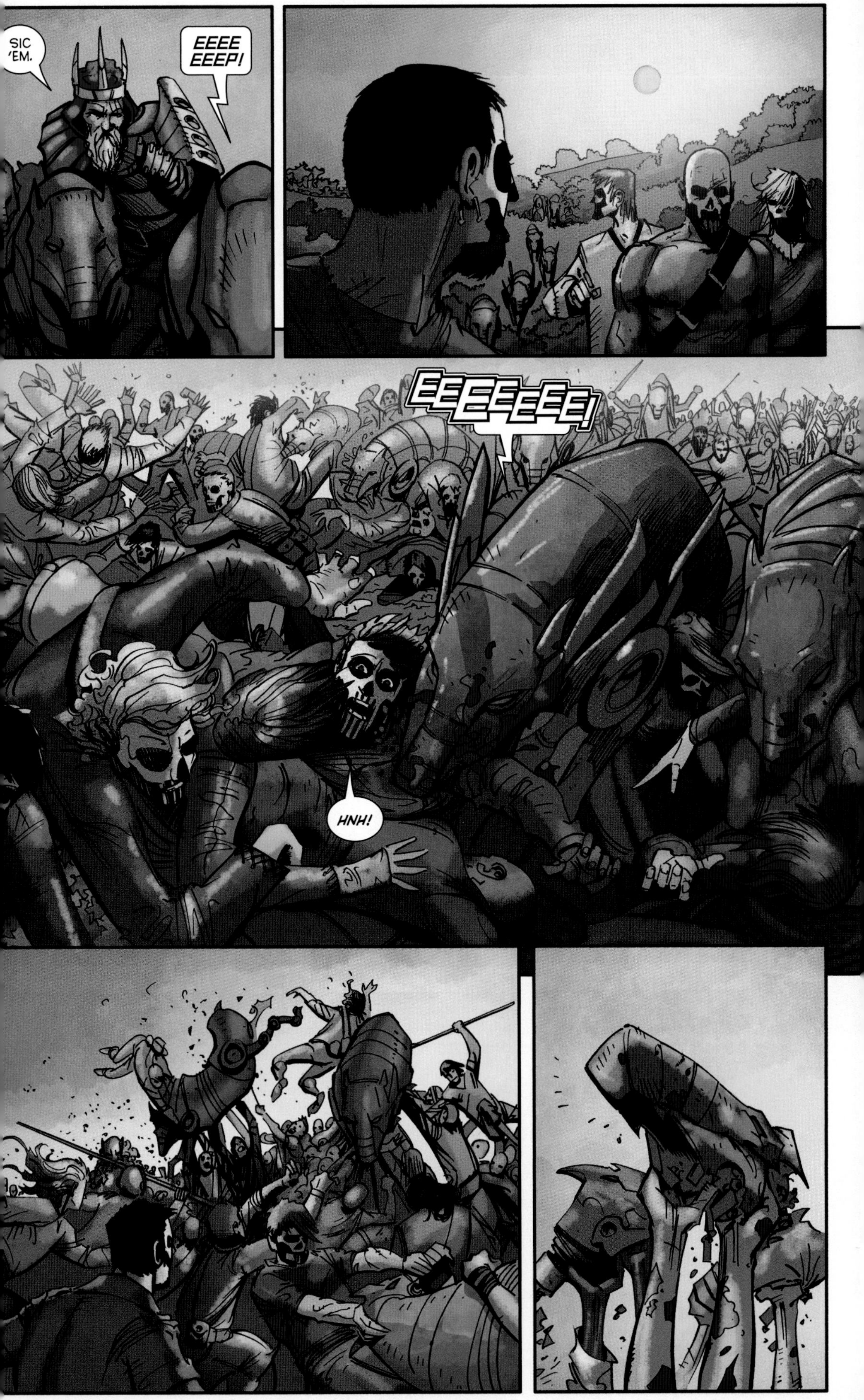
SIC 'EM.
EEEE EEEP!
EEEEEEEE!
HNH!

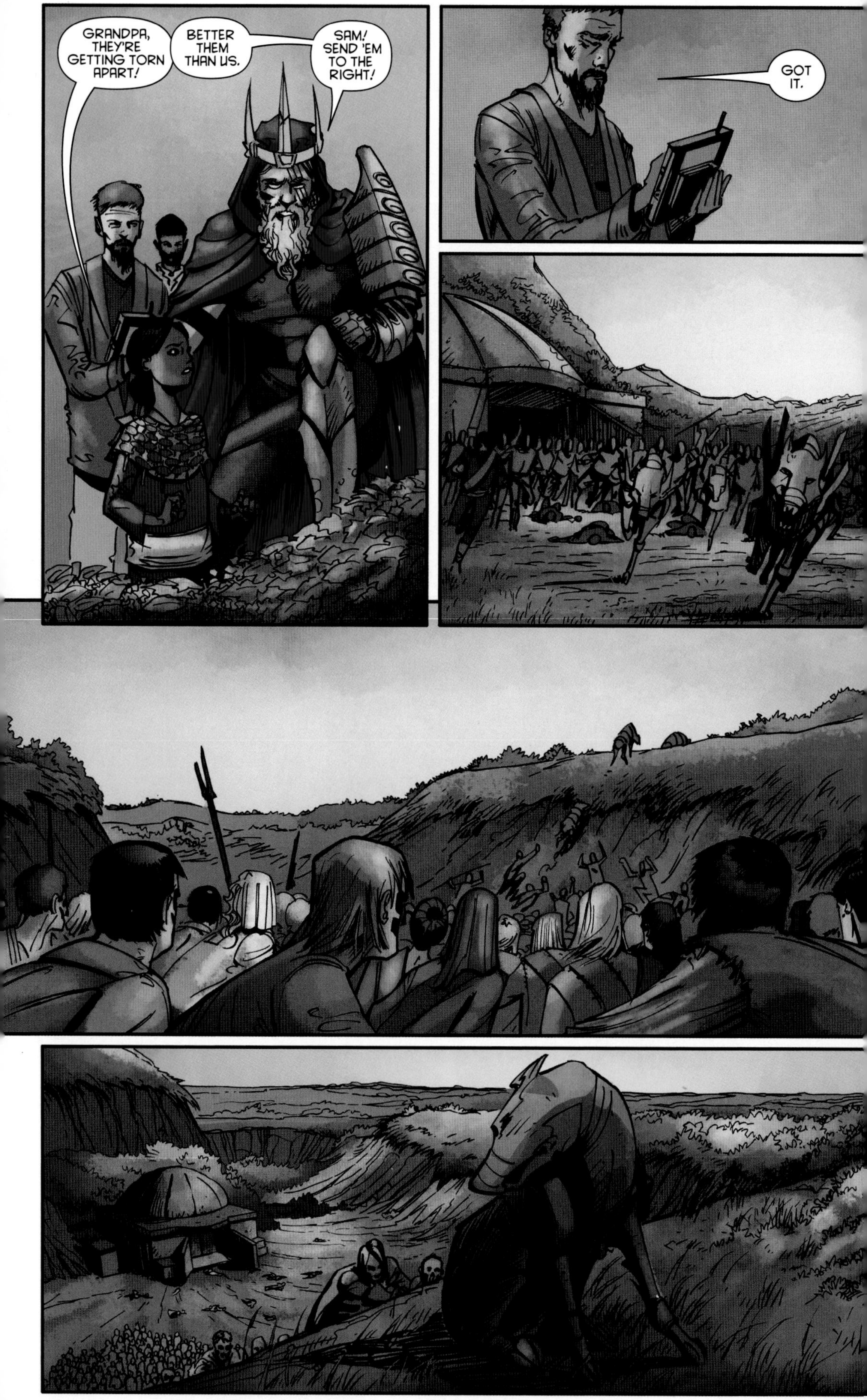

GRANDPA, THEY'RE GETTING TORN APART!
BETTER THEM THAN US.
SAM! SEND 'EM TO THE RIGHT!
GOT IT.

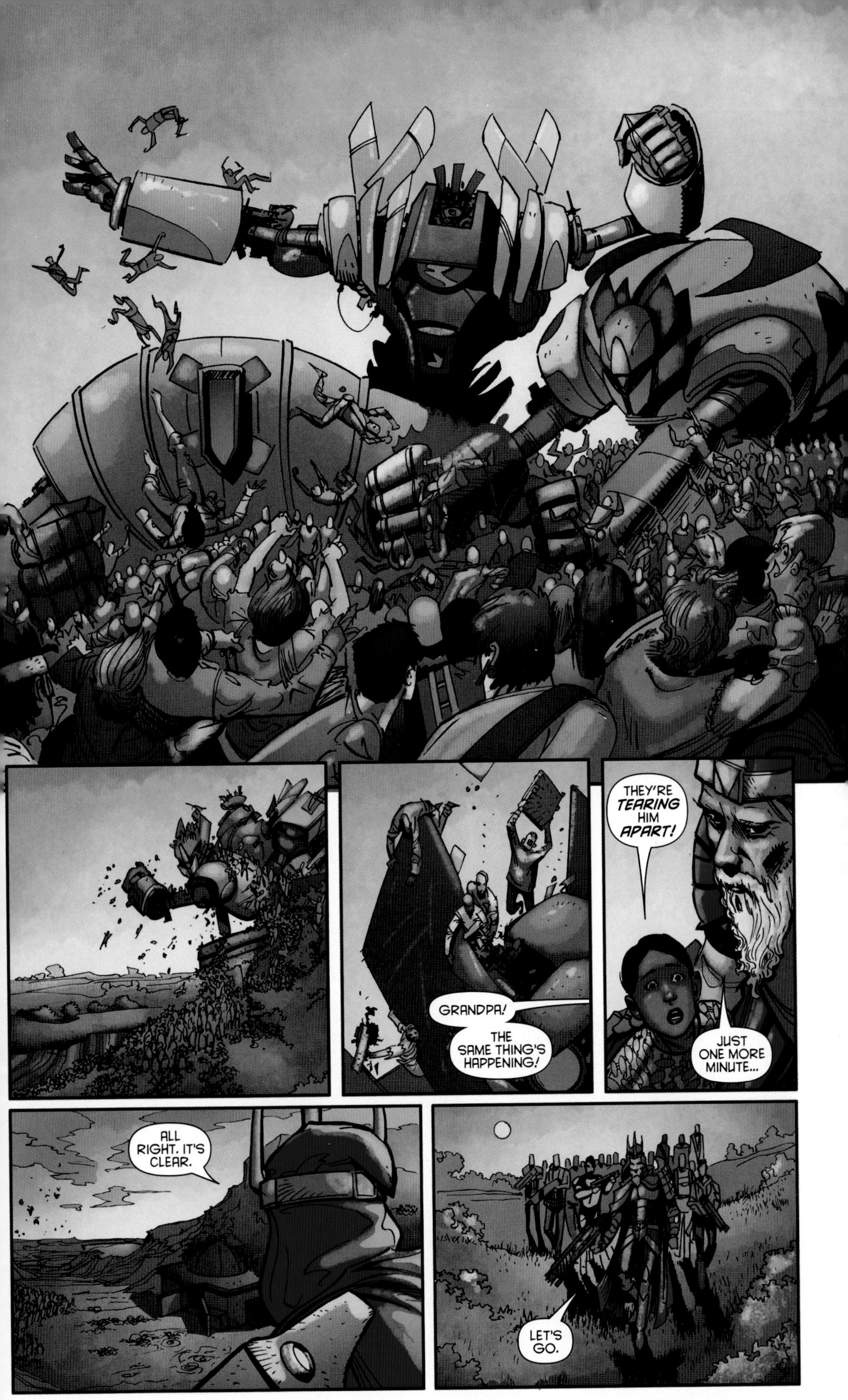
GRANDPA!
THE SAME THING'S HAPPENING!
THEY'RE TEARING HIM APART!
JUST ONE MORE MINUTE...
ALL RIGHT. IT'S CLEAR.
LET'S GO.

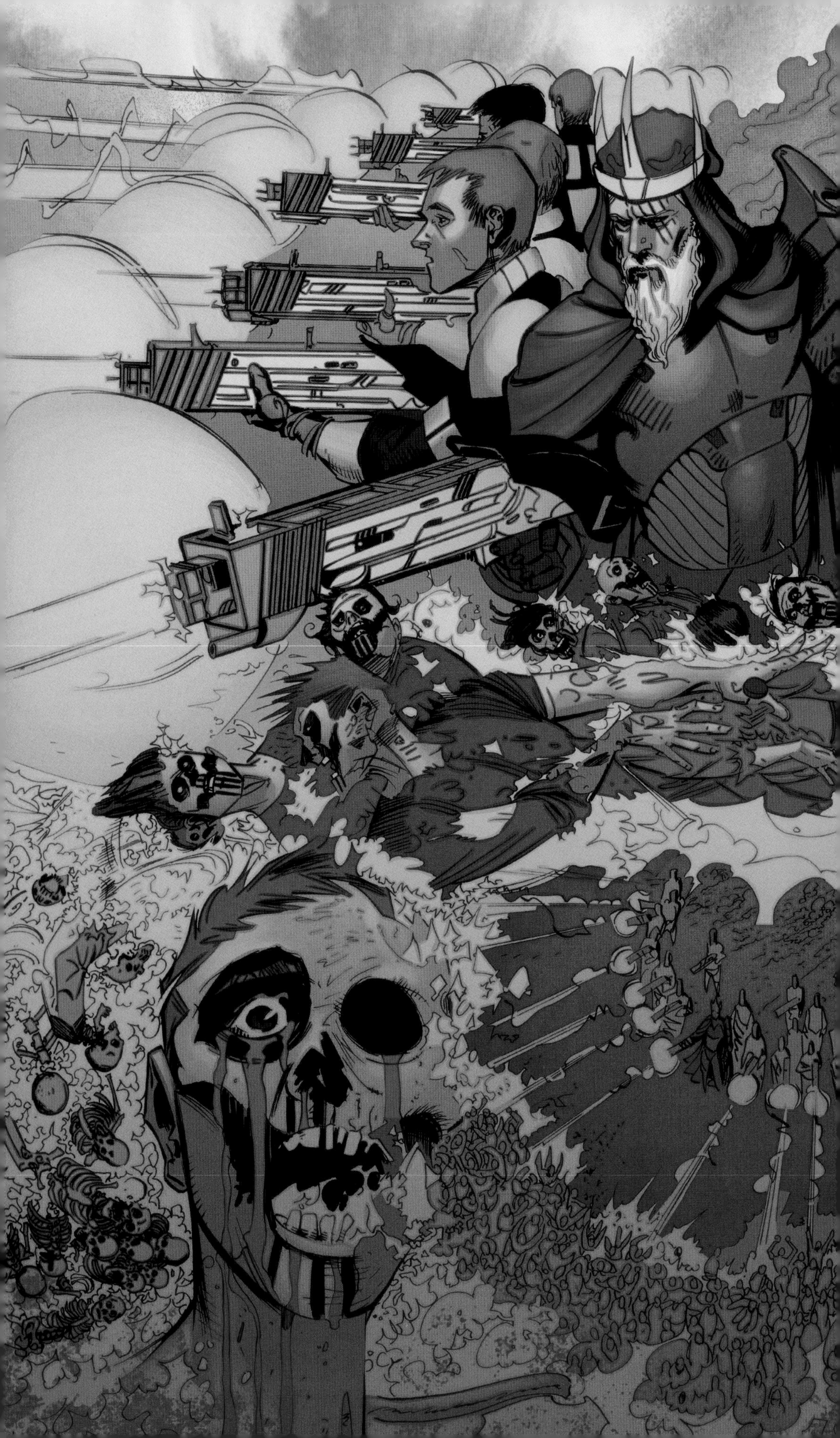

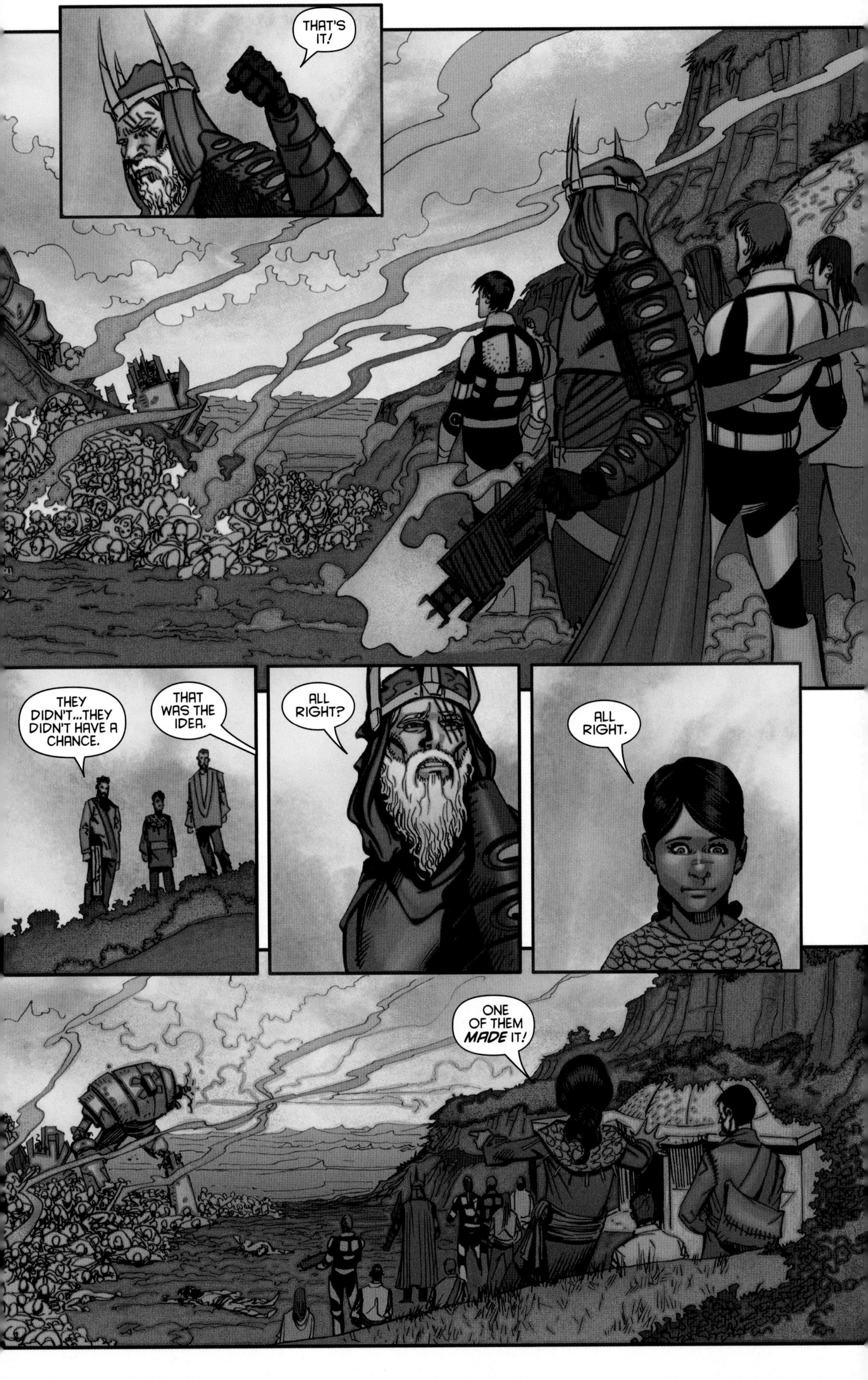
THAT'S IT!
THEY DIDN'T...THEY DIDN'T HAVE A CHANCE.
THAT WAS THE IDEA.
ALL RIGHT?
ALL RIGHT.
ONE OF THEM *MADE* IT!

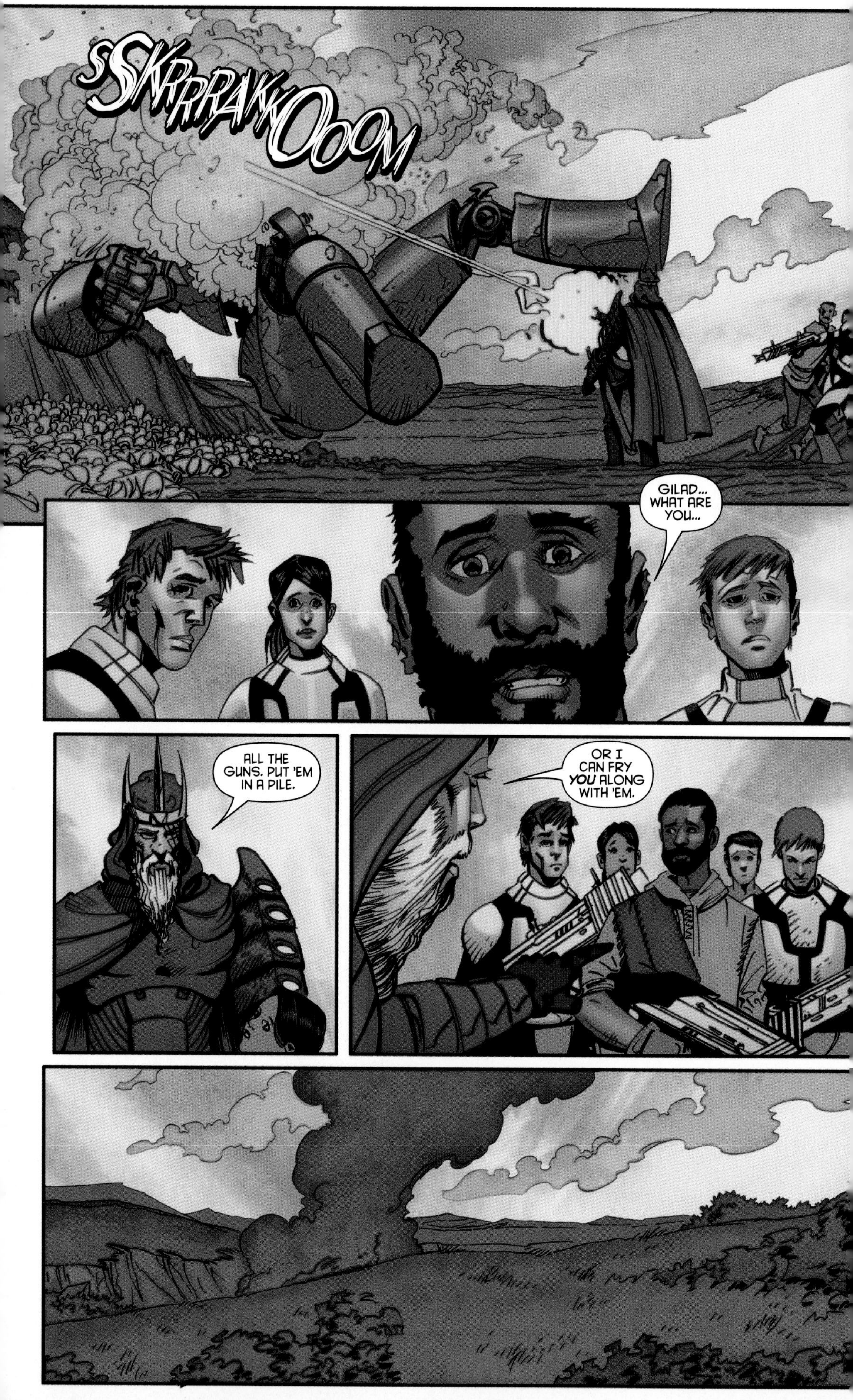
SSKRRRAKKOOOOM
GILAD... WHAT ARE YOU...
ALL THE GUNS. PUT 'EM IN A PILE.
OR I CAN FRY *YOU* ALONG WITH 'EM.

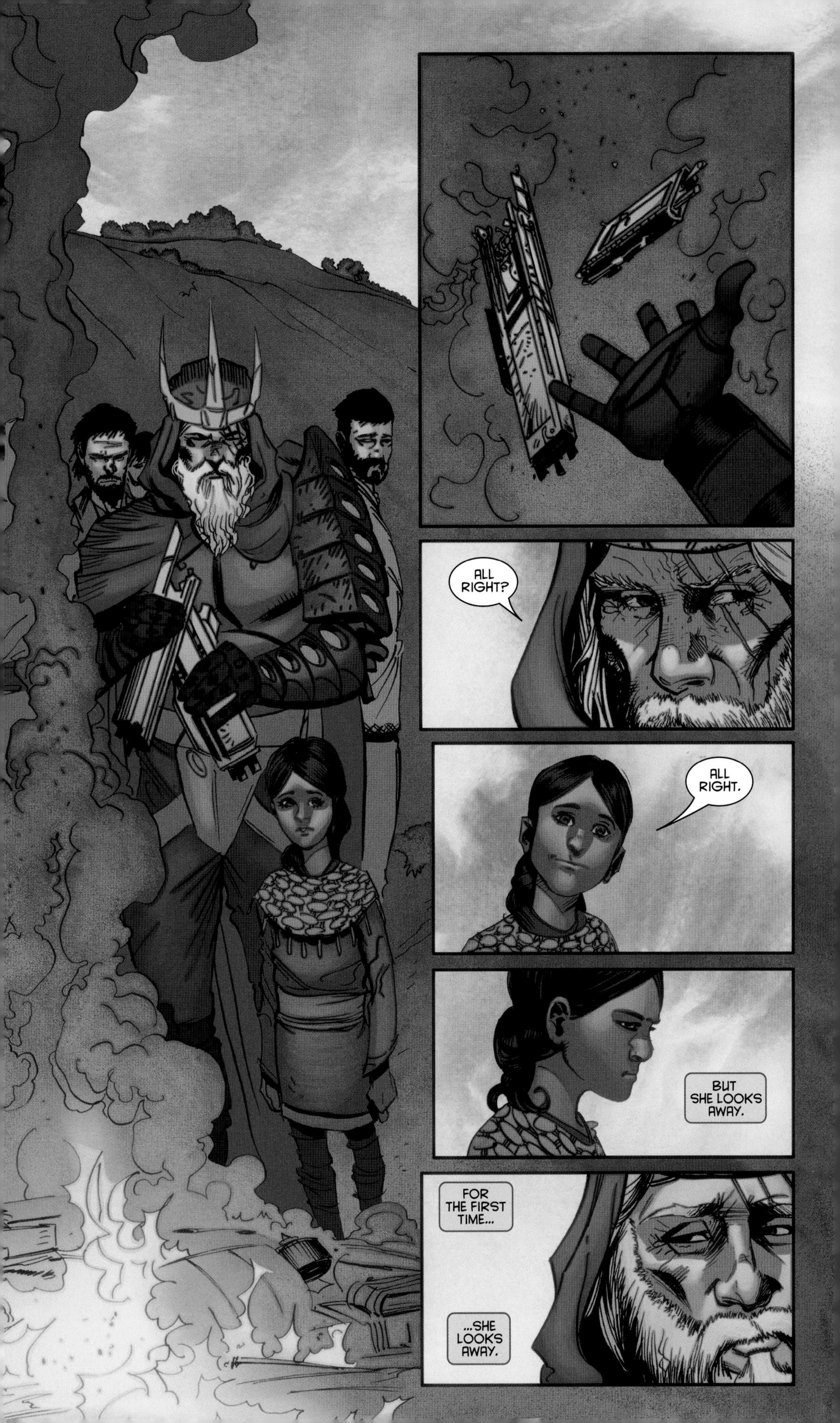
ALL RIGHT?
ALL RIGHT.
BUT SHE LOOKS AWAY.
FOR THE FIRST TIME...
...SHE LOOKS AWAY.

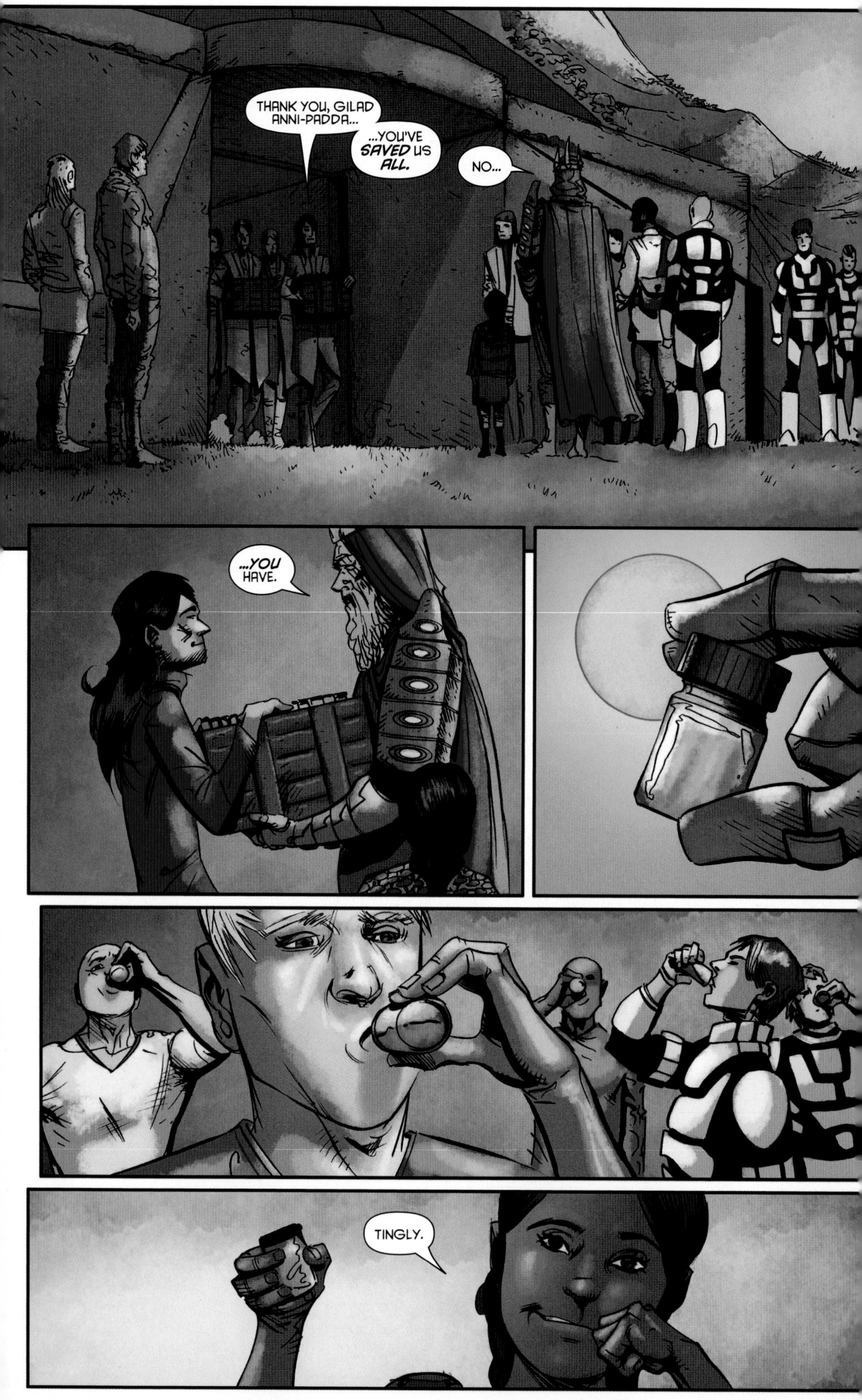
THANK YOU, GILAD ANNI-PADDA...
...YOU'VE SAVED US ALL.
NO...
...YOU HAVE.
TINGLY.

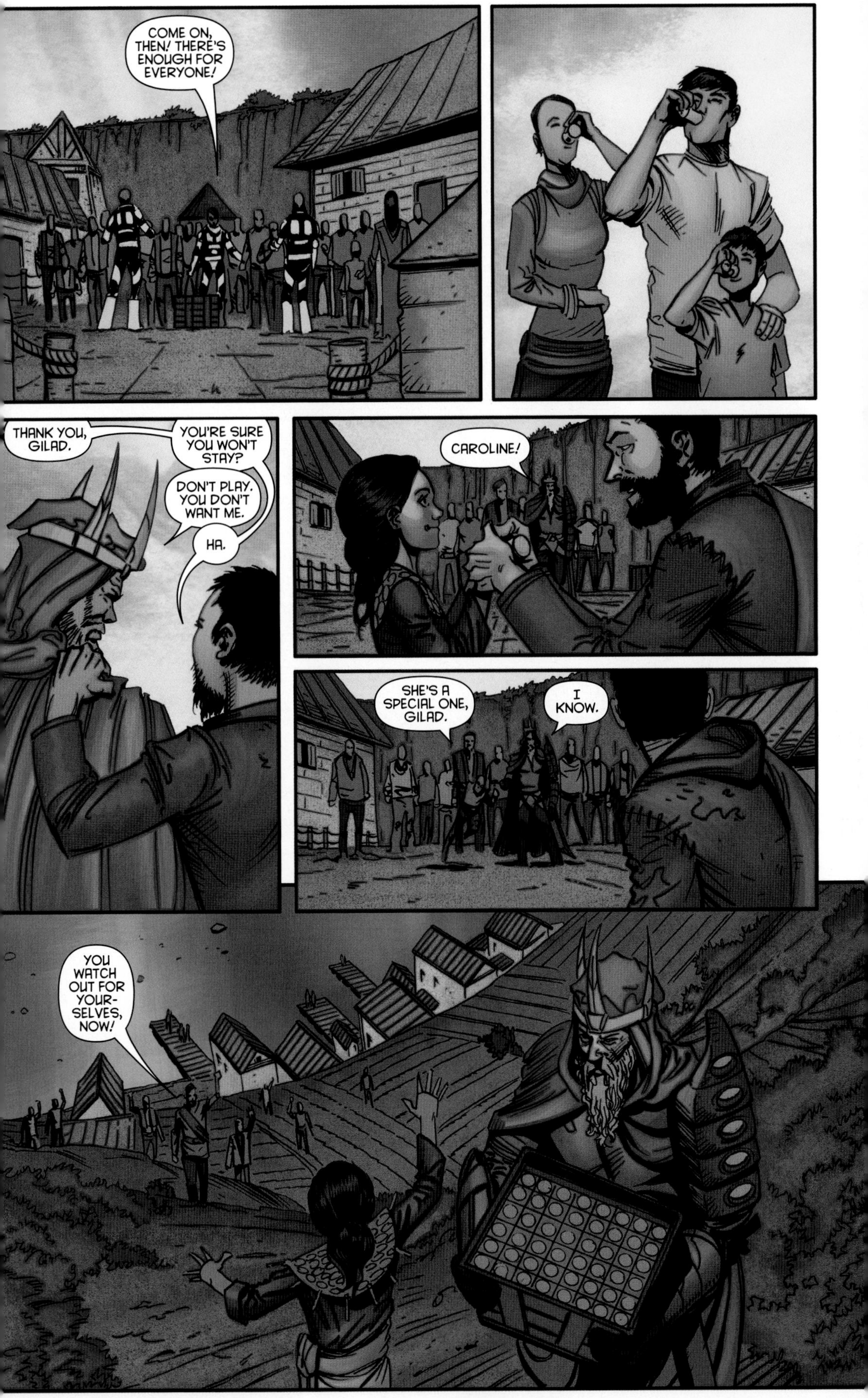
COME ON, THEN! THERE'S ENOUGH FOR EVERYONE!
THANK YOU, GILAD.
YOU'RE SURE YOU WON'T STAY?
DON'T PLAY. YOU DON'T WANT ME.
HA.
CAROLINE!
SHE'S A SPECIAL ONE, GILAD.
I KNOW.
YOU WATCH OUT FOR YOUR-SELVES, NOW!

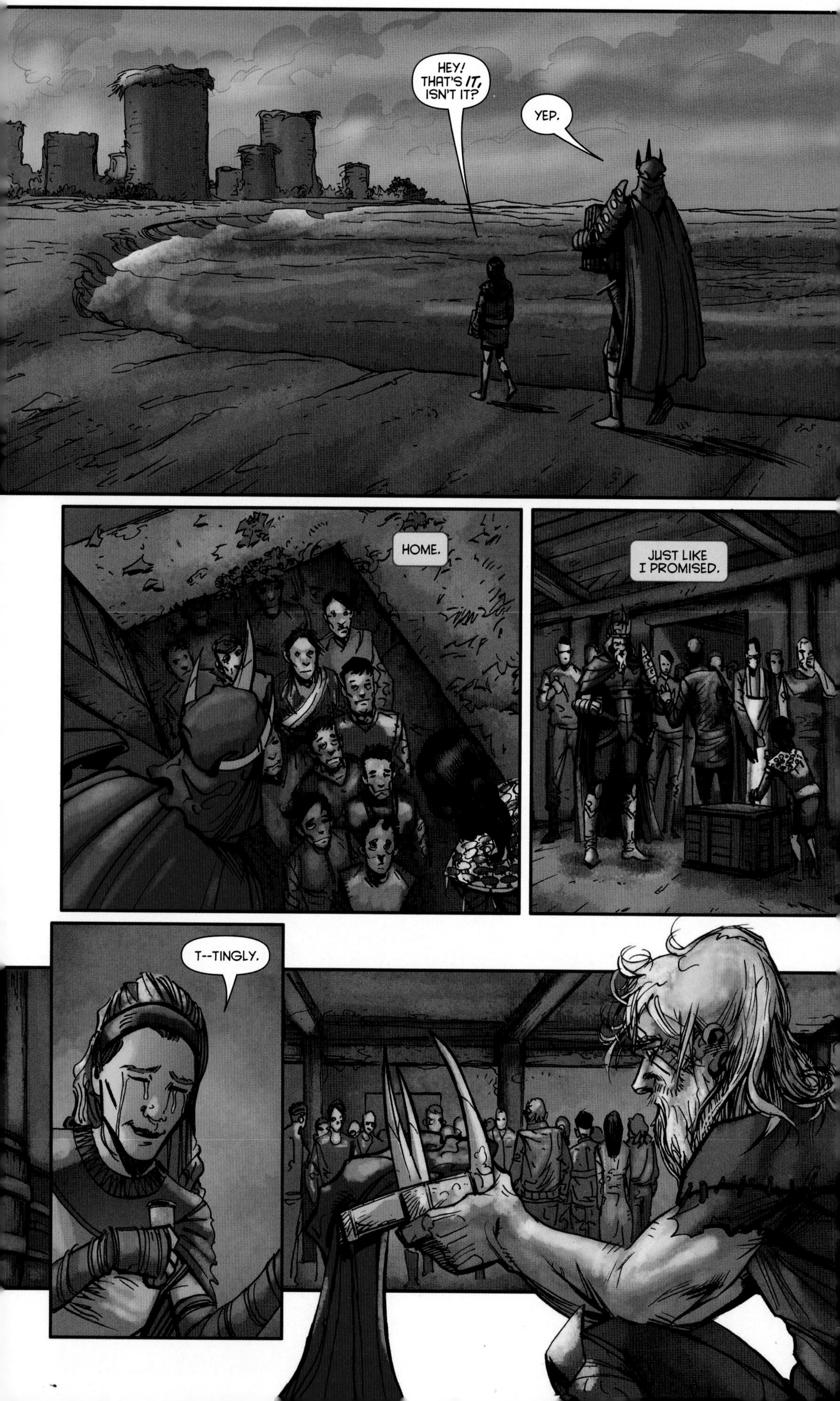
HEY! THAT'S *IT*, ISN'T IT?
YEP.
HOME.
JUST LIKE I PROMISED.
T--TINGLY.

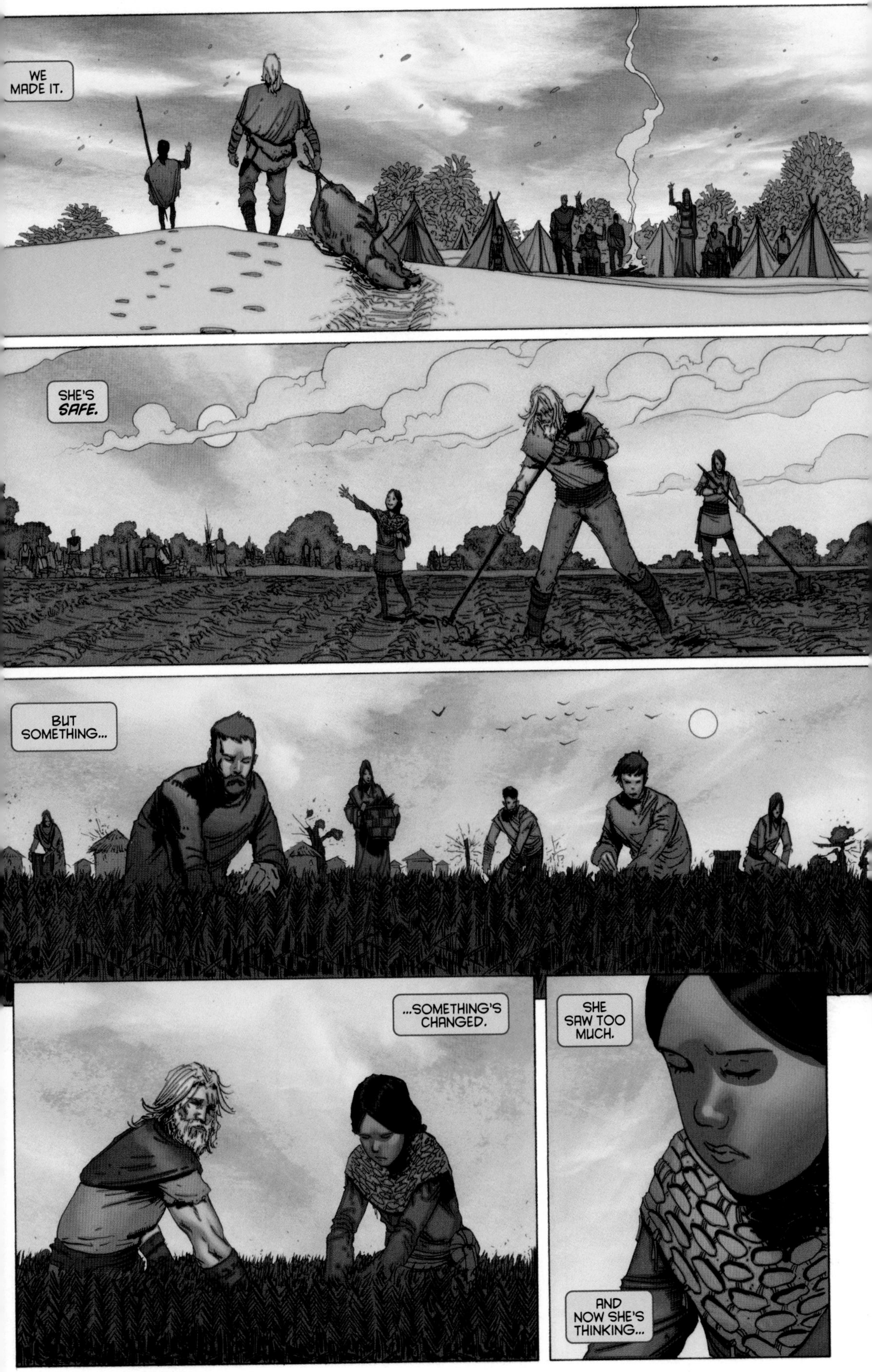
WE MADE IT.
SHE'S *SAFE.*
BUT SOMETHING...
...SOMETHING'S CHANGED.
SHE SAW TOO MUCH.
AND NOW SHE'S THINKING...

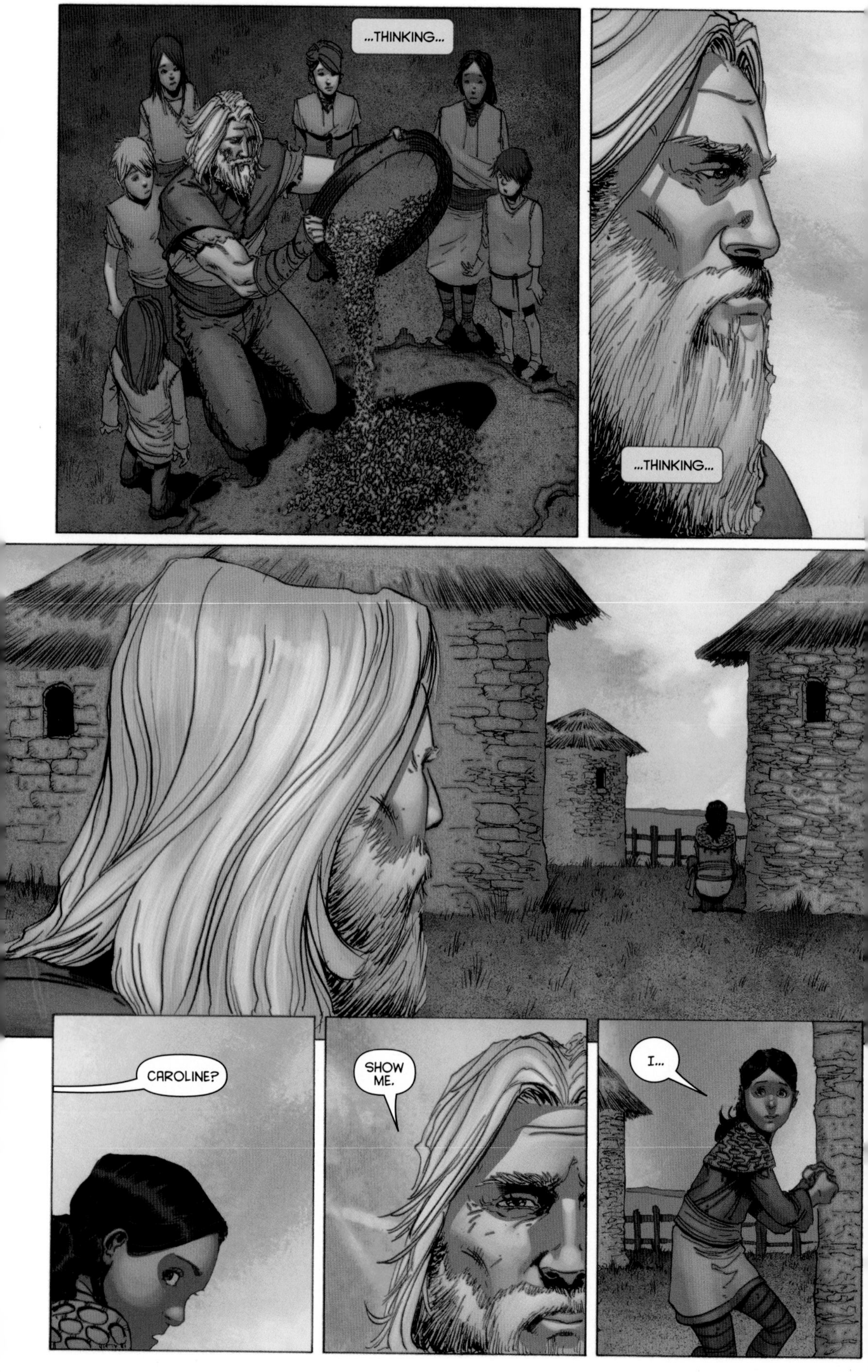
...THINKING...
...THINKING...
CAROLINE?
SHOW ME.
I...

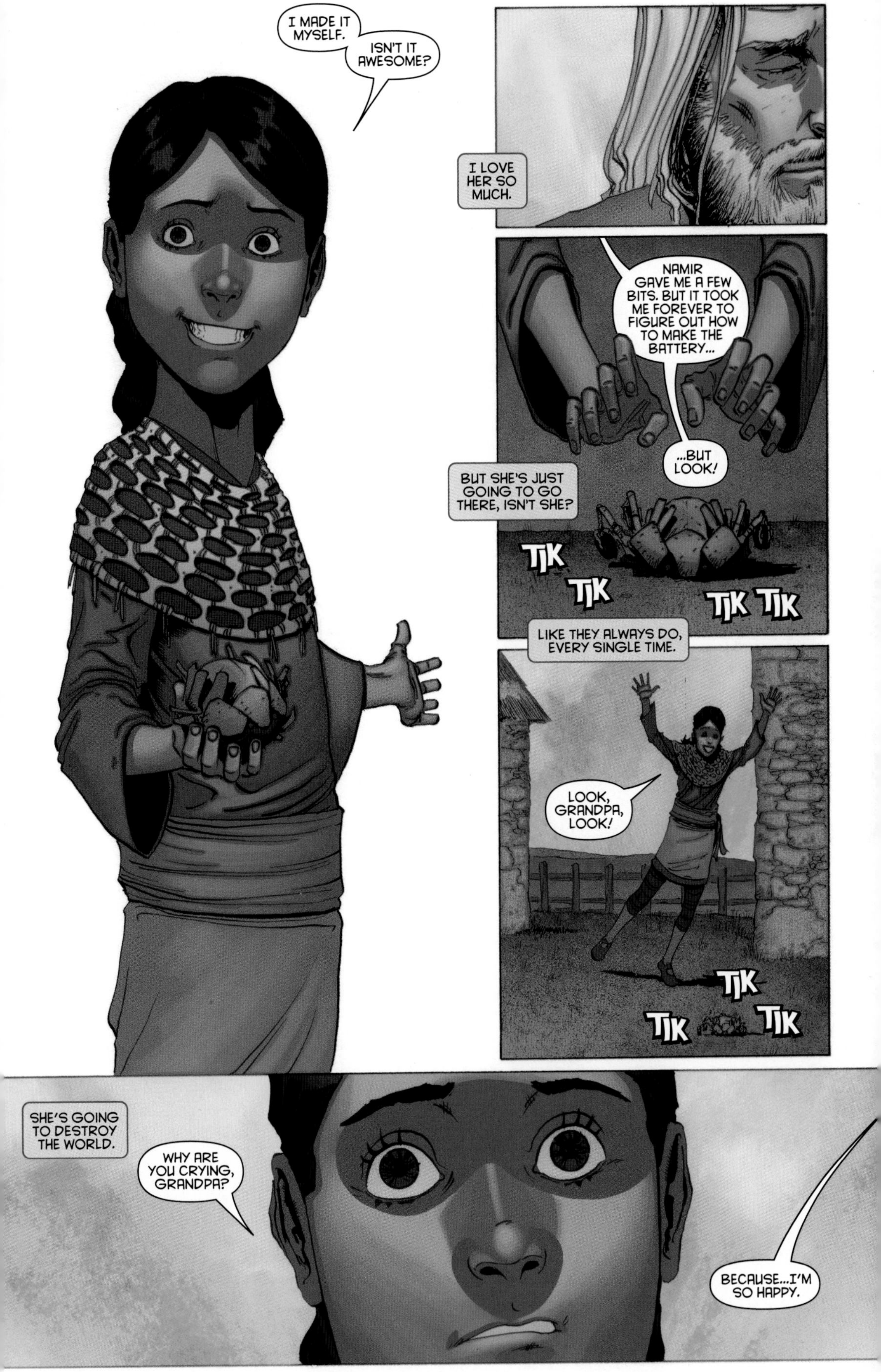
I MADE IT MYSELF.
ISN'T IT AWESOME?
I LOVE HER SO MUCH.
NAMIR GAVE ME A FEW BITS. BUT IT TOOK ME FOREVER TO FIGURE OUT HOW TO MAKE THE BATTERY...
...BUT LOOK!
BUT SHE'S JUST GOING TO GO THERE, ISN'T SHE?
TIK
TIK
TIK TIK
LIKE THEY ALWAYS DO, EVERY SINGLE TIME.
LOOK, GRANDPA, LOOK!
TIK
TIK
TIK
SHE'S GOING TO DESTROY THE WORLD.
WHY ARE YOU CRYING, GRANDPA?
BECAUSE...I'M SO HAPPY.

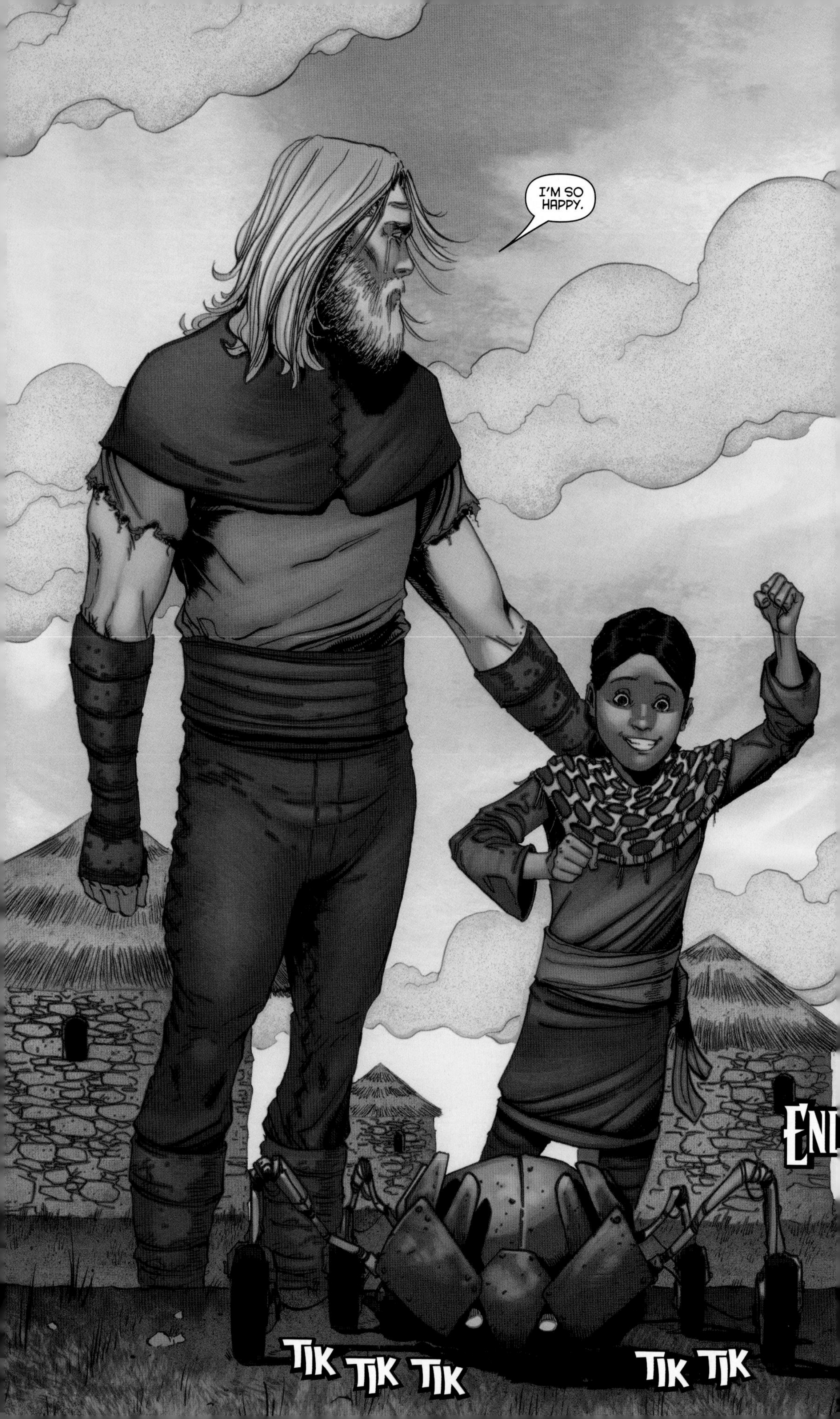
I'M SO HAPPY.
TIK TIK TIK
TIK TIK

GALLERY

ETERNAL WARRIOR #5
PULLBOX EXCLUSIVE VARIANT
Cover by DIEGO BERNARD with
ALEJANDRO SICAT

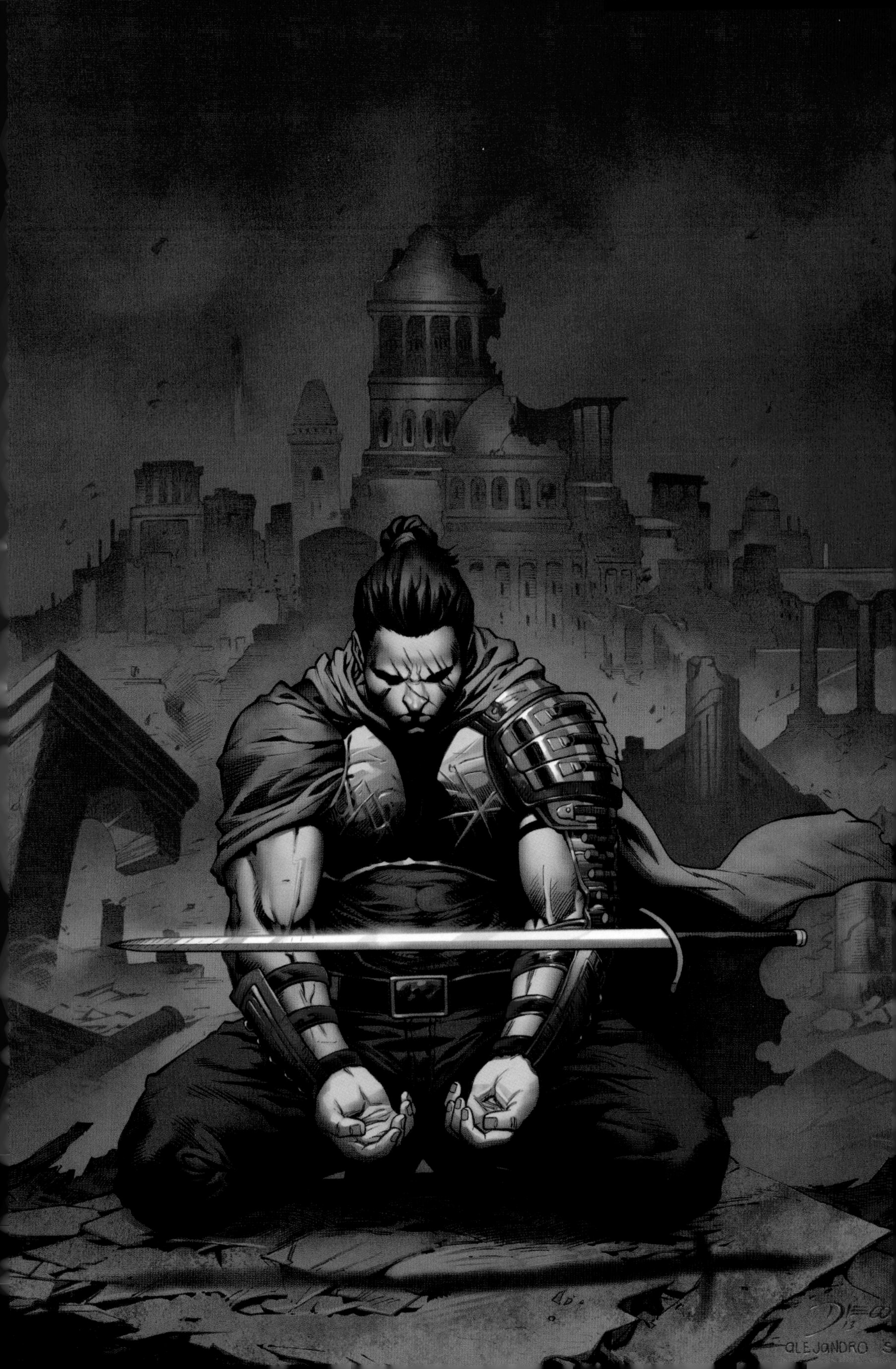

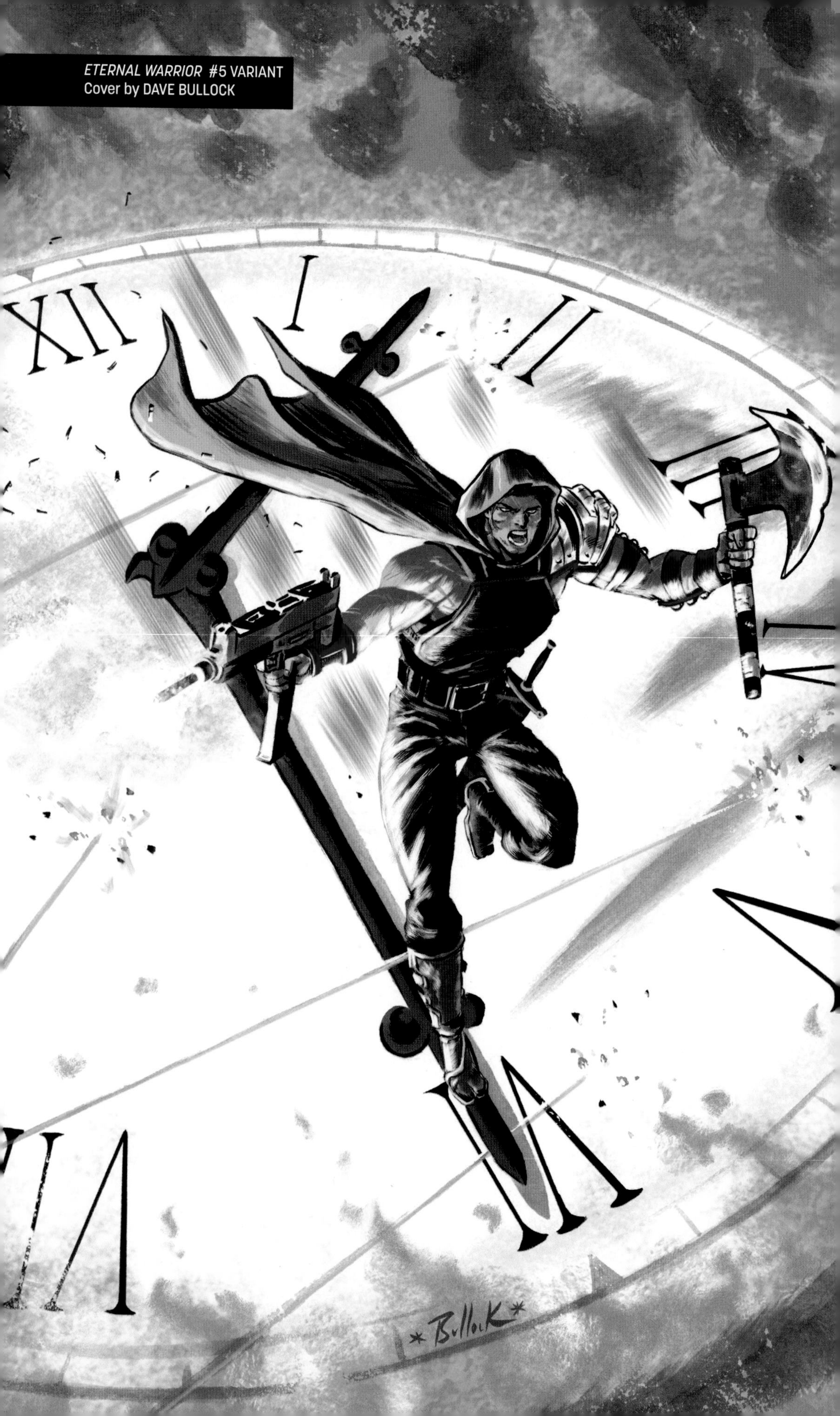
Bullock

ETERNAL WARRIOR #5 VARIANT
Cover by DAVE BULLOCK

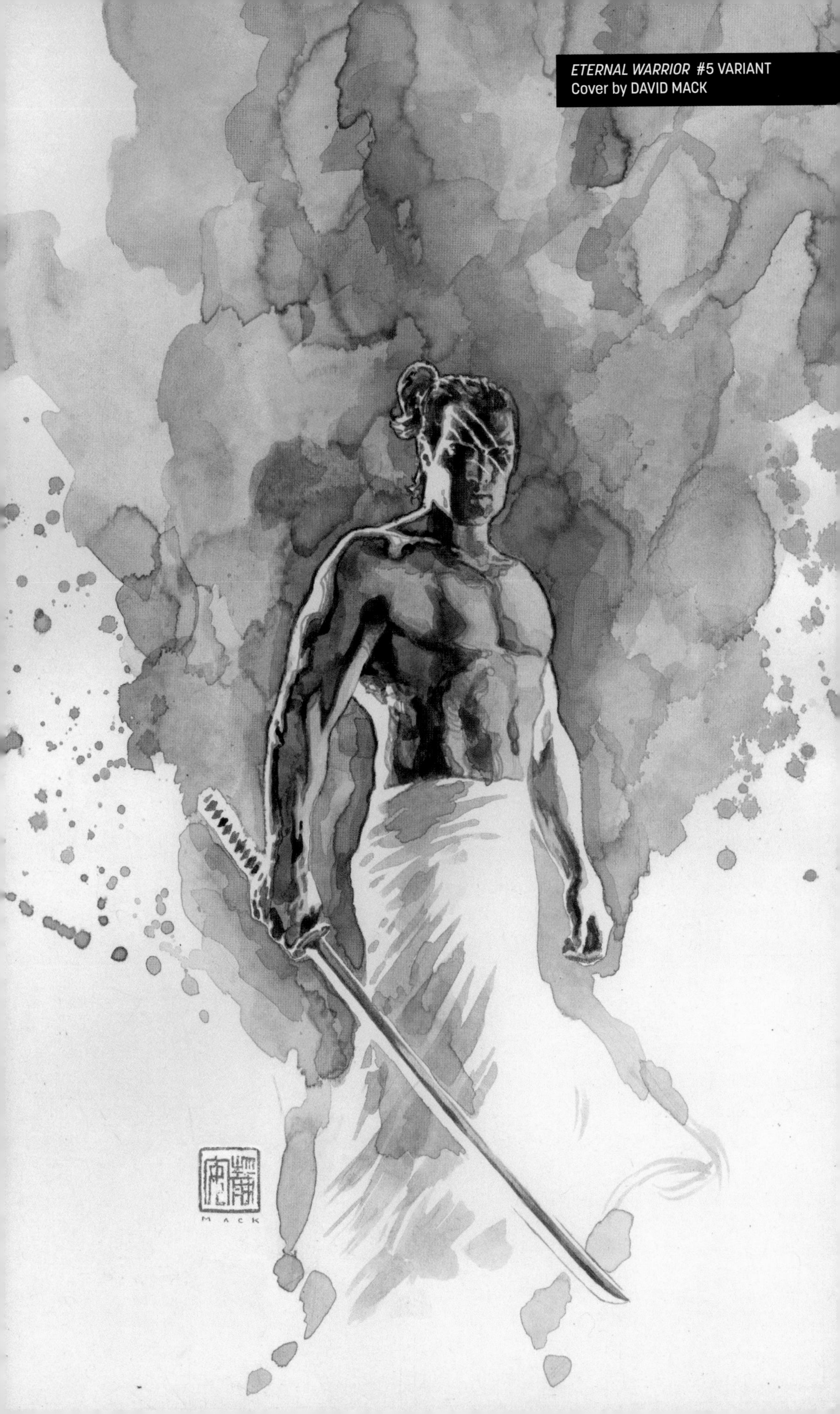
MACK

ETERNAL WARRIOR #5 VARIANT
Cover by DAVID MACK

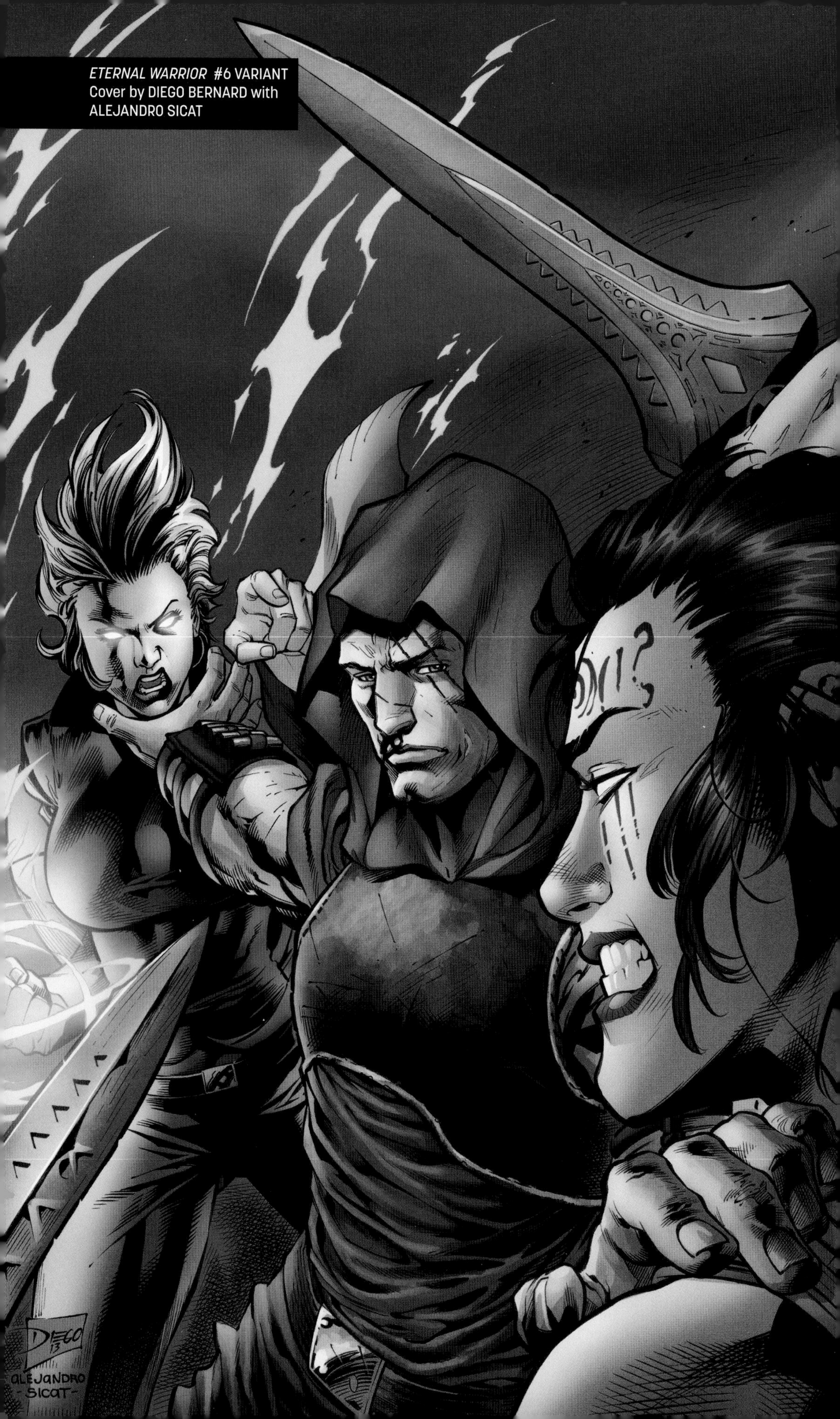
DIEGO 13
ALEJANDRO
-SICAT-

ETERNAL WARRIOR #6 VARIANT
Cover by DIEGO BERNARD with
ALEJANDRO SICAT

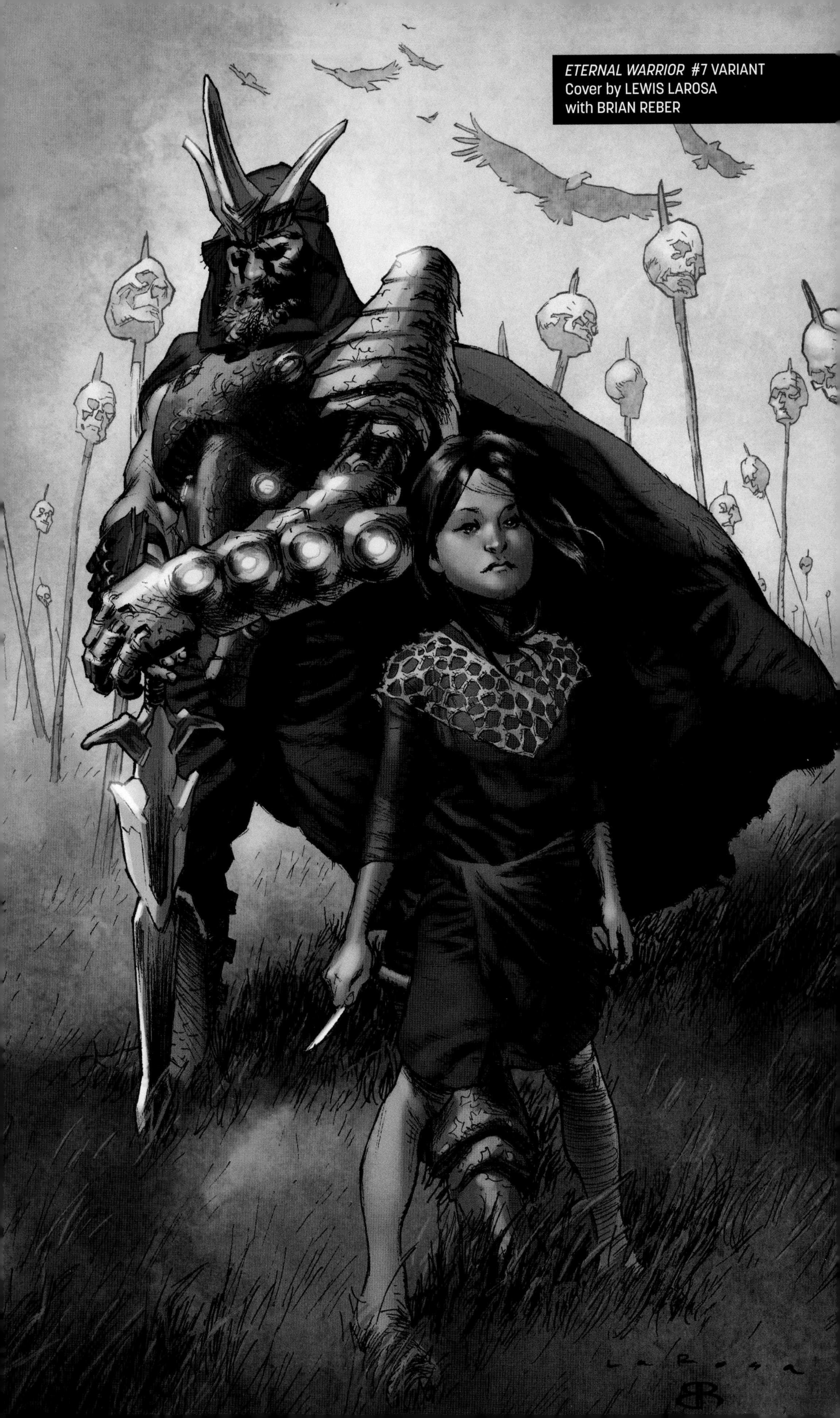

ETERNAL WARRIOR #7 VARIANT
Cover by LEWIS LAROSA
with BRIAN REBER

ETERNAL WARRIOR #8, p. 11
Pencils by ROBERT GILL
Inks by MARK PENNINGTON

ETERNAL WARRIOR #8, p. 12
Pencils by ROBERT GILL
Inks by MARK PENNINGTON

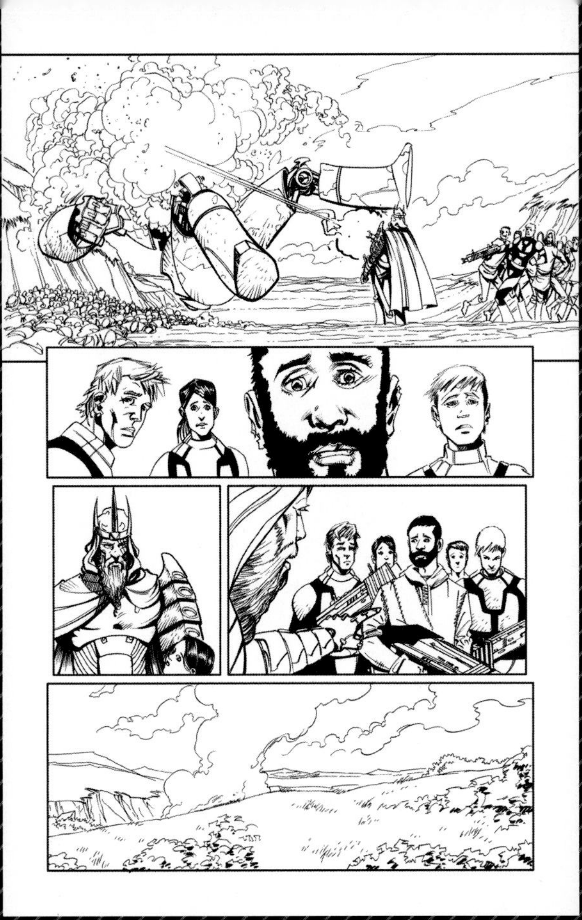

ETERNAL WARRIOR #8, p. 14
Pencils by ROBERT GILL
Inks by MARK PENNINGTON

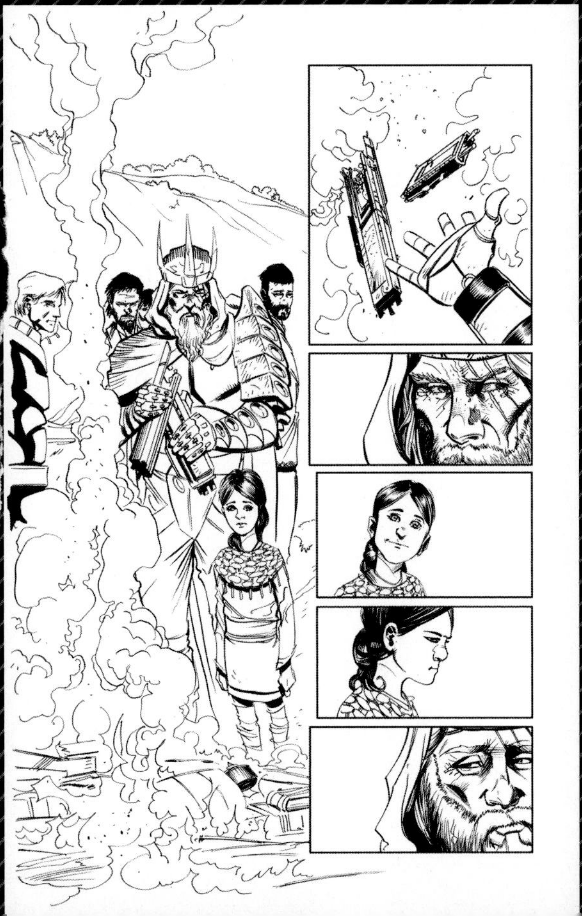

ETERNAL WARRIOR #8, p. 15
Pencils by ROBERT GILL
Inks by MARK PENNINGTON

VALIANT®

DELUXE HARDCOVERS

TREVOR HAIRSINE | STEFANO GAUDIANO | MOOSE BAUMANN
VALIANT
X-O MANOWAR
DELUXE EDITION 1

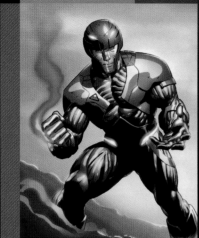

X-O MANOWAR DELUXE EDITION BOOK 1

Writer: Robert Venditti | Artists: Cary Nord, Lee Garbett, and Trevor Hairsine
ISBN: 9781939346100 | Diamond Code: AUG131497 | Price: $39.99 |
Format: Oversized HC

Aric of Dacia, a fifth-century Visigoth armed with the universe's most powerful weapon, is all that stands between the Earth and all-out annihilation at the hands of the alien race that abducted him from his own time. Stranded in the modern day, X-O Manowar's battle against the Vine will take him into the shadows with the lethal operative known as Ninjak–and launch a quest for vengeance that will bring an alien empire to its knees. The Vine destroyed Aric's world. Now he will give them war.

Collecting X-O MANOWAR #1-14 and more than 20 pages of bonus materials!

JOSHUA DYSART | KHARI EVANS | TREVOR HAIRSINE
MICO SUAYAN | IAN HANNIN
VALIANT
HARBINGER
DELUXE EDITION 1

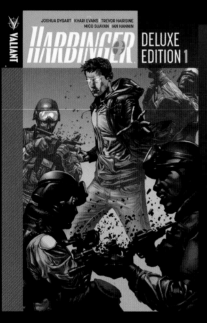

HARBINGER DELUXE EDITION BOOK 1

Writer: Joshua Dysart | Artists: Khari Evans, Trevor Hairsine, Barry Kitson, and Lee Garbett
ISBN: 9781939346131 | Diamond Code: SEP131373 | Price: $39.99 | Format: Oversized HC

Outside the law. Inside your head. You've never met a team of super-powered teenagers quite like the Renegades. Skipping across the country in a desperate attempt to stay one step ahead of the authorities, psionically powered teenager Peter Stanchek only has one option left–run. But he won't have to go it alone. As the shadowy corporation known as the Harbinger Foundation draws close on all sides, Peter will have to find and recruit other unique individuals like himself...other troubled, immensely powerful youths with abilities beyond their control. Their mission? Bring the fight back to the Harbinger Foundation's founder Toyo Harada–and dismantle his global empire brick by brick...

Collecting HARBINGER #0-14 and more than 20 pages of bonus materials!

DUANE SWIERCZYNSKI | MANUEL GARCIA
BARRY KITSON | ARTURO LOZZI | STEFANO GAUDIANO
VALIANT
BLOODSHOT
DELUXE EDITION 1

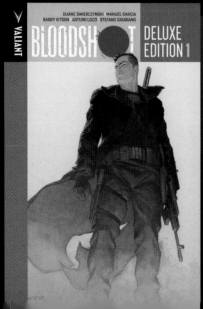

BLOODSHOT DELUXE EDITION BOOK 1

Writer: Duane Swierczynski | Artists: Manuel García, Barry Kitson, Matthew Clark, and Arturo Lozzi
ISBN: 9781939346216 | Diamond Code: JAN141376 | Price: $39.99 | Format: Oversized HC

You have no name, just a project designation. They call you Bloodshot, but the voices inside your head call you "daddy, "sir," "commander," "comrade"–whatever it takes to motivate you to get the job done. But after so many missions and so many lives, you're finally ready to confront your handlers at Project Rising Spirit and find out who you really are. You'd better move quickly, though, because your former masters don't like it when a billion-dollar weapons project goes rogue. And wherever you go, all hell is sure to follow...

Collecting BLOODSHOT #1-13 and more than 20 pages of bonus materials!

VALIANT DELUXE HARDCOVERS

FRED VAN LENTE | CLAYTON HENRY
EMANUELA LUPACCHINO | PERE PÉREZ
ARCHER & ARMSTRONG
DELUXE EDITION 1

ARCHER & ARMSTRONG DELUXE EDITION BOOK 1

Writer: Fred Van Lente | Artists: Clayton Henry, Emanuela Lupacchino, Pere Pérez, and Álvaro Martínez
ISBN: 9781939346223 | Diamond Code: FEB141484 | Price: $39.99 | Format: Oversized HC

Join one of the most acclaimed adventures in comics as naive teenage assassin Obadiah Archer and the fun-loving, hard-drinking immortal called Armstrong unite to stop a plot ten thousand years in the making! From the lost temples of ancient Sumeria to modern-day Wall Street, Area 51, and beyond, Valiant's conspiracy-smashing adventurers are going on a globe-trotting quest to bring down the unholy coalition of cultists known as the Sect–and stop each of history's most notorious conspiracies from remaking the world in their own insane image.

Collecting ARCHER & ARMSTRONG #0-13 and more than 20 pages of bonus materials!

JOSHUA DYSART | DUANE SWIERCZYNSKI | CLAYTON HENRY
BARRY KITSON | KHARI EVANS | TREVOR HAIRSINE
HARBINGER WARS
DELUXE EDITION 1

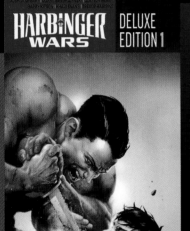

HARBINGER WARS DELUXE EDITION

Writer: Joshua Dysart & Duane Swierczynski | Artists: Clayton Henry, Pere Pérez, Barry Kitson, Khari Evans, Trevor Hairsine, Mico Suayan, and Clayton Crain
ISBN: 9781939346322 | Diamond Code: MAR141422 | **Price: $39.99 |**
Format: Oversized HC

Re-presenting Valiant's best-selling crossover event in complete chronological order!

When an untrained and undisciplined team of super-powered test subjects escapes from Project Rising Spirit and onto the Vegas Strip, Bloodshot and the Harbinger Renegades will find themselves locked in battle against a deadly succession of opponents–and each other. As the combined forces of the H.A.R.D. Corps, Bloodshot, and omega-level telekinetic Toyo Harada all descend on Las Vegas to vie for control of Rising Spirit's deadliest assets, the world is about to discover the shocking price of an all-out superhuman conflict...and no one will escape unscathed. Who will survive the Harbinger Wars?

Collecting HARBINGER WARS #1-4, HARBINGER #11-14, BLOODSHOT #10-13, material from the HARBINGER WARS SKETCHBOOK, and more than 20 pages of bonus materials!

JUSTIN JORDAN | PATRICK ZIRCHER
NEIL EDWARDS | LEE GARBETT
SHADOWMAN
DELUXE EDITION 1

SHADOWMAN DELUXE EDITION BOOK 1

Writers: Justin Jordan and Patrick Zircher | Artists: Patrick Zircher, Neil Edwards, Lee Garbett, Diego Bernard, Roberto de la Torre, Mico Suayan, and Lewis LaRosa
ISBN: 9781939346438 | Price: $39.99 | Format: Oversized HC | COMING SOON

There are a million dreams in the Big Easy. But now its worst nightmare is about to come true. As the forces of darkness prepare to claim New Orleans as their own, Jack Boniface must accept the legacy he was born to uphold. As Shadowman, Jack is about to become the only thing that stands between his city and an army of unspeakable monstrosities from beyond the night. But what is the true cost of the Shadowman's otherworldly power? And can Jack master his new abilities before Master Darque brings down the wall between reality and the otherworldly dimension known only as the Deadside?

Collecting SHADOWMAN #0-10 and more than 20 pages of bonus materials!

VALIANT®

TRADE PAPERBACKS

VALIANT
TO KILL A KING
UNITY

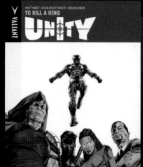

UNITY VOL. 1: TO KILL A KING
ISBN: 9781939346261 | Diamond Code: JAN141356 | Price: $14.99 | Format: TP

UNITY VOL. 2: TRAPPED BY WEBNET
ISBN: 9781939346346| Price: $14.99 | Format: TP | COMING SOON

VALIANT
BY THE SWORD
X-O MANOWAR

X-O MANOWAR VOL. 1: BY THE SWORD
ISBN: 9780979640995 | Diamond Code: OCT121241 | Price: $9.99 | Format: TP

X-O MANOWAR VOL. 2: ENTER NINJAK
ISBN: 9780979640940 | Diamond Code: JAN131306 | Price: $14.99 | Format: TP

X-O MANOWAR VOL. 3: PLANET DEATH
ISBN: 9781939346087 | Diamond Code: JUN131325 | Price: $14.99 | Format: TP

X-O MANOWAR VOL. 4: HOMECOMING
ISBN: 9781939346179 | Diamond Code: OCT131347 | Price: $14.99 | Format: TP

X-O MANOWAR VOL. 5: AT WAR WITH UNITY
ISBN: 9781939346247 | Diamond Code: FEB141472 | Price: $14.99 | Format: TP

VALIANT
SETTING THE WORLD ON FIRE
BLOODSHOT

BLOODSHOT VOL. 1: SETTING THE WORLD ON FIRE
ISBN: 9780979640964 | Diamond Code: DEC121274 | Price: $9.99 | Format: TP

BLOODSHOT VOL. 2: THE RISE AND THE FALL
ISBN: 9781939346032| Diamond Code: APR131280 | Price: $14.99 | Format: TP

BLOODSHOT VOL. 3: HARBINGER WARS
ISBN: 9781939346124 | Diamond Code: AUG131494 | Price: $14.99 | Format: TP

BLOODSHOT VOL. 4: H.A.R.D. CORPS
ISBN: 9781939346193 | Diamond Code: NOV131275 | Price: $14.99 | Format: TP

BLOODSHOT VOL. 5: GET SOME
ISBN: 9781939346315 | Price: $14.99 | Format: TP | COMING SOON

VALIANT
SWORD OF THE WILD
ETERNAL WARRIOR

ETERNAL WARRIOR VOL. 1: SWORD OF THE WILD
ISBN: 9781939346209 | Diamond Code: NOV131271 | Price: $9.99 | Format: TP

ETERNAL WARRIOR VOL. 2: ETERNAL EMPEROR
ISBN: 9781939346292 | Diamond Code: APR141439 | Price: $14.99 | Format: TP

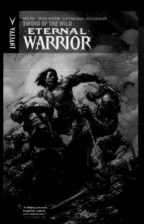

VALIANT

TRADE PAPERBACKS

OMEGA RISING
HARBINGER

HARBINGER VOL. 1: OMEGA RISING
ISBN: 9780979640957 | Diamond Code: NOV121345 | Price: $9.99 | Format: TP

HARBINGER VOL. 2: RENEGADES
ISBN: 9781939346025 | Diamond Code: MAR131332 | Price: $14.99 | Format: TP

HARBINGER WARS (MINI-SERIES)
ISBN: 9781939346094 | Diamond Code: JUL131325 | Price: $14.99 | Format: TP

HARBINGER VOL. 3: HARBINGER WARS
ISBN: 9781939346117 | Diamond Code: JUL131326 | Price: $14.99 | Format: TP

HARBINGER VOL. 4: PERFECT DAY
ISBN: 9781939346155 | Diamond Code: DEC131331 | Price: $14.99 | Format: TP

ARCHER & ARMSTRONG VOL. 1: THE MICHELANGELO CODE
ISBN: 9780979640988 | Diamond Code: JAN131309 | Price: $14.99 | Format: TP

ARCHER & ARMSTRONG VOL. 2: WRATH OF THE ETERNAL WARRIOR
ISBN: 9781939346049 | Diamond Code: MAY131314 | Price: $14.99 | Format: TP

ARCHER & ARMSTRONG VOL. 3: FAR FARAWAY
ISBN: 9781939346148 | Diamond Code: OCT131350 | Price: $14.99 | Format: TP

ARCHER & ARMSTRONG VOL. 4: SECT CIVIL WAR
ISBN: 9781939346254 | Diamond Code: DEC131317 | Price: $14.99 | Format: TP

ARCHER & ARMSTRONG VOL. 5: MISSION: IMPROBABLE
ISBN: 9781939346353 | Diamond Code: APR141438 | Price: $14.99 | Format: TP

BIRTH RITES
SHADOWMAN

SHADOWMAN VOL. 1: BIRTH RITES
ISBN: 9781939346001 | Diamond Code: FEB131168 | Price: $9.99 | Format: TP

SHADOWMAN VOL. 2: DARQUE RECKONING
ISBN: 9781939346056 | Diamond Code: AUG131482 | Price: $14.99 | Format: TP

SHADOWMAN VOL. 3: DEADSIDE BLUES
ISBN: 9781939346162 | Diamond Code: NOV131282 | Price: $14.99 | Format: TP

SHADOWMAN VOL. 4: FEAR, BLOOD, AND SHADOWS
ISBN: 9781939346278 | Diamond Code: MAR141410 | Price: $14.99 | Format: TP

THE WORLD'S WORST SUPERHERO TEAM
QUANTUM AND WOODY!
KLANG.

QUANTUM AND WOODY VOL. 1: THE WORLD'S WORST SUPERHERO TEAM
ISBN: 9781939346186 | Diamond Code: SEP131374 | Price: $9.99 | Format: TP

QUANTUM AND WOODY VOL. 2: IN SECURITY
ISBN: 9781939346230 | Diamond Code: JAN141365 | Price: $14.99 | Format: TP

VALIANT

RAI 霊

VOLUME ONE: WELCOME TO NEW JAPAN

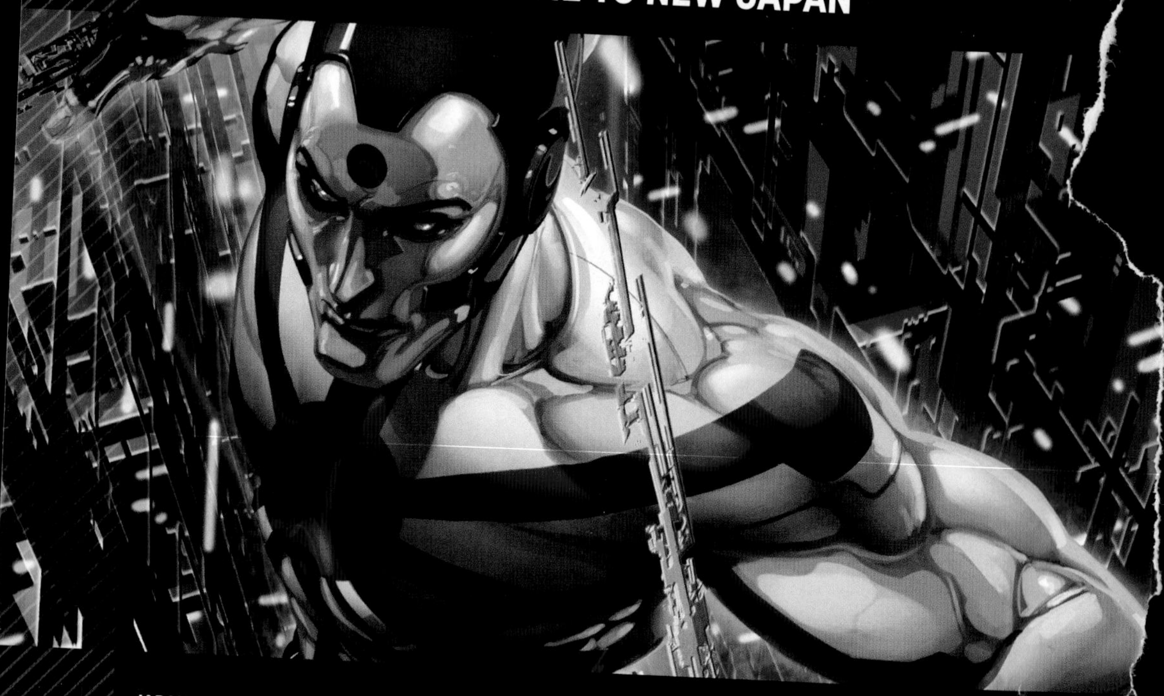

JAPAN IN THE 41st CENTURY!

The year is 4001 A.D. - led by the artificial intelligence called "Father," the island nation of Japan has expanded out of the Pacific and into geosynchronous orbit with the ravaged Earth below. With billions to feed and protect, it has fallen to one solitary guardian to enforce the law of Father's empire - the mysterious folk hero known as Rai. They say he can appear out of nowhere. They say he is a spirit...the ghost of Japan. But when the first murder in a thousand years threatens to topple Father's benevolent reign, Rai will be forced to confront the true face of a nation transformed...and his own long-lost humanity...

Collecting RAI #1-4 by New York Times best-selling writer Matt Kindt (*Unity, Mind MGMT*) and superstar artist Clayton Crain (*X-Force, Carnage*), start reading here to discover an astonishing new vision of the future that Comic Book Resources calls "an immersive experience... unlike anything else in comics."

TRADE PAPERBACK
ISBN: 978-1-939346-41-4

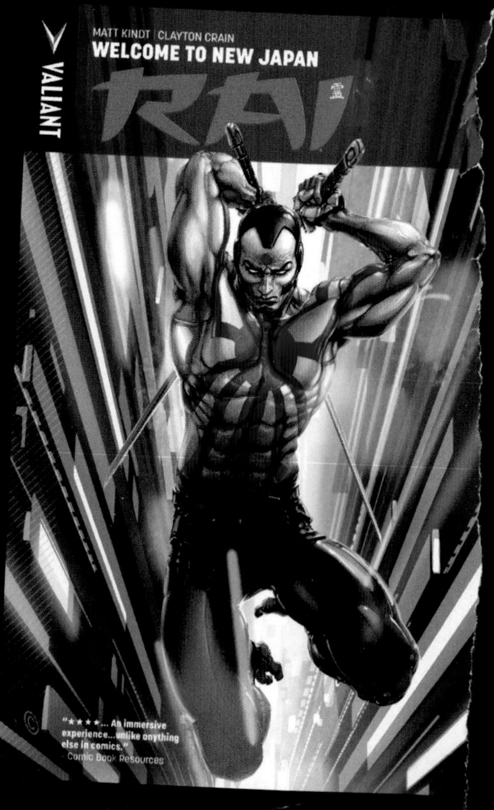
VALIANT
MATT KINDT | CLAYTON CRAIN
WELCOME TO NEW JAPAN
RAI
"★★★★... An immersive experience...unlike anything else in comics."
- Comic Book Resources